Lost in Space

Lost in Space
The Criminalization, Globalization, and Urban Ecology of Homelessness

Randall Amster

LFB Scholarly Publishing LLC
New York 2008

Library of Congress Cataloging-in-Publication Data

Amster, Randall.
Lost in space : the criminalization, globalization, and urban ecology of homelessness / Randall Amster.
p. cm.
Includes bibliographical references and index.
ISBN 978-1-59332-297-7 (alk. paper)
1. Homelessness. 2. Homelessness--Arizona--Tempe. 3. Urban ecology. 4. Public spaces. 5. Homeless persons. 6. Crime and globalization. I. Title.
HV4493.A57 2008
362.5--dc22

2008021805

ISBN 978-1-59332-297-7 (paperback)

Printed on acid-free 250-year-life paper.

Manufactured in the United States of America.

CONTENTS

FIGURES AND ILLUSTRATIONS

FOREWORD

With *Lost in Space*, Randall Amster offers us a beautifully incendiary book, a book that burns with outrage, erudition, and human engagement.

The erudition is evident throughout *Lost in Space*; each chapter of this fine book incorporates an evocative mélange of intellectual innovation and reasoned critique. Gleaning insights from a remarkable range of perspectives – cultural geography, sociology, cultural and critical criminology, urban studies, social history – Randall Amster builds throughout these chapters an elegant analysis of the late modern city and its spaces. As he demonstrates, knowing the political and cultural coordinates of urban space is essential to understanding the social conflicts that emerge as that space is traversed, occupied, and controlled. As he also shows, knowing something of anarchism is important, too, since anarchic sensibilities often animate such spaces, providing street people and urban scholars alike ways of resisting spatial domination.

Amster intertwines this analysis with a revealing case study, a close account of a city, an avenue, and the social and economic forces circulating there. As he takes pains to point out, this single case incorporates the global predations of late capitalism and the pervasiveness of contemporary social control – but it also incorporates human beings and human agency. And so Amster lets us hear from the individuals involved, lets them make their case: politicians, newspaper reporters, businesspeople, and especially the homeless folks whom the local authorities wish most to silence. Amster lets us hear from himself as well; after all, as the reader soon discovers, he's as much a part of the case, of the spatial conflict he documents, as anyone else. Put differently, Randall Amster didn't just write this book, he lived it – and has continued living it for years. Because of this, because of his own integration of erudition and human engagement, he accomplishes something seldom seen, even in the best of scholarship: he takes us from a little patch of Arizona sidewalk to the largest of social concerns, to the very heart of contemporary society and its constructions of crime and social control.

And it is here that the outrage emerges – and rightly so. Amster meticulously documents the insidious erosion of public space in society and with it the undermining of the spatial foundations on which democracy and community are built. He unflinchingly records the mean-spirited strategies by which public space is today cleansed of the homeless, the marginalized, and the itinerant; as he shows, the contemporary political economy of urban space is not a pretty one, no matter how many flowers are planted, no matter how many high-end shops are erected. Most revealingly, he exposes the campaigns of obfuscation through which political and economic authorities go about this work, exposing also those powerful groups and individuals who lack even the courage to acknowledge what they seek to accomplish. In all this, Amster pulls down the cheap facades of 'civility' and 'urban redevelopment' that the powerful have erected in today's urban spaces, revealing instead emerging configurations of inequality and injustice that stretch from the cities of Canada to those of South Africa.

Together, this mix of erudition, engagement, and outrage makes *Lost in Space* a model of critical scholarship – and one of the very best analyses of contemporary spatial control that I have seen. But while a scathing indictment of economic domination and anti-democratic public policy, the book is at the same time a handbook of hope, a chronicle of direct resistance to a tightening circle of enforced conformity. You see, as it turns out, Randall Amster wasn't only a participant in the case he documents; he was a primary force in organizing resistance, in turning a case of urban control into a defense of public space. If reading *Lost in Space* doesn't get you in the mood for hope and resistance, doesn't encourage you to think hard about the very nature of spatial democracy and social justice, then I'd suggest you read it again, this time with an eye toward outrage.

Jeff Ferrell
March 2008

PREFACE

This is both a new book and an old book at the same time. It is new in the sense that the processes and phenomena described here are, to greater or lesser degrees, now happening in nearly every city across the United States and the world over. Exploring a decade of events in one particular locale (namely Tempe, Arizona) gives insight into processes taking shape nearly everywhere, indicating that an investigation of a single piece of a whole reveals something of the nature of that whole. While they may not hold true all the time, lessons learned from a micro-exploration illuminate our understandings of macro trends. Indeed, indigenous cosmologies often devolved upon such a vision of the world, and now modern physics has traced back to the same conclusion: the workings of the entire universe are related to and reflective of the life of a single particle. By analogy, a case study of one city would tell us something about cities in general, and to that end cities across the U.S. and around the globe are compared in this new work. Furthermore, an investigation of any particular social issue will suggest ways of understanding all social issues, and while this is not to imply a literal one-to-one mapping across a range of problems – for instance, racism and littering may appear to be quite different matters – there are still common threads to be explored, analogies to be drawn, and reflexive relationships to be found. This to me is the essence of an *ecological* perspective, and its teachings form the framing of this work.

Having said that, it is also the case that this is in some ways an old book. I have been investigating the particular issues that are front and center here – the proliferation of homelessness, the privatization of space, the criminalization of status, and the globalization of these processes – for the better part of a decade. I titled my dissertation *Spatial Anomalies: Street People, Sidewalk Sitting, and the Contested Realms of Public Space*, and completed it in 2002. Two years later, it became a book called *Street People and the Contested Realms of Public Space*, in which I updated the research and broadened the focus to include both additional locales and more voices. Now, with four more years having passed, I return to these familiar spheres of inquiry with renewed vigor and a simultaneous sense of trepidation and hopefulness, with the former due to a profound feeling that the problems I consider here have largely gotten worse, and the latter reflecting my strong sense that an awareness of this is now well known across a range of academic disciplines and in nearly every corner of the globe. While I am grateful that earlier versions of this work have played some small role in the dissemination of a critical perspective on these important social issues, I am also aware that we need new ways of looking at old problems and that the map of the world quite literally keeps changing. Here then is my attempt to connect the dots of the old with the needs of the new.

The world has undergone profound changes in the last few years. The full implications of the so-called 'war on terror' have begun to sink in, with war economies, surveillance societies, crackdowns on dissent, and hostilities toward 'others' now prevalent. Similarly, the full dimensions of 'corporate globalization' are being felt by people everywhere, including the dismantling of social safety nets, the loss of unique cultural identities, the relentless extraction of natural resources, and the ongoing immiseration of low-wage (or even no-wage) workers. Further, global awareness of environmental issues has been aroused by phenomena including the ubiquity of 'climate change' as a potentially apocalyptic scenario, the increasing shortages of basic resources such as water, the regular extinctions of animal species, and the worldwide health threats posed by toxins. The simultaneity of these three dominant examples of an emerging consciousness – militarization, globalization, and environmental degradation – is most definitely *not* coincidental. Indeed, the issue of homelessness is one moment where they all connect: veterans returning from war sometimes wind up on the streets; neoliberal economics pushes people to the margins; and global warming contributes to hurricanes and tsunamis that uproot people. All of this suggests the value of an ecological perspective on homelessness.

And that brings me back to the gist of this work, where I strive to maintain a perspective that focuses upon interconnections, reflexive relationships, and root causes (a deeper meaning of the word 'radical'). In the life story of a single homeless person, there is a kernel that speaks to the global forces noted above. Likewise, in one parcel of public space becoming private there is a metaphor for what is happening to the entire planet itself. When franchised 'chain stores' take over the downtown of a particular city, it renders that place largely indistinguishable from all other places where the same has occurred. And when a local contingent resists these processes, they are in fact confronting forces of oppression and totalization that occur the world over. It is in this spirit that I offer this small work for your consideration and, hopefully, your inspiration to continue the struggle.

ACKNOWLEDGMENTS

Many are due thanks for their assistance and support in sustaining this project over the past decade, and while I forbear to list everyone here, a few are notable for their unique contributions. Pat Lauderdale helped set the tone and establish the framework for the study, sharpening queries and checking realities throughout in ways for which I remain deeply grateful. Jeff Ferrell's gracious agreement to write the foreword to this volume is deeply appreciated; his words and deeds continue to inspire the intellect and incite the imagination. Luis Fernandez and Mare Schumacher contributed many insights along the way that added numerous dimensions to the project. Gabriel Kuhn read drafts of many of the chapters in various forms over the years, offering new perspectives and positive encouragement. Leo Balk and the editors at LFB provided invaluable assistance in bringing this work to fruition. The Center for Urban Inquiry at Arizona State University generously provided funding during the crucial early research phases of the project. My parents, sister, and brother-in-law all provided support and sounding-board moments throughout the duration. Kathleen Halbert shared in the tribulations of the writing, graciously edited the final manuscript, and lovingly endured the all-consuming nature of the process. My children, Arlo and Zeno, are the reason I write at all.

Parts of this work have appeared in journals as earlier versions and works in progress, for which I am grateful to the respective editors and reviewers. Portions of Chapter Four appeared in the *Humboldt Journal of Social Relations*, while aspects of Chapter Two were initially inspired by articles appearing in both *Anarchist Studies* and the *Contemporary Justice Review*. A significant part of Chapter Three comprised an article for *Social Justice* and was further honed in talks sponsored by the Free to Camp Coalition and the Arizona Coalition to End Homelessness, while aspects of Chapter Seven were developed in a keynote address for the Local to Global Justice annual teach-in. Finally, the emerging *urban ecology* framework suggested throughout this volume was partly cultivated in a workshop facilitated at the Master of Arts Program colloquium at Prescott College.

Notwithstanding the generous support and encouragement offered and received throughout, any omissions, errata, misconceptions, or other shortcomings are the author's responsibility alone.

CHAPTER ONE

Facing the 'Homeless Problem'

Subsistence, Survival, and Skid Row

This introductory chapter explores the historical and contemporary implications of homelessness as both a social and spatial problem. This construction implicates a wide range of academic disciplines and public policy concerns, including fields ranging from urban sociology to social problems inquiry to community dynamics. Studies of particular cases will be introduced here, and will be carried through the balance of the text as grounded examples that will serve to promote continuity across the chapters. Guiding questions will be posed here as well, including why homelessness is often coded as a 'problem' in society, and what we might learn from the lived experience of homeless people and the communities they often create.

Introduction: What's Your Problem?

Scholars, commentators, and activists alike have at times lamented the steady erosion of public space, charting its decline along with the concomitant rise of forces of development, commercialization, and privatization. An important and pervasive implication of these processes can be seen in the ongoing trend toward the criminalization of homelessness, evidenced by the scores of cities and municipalities in the United States that have enacted anti-homeless laws in the last decade, including ordinances prohibiting 'urban camping,' 'aggressive panhandling,' and sitting or lying on public sidewalks, often adopted at the behest of commercial interests. Why would a marginalized and often politically disenfranchised group such as homeless people be the subject of such fervent regulatory efforts? Is there something in particular about this class of individuals that constitutes a threat to society? And who do we mean when we talk about 'the homeless'?

Situated among the spheres of legal geography, critical criminology, and urban sociology, this work seeks to address these queries by exploring interconnections among: (i) the lived experiences of homeless people, (ii) the impetus of development and gentrification; (iii) the material and ideological erosion of public space; (iv) the enactment of anti-homeless ordinances and regulations; and (v) emerging forces of resistance to these trends. Looking at examples from across the United States (and internationally as well), including an in-depth exploration of these issues in one particular community (namely Tempe, Arizona, a 'college town' in the Phoenix metropolitan area with a population of around 200,000), it is the purpose of this investigation to describe and document how processes of geographic regulation and homeless criminalization are interlocking and mutually-reinforcing facets of a larger frame of social and spatial control often loosely grouped under the emerging rubric of *globalization.* By shining a light on these issues, it is hoped that this work will be useful in amplifying a generalized critique of the processes of globalization and development and in promoting action undoing the same, as well as encouraging the homeless and their advocates to contest policies of social and spatial exclusion. In order to do so, it is necessary at the outset to understand just who 'the homeless' are and to begin to explore why they are most often viewed in terms of comprising a 'problem.'

Vagabonds and Transients in History

> "I am truly a 'lone traveler,' and have never belonged to my country, my home, my friends, or even my immediate family, with my whole heart; in the face of all these ties, I have never lost a sense of distance and a need for solitude – feelings which increase with the years. One becomes sharply aware, but without regret, of the limits of mutual understanding and consonance with other people. No doubt, such a person loses

> some of his innocence and unconcern; on the other hand he is largely independent of the opinions, habits, and judgments of his fellows and avoids the temptation to build his inner equilibrium upon such insecure foundations."
>
> -- Albert Einstein (1954:9)

In the quest to understand the origins of homelessness and its construction as a social problem, it is instructive to consider the historical archetypes of the *vagabond*, the *transient*, and the *stranger*. Infused with an aura of subversiveness (Miller 1991:154), these avatars provide a pertinent bridge between the ways in which 'identity' is conceived in the postmodern age and how certain categories come to be defined as dangerous and problematic. Vagabonds throughout history have been seen as 'indeterminate' in the sense that they do not exist in fixed social or spatial locations. Zygmunt Bauman (1993:240) has done much to bring this archetype to light:

> "The vagabond does not know how long he will stay where he is now, and more often than not it will not be for him to decide when the stay will come to an end. Once on the move again, he sets his destinations as he goes and as he reads the road-signs, but even then he cannot be sure whether he will stop, and for how long, at the next station. What he does know is that more likely than not the stopover will be but temporary. . . . The vagabond is a pilgrim without a destination; a nomad without an itinerary. The vagabond journeys through an unstructured space; like a wanderer in the desert, who knows only of such trails as are marked with his own footprints, and blown off again by the wind the moment he passes, the vagabond structures the site he happens to occupy at the moment, only to dismantle the structure again as he leaves. Each successive spacing is local and temporary – episodic."

The vagabond is an avatar of chaos, indeterminacy, and unbounded freedom, suggesting a spirit of subversiveness (see Bauman 1996:28; cf. Lofland 1998:153). Indeed, as Norval (1994:132-33) observes: "For Bauman, then, the indeterminate has a subversive potential precisely because it undermines the very logic of identity upon which the order-chaos polarity is found. Indeterminacy resists reduction to either of the categories, and thus subverts the very principle upon which oppositionality and, as others might argue, the whole of Western metaphysics is based. . . . A crisis, on this view, can be described as a situation in which the horror of indetermination has manifested itself. That is, a situation in which the dominant discourse is unable to determine the lines of inclusion and exclusion according to which the identity of the social is constituted." Historically, "the vagabond was the bane of early modernity, the bugbear that spurred the rulers and the philosophers into an ordering and legislating frenzy. . . . The vagabond was masterless, and being masterless (out of control, out of frame, on the loose) was one condition modernity could not bear and thus spent the rest of its history fighting" (Bauman 1996:28). Often identified as *deviant*, *diseased*, *dangerous*, *disaffiliated*, and *undesirable*, the vagabond or vagrant has since at least the 14th century been the subject of punitive and legislative efforts aimed at limiting and/or eliminating their presence in cities and towns (Miller 1991; Barak 1991; Simon 1992; May 2000). Nonetheless, a strange affinity remains for the vagabond, existing alongside equally strong feelings of repulsion: "On the one hand, the vagrant is viewed as an enemy, a disrupter, a menace to established order, a parasite – he or she is someone to be shunned, stigmatized, or even killed. But the vagrant is also celebrated; he or she is sometimes perceived as the embodiment of all that is good in [hu]mankind. And the vagrant is romanticized as a vagabonding, unfettered, free spirit" (Miller 1991:xiii). While most of us seek homes and other structures as hedges against the horrors of indeterminacy and impermanence, the vagabond acknowledges this condition of fleeting fragmentation, "cherishing out-of-placeness" (Bauman 1996:29).

More than all of this, the vagabond is a social critic, a commentator on life in the postmodern era: "The hub of postmodern life strategy is not identity building, but avoidance of fixation" (Bauman 1996:24). Driven by the fragmentary and contingent vagaries of life in an era of deconstruction and dislocation, the vagabond renounces bounded place in favor of infinite space, wearing her indeterminacy as a badge of resistance. In this vein, David Harvey (1990:302-03) observes that "the capacity of most social movements to command place better than space puts a strong emphasis upon the potential connection between place and social identity. . . . In clinging, often of necessity, to a place-bound identity, however, such oppositional movements become a part of the very fragmentation that a mobile capitalism and flexible accumulation can feed upon." It is precisely because the vagabond denies place that her fragmentation is a form of resistance and not unwitting complicity. As Nietzsche (1996:266) intimates, "He who has come only in part to a freedom of reason cannot feel on earth otherwise than as a wanderer – though not as a traveler towards a final goal, for this does not exist. But he does want to observe, and keeps his eyes open for everything that actually occurs in the world; therefore he must not attach his heart too firmly to any individual thing; there must be something wandering within him, which takes its joy in change and transitoriness."

In this sense, "[w]herever the vagabond goes, he is a stranger" (Bauman 1996:28; cf. Baudelaire 1974), a displaced figure for whom "established values have no meaning or attraction whatsoever, [who] embraces the mutability, deprivation, and exteriority of a world without borders and without permanent form" (Stamelman 1993:118):

> "The Baudelairean stranger, at once mysterious and extraordinary, inhabits a world that from the perspective of his bourgeois interlocutor is one of lack. For the stranger is a being who lives in deprivation, who has either refused or been refused the conventional realities of social order: home, family, community, society itself. The stranger, a creature of loss, lives in a continual state of exteriority and absence. Continually on the move, contained by no frontiers or boundaries, the stranger has for 'home' only the changing landscapes of his wandering, for 'companions' only the echoes of his own footsteps, for 'possessions' only the absence of possessions. The stranger is a nomad, a pariah, an exile, a man or woman on and of the Outside, to whom all communal acts, all common activities, the most simple human verbs – to have, to belong, to speak – are foreign" (Stamelman 1993:119).

Who is this stranger? Of course he is us, both self and other, "for indisputably, we are all strangers. In that, we are, all of us, different and, all of us, the same" (Stamelman 1993:134). As Julia Kristeva (1991:1) similarly asserts, "the foreigner lives within us: he is the hidden face of our identity, the space that wrecks our abode, the time in which understanding and affinity founder. By recognizing him within ourselves, we are spared detesting him in himself. A symptom that precisely turns 'we' into a problem, perhaps makes it impossible, the foreigner comes in when consciousness of my difference arises, and he disappears when we all acknowledge ourselves as foreigners, unamenable to bonds and communities." More succinctly, a homeless woman in downtown Phoenix, Arizona displayed a sign saying, "I am a stranger in a strange land" (Fitzpatrick 1993). This, then, is what the vagabond portends (cf. Bauman 1999:77), a life of unbounded choice and relentless change, and explains in part why he often frightens us. Indeed, when we consider the modern nomenclature of 'homelessness' (a label that has been in use for a mere few decades), it becomes apparent how intertwined our notions of identity are with the stability of 'place,' or more precisely with things being in the 'right place.' Homeless people now and throughout history have quite literally been defined as people without a 'right place' to be, often creating an uncomfortable reminder of our own vulnerability and transitory qualities. Perhaps even more than other 'social problems,' homelessness thus strongly suggests an ecological outlook that deeply explores the nexus of "person-environment relationships" (Fitzpatrick & LaGory (2000:48). How does the environment (built and natural) impact people's behaviors and choices? How do people's choices in turn affect the environments in which we live? These questions speak to the condition of homelessness as well as to the utility of an ecological perspective that will be developed throughout this work.

Transient Voices, Conscious Choices

> "It is the epitome of despair, to be homeless. It is the cold, dank surface at the bottom of the spiral that begins with a drinking problem, a husband running out on his family, or a debilitating mental illness. It is the endgame of abandonment, of social rejection."
>
> -- *Arizona Republic* editorial, 12/10/01

The above passage adequately states what might be termed the 'traditional' or 'classical' definition of homelessness. That it is the opening to an editorial published as recently as December of 2001 is a testament to the pervasiveness and enduring power of such standard mainstream assessments. It is equally instructive to note that a substantially similar definition to that noted above passes as the sociological standard as well. As one writer opines, "more often than not, the homeless are studied as a sociological problem and the dynamics of power on their part . . . are not studied" (Arnold 1998:14). In this lexicon, homelessness is generally considered a pathological condition at worst and a state of victimization at best (see generally Wagner 1997; Ropers 1988). At one extreme is the conservative, cartoon-like definition of 'street people' as "an almost unclassifiable mix of the sick, the desperately poor, the untreated mentally ill, drug and alcohol addicts, runaways, and aggressive ne'er-do-wells" (Conner 1999; cf. Ellickson 1996; Teir 1998). At the other end is the more liberal view of homelessness as mainly a structural phenomenon bound up with unemployment rates, housing markets, mental health clinic overcrowding, and lack of treatment options for substance addictions (e.g., Ropers 1988; Marcuse 1988; Hopper, et al. 1985; Hafetz 2003; Baron 2004). Indeed, it is clear that the dominant perception of the homeless as presented by the media, merchants, law enforcement, city officials, and sometimes even social workers and sociologists, is one of abjection, pathology, and/or victimization – in other words, the homeless are generally viewed as a problem in need of a solution.

And undoubtedly, homelessness as a social issue *is* problematic. Rates of people considered to be homeless (defined as lacking a fixed residence for some specified period of time) continue to rise, with more vulnerable populations such as children and families showing rapid increases (see, e.g., Harter, et al. 2005:306; Eaton-Robb 2007). Still, what is generally lacking in these formulations is any regard for *agency* in relation to actual homeless individuals and communities (cf. Ruddick 1996; Hill & Bessant 1999; Arnold 1998, 2004; Waldron 1991). In this sense, portraying the homeless as either defective units to be repaired or removed, or as unwitting victims of social circumstance, both accomplish the result of stripping homeless individuals of rights of agency and autonomy (Barak 1991; Ruddick 1996; Mitchell 2003). Homeless people may indeed at times be constrained to choose from among a limited and unappealing range of options, but to deny their capacity to exercise choice and construct their identities is to deny them status as full human agents (cf. Waldron 1991; Mitchell 2003:183). Moreover, the dominant portrayals belie the actuality of street life, where homeless people are not simply passive victims or irrational subjects but make many choices in areas as basic to survival as food, shelter, hygiene, and in numerous encounters and confrontations with authorities, merchants, and passersby. As Ruddick (1996:61) notes, "far from being dupes – impassive in their stigmatization – the homeless constantly and consciously negotiate these meanings, attempting to transform their relationship to those around them."

In addition to the negotiation of complex choices of survival, there is also a macro-level to the exercise of individual agency that often expresses itself as a form of *resistance* (see Wagner 1993:58). To take an example from history, the Cynics of ancient Greece resisted the dominant culture of their time, leading lives of voluntary poverty, begging for alms in the agora, and sleeping in the open alongside roads and byways. In tracing the origins and evolution of vagabonds, vagrants, and street people from the classical era to modern times, Henry Miller notes that "every society in every age has had its share of people who live on the margins of conventional life" (1991:xii), and that generally "they were quite contemptuous of established society" (1991:xvi). Among the exemplars that Miller analyzes are the "mendicant friar" of the Medieval era who took "vows of poverty" and for whom "begging was common" (1991:2), as well as "the hippie" who "solicited without self-abnegation. There was no groveling, no self-pity, no hint of despair. 'Any spare change?' was accompanied by a smile, Mona Lisa-like in its inscrutable wisdom, and a demeanor that conveyed a sense of wholeness and good fortune" (1991:101).

Searching for common threads among these antinomians, Miller observes that "they all arise in periods of cultural crisis; they share a rejection of and contempt for orthodoxy; for the most part, they celebrate the primacy of the free and unencumbered spirit; and they frequently exalt the virtues of poverty and simplicity" (1991:79). In addition to voluntary poverty, he locates common values including: self-expression, paganism, living for the moment, liberty, women's equality, mystic insight, and love of the exotic (1991:85). With the hippies in particular (precursors to today's young urban homeless), Miller notes their disenchantment and disaffiliation with 'civilization': "They were nurtured and nourished on a fraudulent promise and they perceived the sham. Having seen the sham, they found themselves in an impossible situation. It was no longer possible for them to continue on with their lives – working toward such orthodox objectives as higher education and a career – with the knowledge that such goals brought nothing but emptiness and superficiality" (1991:104).

This sense of inherent *intentionality*, of conscious resistance, is reflected today in a number of urban homeless enclaves, including that of the 'Mill Rats' of Tempe – so named because the 'main drag' in town is Mill Avenue – who are seen as "self-styled, freewheelin' hoboes-by-choice" (Gilstrap 1993; see also Holthouse 1998a, 1998b). Interestingly, the homeless youth in Tempe have largely embraced the Mill Rats label, ostensibly "in order to claim marginality as a political strategy in the ongoing struggle for space and identity in the city" (cf. Lees 2003:625, discussing similar tactics by 'The Undesirables' in Portland, Maine). Perhaps prompted by history's call, there remain people who would rather live in the margins than partake of a culture whose central premises often appear to be the destruction of human freedom and the consumption of the natural world. For instance, an article on 'Young Urban Squatters' in the homeless paper *Street Spirit* (Burch 1998) notes that "what they are rebelling against is the kind of oppression that traps most people into those 'lives of quiet desperation'" that Thoreau warned of in the early days of industrialization, and further notes that for many of these street kids, 'spanging' (i.e., spare-changing) represents "a more ethical way to get food and pocket money than working for a corporation." An article about street life in Austin, Texas (Duff 1999) quotes 'Meek' saying that "he lives outdoors by choice, and likens the homeless society to a 'self-sufficient Utopia' whose members rebel against mainstream norms." Likewise from a 1997 article on street people in Santa Cruz, California (Herman 1997): "Gary, a self-described gypsy, told me that he was rebelling against the consumer culture. He played a Japanese flute badly and claimed devotion to a monk's lifestyle: 'The path of the monk is to give up his own self-interest,' he had said. 'Are anybody else but the homeless doing anything around here that's not related to a paycheck?'" The same article quotes 'Rainbow,' 24: "We choose this; we like the nomadic life, the culture of a gypsy population."

Academic treatments of the subject are replete with confirmatory sentiments. In a study of street people in Toronto, Ontario, Morris & Heffren note that in response to being asked "What's the best thing about street life?" the response of "freedom" topped the list, beating out "just still being alive," "hope," and "friends" – with freedom defined as "the freedom to come and go as they please, and to be themselves" (1988:39). Based on a three-year participant observation study of one of the most intractable homeless enclaves, New York's Bowery, Grunberg (1998:241-42) observes that a sense of "homelessness as a lifestyle" exists there in the spirit of preserving "the idea to stay homeless." In a two-year study of street people in a northeastern American city, David Wagner (1993:32-34) recalls how "the subjects' own accounts of how they became homeless stress personal issues and often their own actions in deciding to live in the streets," and how "homeless subjects, particularly street kids and battered women, often took the position, against the conventional wisdom of liberals, that homeless people chose the street. Many asserted that the streets were far better than their previous lives, and that they preferred independence to family life" (1993:60; cf. Twaddell 2007).

In a classic study of 'urban nomads,' Spradley (1970:72,253) further observes that "some men enter this way of life by choice," and reports that in some cases "these are men who don't want a steady job, no desire to compete in the rat race. Society looks on him as a man who can't keep up when he is one who doesn't want to keep up." Analyzing "single homelessness" in England, May (2000:741) notes an "important connection between travelling and homelessness," and argues that in many cases the homeless are "those who have 'chosen' a life of mobility rather than a more settled existence." Among a sample of homeless teenage girls in San Francisco, Solomowitz (1997:186) discerns that many "have strong roots in anarchism, often seeking disapproval from the 'mainstream' and challenging the basic tenets of white, middle-class adult culture. They have challenged basic norms of cleanliness, gender roles, distribution of wealth and property, American imperialism, biological family networks and the geographic and social place of youth in adult culture." And in a more theoretical turn, Arnold (1998:176-77) explores a type of homelessness that "is situated in autonomy and is willed," representing a form of "voluntary uprootedness." On the other hand, Snow & Anderson (1993:253-55) assert that the "voluntaristic explanation . . . is not one of the favored or frequently articulated reasons the homeless give for being on the streets." Hil & Bessant (1999:42) likewise maintain that "it is inaccurate to regard [them] as romantic heroes or purposeful rebels." And VanderStaay (1992:82) admonishes that, "contrary to lingering notions of street kids as Huck Finn prototypes or anachronistic hippie rebels, the vast majority of street youth eke out lives of violent desperation." Nevertheless, Don Mitchell (1997:321) maintains, and I obviously concur, that it is "crucial to show the voluntary nature of homelessness [since] the public sphere is a voluntary one," and thus images of the homeless as purely involuntary actors undermine notions of citizenship and democratic participation in the public realm.

The street people of Tempe reflect these trends in abundance. An *ASU State Press* article (Zawicki 2000c), for instance, depicts Tempe's street kids as "the perfect picture of freedom and brutal independence," since many "proclaim they are there by choice" as a response to an "organized society which is decadent and depraved." The lead editorial in the same issue of the *State Press* (2000b), in arguing against criminalization and for more services, observes that "some of the homeless people on Mill Avenue, the young 'Mill Rats,' are largely there by choice. . . . These kids are living a lifestyle that might seem foreign to most of us, but they're doing it by choice." And as Jeff Ferrell (2001:168) observes in connection with Mill Avenue's 'gutter punks': "They define themselves more by their willingness and ability to live on their own terms, and to find among themselves the ability to survive on the margins. Traveling around the country by freight train or Greyhound bus, squatting together in abandoned buildings, hanging out on the streets, gutter punks practice the anarchic, do-it-yourself, anti-authoritarian politics of punk with a remarkable sense of purpose."

The interviews I conducted in downtown Tempe are similarly indicative. 'Piper,' 20, for example, described his views in April 2000:

> "We live different lifestyles – I go through some tough times sometimes, and there's a lotta wild shit that happens and all, but I'm really content. I got more love now, I got more of a family type of thing than with my own family . . . and I really do think that like all these people that look at us like that, maybe subconsciously they are jealous, cuz like we're sitting here happy-go-lucky and they're not really content with their lives – they got all these responsibilities, but we don't have a boss to check in with, we don't have parents, or a wife or a husband . . . The city's goal is to get the homeless off the streets, but there's like a lot of homeless that wanna be on the streets cuz they enjoyin' life at the time, some travelin' through cuz they wanna see the country. . . ."

Analogous sentiments were echoed in the same time frame by 'Dante,' 23, who intimated that "we choose a different lifestyle, we travel as free spirits, we live as sovereign citizens," and 'Melee,' 19, who stated that she didn't "like how bureaucracy works [since] people are becoming plastic," and sees herself as "an entertainer who exists to make people think." A week later, also in April 2000, 'Bill,' 46, stated: "I choose to be poor and on the street right now. I'd rather die than give them the power – the landlords, corporations, police." Julie Cart, formerly of the Tempe Salvation Army (2000), which mostly sees the older homeless in Tempe since "many of the youths fear service institutions and shelters," noted that the reason most of her clients were homeless was "usually not a choice, but the end result of an emotional breakdown, losing one's job, alcoholism, [or] the elimination of affordable single occupancy housing;" nevertheless, Cart did relate that some of the homeless she sees cite "positive aspects" of their lifestyles, including "that there are few responsibilities, that it's easier than 'regular' life, that they can avoid the repetitiveness of 'work,' that they are 'doing fine' making crafts, that they enjoy rejecting institutions."

Still, it would be remiss of me not to address the problematic nature of the concept of *choice* as applied to marginalized people such as the homeless. Politically speaking, the reality is that voluntaristic explanations of homelessness have been invoked by conservatives in maintaining the pathological view focusing on personal depravity, and likewise that such explanations are disdained by liberals as unhelpful to the quest to secure more and better social services (cf. Hafetz 2003; Baron 2004). To take a particular example with relevance here, it has been observed that "Tempe's mayor supports individual culpability for homelessness, identifying the homeless problem in Tempe as primarily related to 'packs of kids' choosing to be homeless and frequenting the downtown area. . . . Business organizations also emphasize the individual deviancies of the homeless and actively pressure public officials to reduce homeless access and resources" (Brinegar 2000:510). In an earlier interview with the *Phoenix New Times* (Holthouse 1998a), former Tempe mayor Neil Giuliano expounded on the troubling implications of the 'individual culpability' perspective:

> "I don't feel badly at all for the pack kids, the ones that hang out in clusters around Coffee Plantation, who have chosen to live this way and chosen to elicit fear from citizens, and I will be very aggressive in making Tempe a less friendly place for them. . . . I feel the existence of these kids is a very sad, dangerous commentary on the state of society, and the reality is if these kids stay on the streets, eventually they're going to be forced into a society where 'the system' is going to have to

deal with them legally, and that's too bad, but for most of them, it's their choice. Ultimately, it's their choice."

In the face of such overt animus from powerful public figures, I am somewhat comforted that the 'third way' position I have attempted to develop here, one that credits structural explanations yet seeks to preserve individual autonomy and promote a spirit of contestation, is primarily seen as a position that "argues existentially (or anarchistically) that the freely marginal should be allowed a place to exist" (Barak 1991:14). Indeed, it is mildly shocking to discover that the 'radical' position on the condition of the homeless is one that argues for their right simply to exist! And yet, as will be explored herein, sometimes the mere existence and presence of homeless bodies in public places can be among the most revolutionary statements of all.

In furthering this eventuality, I am guided by the related understandings that "homeless individuals do make decisions about their lives, and it is fruitless and perhaps harmful to assert otherwise" (Daniels 1997:715), and that "homeless individuals, for the most part, are not unwitting, passive actors but relatively active agents in negotiating and reacting to the spatial and political constraints they encounter" (Snow & Mulcahy 2001:165). Nevertheless, it is not lost on me that despite the fact that "for many, homelessness is at some level voluntary," it is equally clear that in many cases "the range of choices available to homeless individuals may be so narrow and unsatisfying that a condition many of us cannot imagine being freely chosen is indeed the least of all possible evils" (Daniels 1997:715), and that part of the task is to "acknowledge the autonomy that homeless individuals exercise in a world of frighteningly limited and inadequate choices" (Daniels 1997:733). Extending this sentiment, Blomley (2006:4) opines that "advocates for the homeless are often forced to advocate for their rights to more humanely continue to occupy public space. While politically necessary, sustaining the right to beg, for example, or to sleep in public, is hardly sufficient." Still, Wagner (1993:34) notes that "it is a disservice to the poor to deny them any choice within these structural alternatives [of] living literally on the streets, living within the shelter system, staying with friends or family, or living out of a car." A letter to the editor in the *Arizona Republic* (April 29, 2000) from a homeless man is revealing: "Some of us have chosen homelessness. In my case – and I am not the only one – I have chosen homelessness as the only decent alternative to accepting the unrelenting free decisions of others." And yet, as Jeremy Waldron summarily intones in 'Homelessness and the Issue of Freedom' (1991):

> "If we value freedom . . . because of the importance of choice and of not being constrained in the choices one makes, then that value ought to lead us to pay some attention to how many choices a person has left after each constraint has been exercised. From any point of view that values choice and freedom of action, it ought to be a matter of concern that the choices left open to a person are being progressively closed off, one by one, and that he is nearing a situation where there is literally nowhere he can turn."

Spradley's study of 'urban nomads' (1970:261) led him also to conclude that "the choice to remain a tramp and the choice to become something else must both be live options if we are to extend freedom to these men." Noting that under such conditions there are some people who "will always be tramps," Spradley wonders: "Is American society large enough to tolerate and even welcome such diversity? Can we guarantee citizens the right to be different when this means some will choose to be tramps?" (1970:261). Concluding on a hopeful note, Spradley longs for a time when society will "recognize the creative skill and dignity" in homeless culture as a "small but important step" in creating a "multicultural society based on the acceptance of difference" and, ultimately, "a world of strangers who are friends" (1970:262). Unfortunately, as Sarah Brinegar's study (2000:511) of government policies toward the homeless in Tempe concludes, Spradley's hope remains unrealized three decades later: "Social diversity may have gained value recognition in our society, but it is clear that this value does not extend to the homeless in the current social order."

Brick by Bricolage: Subsistence, Survival, and Social Services

Whether deliberate or compelled, desperate or utopian, nomadic or stationary, the experience of being homeless often revolves around addressing basic questions of survival. "Like people everywhere, the homeless must eat, sleep, eliminate, makes ends meet, socialize, and secure a measure of meaning and self-respect" (Snow, et al. 1996).

Options presented and choices made in these essential areas can be among the most difficult and dangerous ones a street person makes (cf. Lefer 1999), and their practical resolution goes to the very core of what it means to be homeless in a 'homeful' society and to how homeless people construct their identities. In a manner that is also reflected in mainstream society, the answer to the question of how one sustains their material and corporeal existence becomes fundamental to one's persona and presentation of self. Within the homeless milieu, the method of attaining subsistence often marks the line between sub-sub-subcultures such as 'hustler,' 'hippie,' 'slacker,' and 'tramp.' And while the intermittent appearance of possibilities such as 'services,' 'shelters,' and 'centers' can buffet the pain somewhat, it soon becomes apparent that even these prospects can be problematic in ways such that, "given the restraints and often dangers of such places, many choose to avoid them altogether" (Kawash 1998:327).

One of the remarkable aspects of studying cultures confronting issues of poverty and subsistence is the inevitable discovery of the elegant and efficient solutions the local denizens seem to fashion to sustain themselves. As Snow & Anderson (1993:316) conclude:

> "What has impressed us most about the homeless we came to know and whose stories we have endeavored to tell is their resourcefulness and resilience. Confronted with minimal resources, often stigmatized by the broader society, frequently harassed by community members and by law enforcement officials, and repeatedly frustrated in their attempts to claim the most modest part of the American dream, they nonetheless continue to struggle to survive materially, to develop friendships, however tenuous, with their street peers, and to carve out a sense of meaning and personal identity. To emphasize this is not to romanticize the homeless and their lives but simply to recognize the many ways they confront their often brutalizing circumstances."

Indeed, the power of developing a *subsistence perspective* can be found across a wide spectrum of spaces and communities. Jeff Ferrell's (2006:178) recent auto-ethnographic foray into the world of 'scroungers' is highly illustrative, observing that the "widespread involvement of homeless folks . . . and independent scrap haulers in urban scrounging, and the sense of dignity and autonomy I found so often among them, suggest something of scrounging's value for individual sustenance." A particularly pointed application of these trends is realized in the homeless experience, where a definite sense of being a 'bricoleur' becomes quickly evident (Snow, et al. 1996:93):

> "Bricoleurs are persons who are 'adept at performing a large number of diverse tasks.' [T]hey do so with whatever resources and means are at their disposal. . . . Used metaphorically, bricoleur can designate any individual who devises unconventional but pragmatic solutions (bricolages) to pressing problems. We think the homeless – at least many of them – qualify for such designation because of their inventive and opportunistic cobbling together of a mix of income sources and survival routines from limited possibilities. It is this repertoire or bricolage that enables them to make do under very trying circumstances. . . . To understand the homeless as bricoleurs is not only consistent with the character of material survival on the streets, but shifts attention from their widely chronicled disabilities to the practices by which they survive. Viewed this way, homeless people look more like resourceful, fully human actors than mere incompetents."

Likewise, a journalistic account of homeless 'river-dwellers' in Tempe (MacDonald 2001) specifically notes that "these survivors constructed shelter from anything and everything they could find, including camp tents, tarps, wood, rocks, and even sun-baked mud" (see also Hopper, et al. 1985:194, analyzing the homeless' "adaptation practices," "improvisation," and "resourcefulness and resiliency").

Seemingly taking these lessons seriously, homeless lives "are mostly possessed with the details" (Herman 1997) of securing food, shelter, work, health, sanitation, and sleep. Such "survival strategies" (Ruddick 1996:43) and "subsistence activities" (Barak 1991:83) of the homeless have been frequent subjects of scholarly study and analysis (e.g., Wright 1997; Snow & Anderson 1993; Waldron 1991; Morris & Heffren 1988; Foscarinis, et al. 1999; Smith 1994). One of the more excruciating areas of investigation concerns the implications of the "unavailability of toilets open to the public" in many urban spaces (see Smith 1994:n.29); as Mike Davis (1992:163) notes, "public toilets have become the real frontline of the city's war on the homeless." It is apparent that, where the homeless are concerned, "few communities provide enough toilets" (VanderStaay 1992:2), and that "public toilets with unrestricted access have all but disappeared from the urban landscape" (Kawash 1998:332). Of course, as the chapter entitled 'When You Gotta Go' in Mitchell Duneier's quirky *Sidewalk* (1999) implies, and as Samira Kawash (1998:333) confirms, "because of the virtual absence of toilets, street dwellers are often forced to relieve themselves any way they can. Elimination becomes a crucial focus of street dwellers' activities." As some analyses have pointed out, even the weight of crime and punishment is not dissuasive when it comes to such basic bodily functions (see Smith 1994; Foscarinis, et al. 1999; Wachholz 2005), since there can be no deterrent effect in criminalizing basic *survival* (see Davis 1992:166). In a classic 'double bind' scenario (Arnold 1998:208; 2004), it appears that both the voluntary *and* involuntary acts of homeless people generate equivalent antipathy from the larger society, leaving them without viable domains of personhood.

Another basic aspect of survival, even (or perhaps more aptly, *especially*) for street people, is *work*, or more broadly, the method of maintaining one's material existence. For obvious reasons, homeless people often subsist by way of 'shadow work,' which includes day labor, panhandling, scavenging, peddling, selling plasma, dealing drugs, theft, prostitution, and 'dumpster-diving' (see Snow & Anderson 1993:145-170; Snow, et al. 1996; Fitzpatrick & LaGory 2000:143; Ferrell 2006; Borchard 2005:134; cf. Hopper, et al. 1985:211-14, on the "underground economy"). Other resources reported include social security, veteran's benefits, unemployment, welfare, and food stamps. Of course, resort to more institutional forms of income generation carry greater risks, perhaps explaining why surveys conducted by Snow, et al. (1996:90) reveal that nearly 60% of their homeless informants report engaging in some form of shadow work within a month. This parallels the suspicion street people often hold for shelters, drop-in centers, and other institutional sources for social services, at times viewing such options as involving "humiliating degradation rituals," and sometimes refusing any involvement with systemic services altogether (Wagner 1993:64; Wagner 1995:138); as Talmadge Wright (1997:221) similarly observes, "for many homeless, using social services . . . involved a humiliating process." In this light, Wagner (1993:64) perceives that even among the homeless willing to rely in part on social service agencies, they were mainly "involved in a complex pattern of resistance to bureaucratic institutions, tempered by occasional accommodation, moving back and forth from avoidance to manipulation."

Events in Tempe, interviews with its street people, and observations of its few service providers illustrate all of these trends, and add a few new wrinkles toward developing an understanding of subsistence, survival, and services in relation to the homeless. To take the last point raised above – resistance to services – an *ASU State Press* article (Zawicki 2000c) notes the inherent ambivalence: "While they speak of the benefits of outreach groups, the street kids do not reveal any need to be helped or changed." The same article quotes 'Doe,' 16, as saying, "I just don't trust the HomeBase people; they want to know all this stuff about you and write all this stuff down." HomeBase Youth Services is generally viewed as one of the more benign service entities, reflected in the remark from 'Kevin,' 15, that "they treat us like human beings when most people around here just ignore us" (in Beaver 2000). In evidence here again is that sense of ambivalence toward acceptance of services on the street.

It should be noted that HomeBase volunteers visit some of the most intractable locales in the Phoenix metropolitan area, including the spot infamously known as 'BoysTown' for its young male prostitution, CASS (Central Arizona Shelter Services) in downtown Phoenix, and Tempe's Mill Avenue (see Bland 1998). While there, in addition to doing some documentary casework to 'track' particular homeless youths' progress and/or regress, volunteers distribute free food, blankets, medicine, and bus passes to visit their drop-in center in Phoenix, where it is hoped that more permanent solutions than "crisis management" can be achieved. On the day that I participated in an outreach ride-along with HomeBase volunteers (June 13, 2001), we visited all of the locales noted above. In BoysTown, one of the volunteers remarked that "prostitution is a survival strategy" for many of the young homeless males there. At CASS, there was an ironic sidelight involving a prominent sign on the street near the facility warning that 'THE SERVING OF FOOD IN THIS AREA IS PROHIBITED!' And while on Mill Avenue, it was emphasized that the volunteers "don't do the work of the police," and that the food and supplies they provide come with no strings attached; it was also noted by one of the volunteers, however, that some of the Tempe merchants' groups who had donated money to HomeBase – most notably, the pro-business organization Downtown Tempe Community, Inc. (DTC) – had "made it clear that the money was given so that we would help move the street kids from the downtown area."

Nonetheless, Tempe more recently has slowly shifted its rhetoric and policies, hiring a 'Homeless Coordinator' and launching a pilot program called HOPE (Homeless Outreach Program Effort). Modeled after HomeBase's mobile service, the program includes consultation with area service providers and "referrals, advocacy, and transportation to services" (TCC 2006; James 2008). A number of other groups have begun operating in the city, including the Tempe Youth Resource Center, Project Homeless Connect, CAP (Community Action Program), and I-HELP (Interfaith Homeless Emergency Lodging Program). While these are indeed positive developments, and while the motivations of the people supporting these efforts are no doubt sincere and well-intentioned, it is still the case that the prevailing mood over the years among the city's policymakers generally has not been one of accommodation. In the three years that I collected articles and conducted interviews (1998-2001), there were many accounts revealing the city's basic hostility toward the street people in the downtown area, a phenomenon succinctly dubbed by one of my informants ('Leon' 2000) as "a crusade of demonization." For example, by early 1999, the *State Press* had reported that the last restroom on Mill Avenue open to the general public had been officially closed (Aas 1999; Boos 1998). One article (Boos) noted that the remaining "restrooms on Mill Avenue are located within places of business and are only for customers," while the other (Aas) quoted a 22-year old homeless man saying, "I think there should be a public bathroom here . . . when you've got to go, you've got to go." My own interview notes include Bill (2000) observing that "there ain't no public restrooms in this town nowhere;" Dante (2000) boasting about being able to use the Jack-in-the-Box bathroom once in a while; and Julie Cart (2001) noting that in addition to using Salvation Army bathrooms by day, some of the homeless had taken to using the restrooms at the Tempe Police station!

In terms of sleeping options, it remains the case that "there are no shelters anywhere in the city of Tempe" (Cart 2001). By late 1999, the sleeping and toilet issues for the downtown homeless had so intensified that it prompted me to write a guest column for the *State Press* entitled 'Sleepless in Tempe? Try the City Jail,' arguing that "while the City is busy cracking down on homeless people and transients, there's (literally) no place else in Tempe for them to go. . . . The combined net effect of these ongoing police crackdowns and the complete lack of homeless facilities in Tempe is that street people are punished for engaging in behavior (such as sleeping, procuring food, and going to the bathroom) that is essential to their survival. Moreover, in a perverse turn of public dollars at work, the Tempe City Jail has become a de facto shelter of last resort for some (un)lucky street people." The column concluded that "the City has deemed it more desirable to criminalize than socialize, more effective to lock up than provide shelter, and better policy to crack down than coddle. Compassion is seen as a sign of weakness and a plainly unprofitable endeavor."

As the year drew to a close, it was reported that Tempe was considering allocating $13,000 "for a study to find out how many homeless people are in the city and what they need" (Diaz 1999). The same article appropriately quotes 'meek' who noted that it shouldn't be that hard to figure out what the homeless need: "How about a shelter? That would be nice." Likewise interviewee Bill (2000): "How 'bout a 24-hour shelter with showers? They spent $200 million on an artificial lake but we can't get no shelter or showers?" Ditto 'Kevin' (2000): "So they spend fucking $88 million on a lake, but they can't put the money on a shelter or a shower or a bathroom?" Melee (2000), however, said that she wouldn't use a shelter, but that the city should just legalize urban camping, a sentiment echoed by Piper (2000) as well: "Sleeping?! In Tempe?! They don't want us to sleep here, they don't want us to sleep there – well, it's changed a lot, they put that fucking lake in, what the – a man-made lake right in the middle of a fucking desert! I think they put that lake in to get rid of us, to get rid of all the squatters. You know, every city, Tempe or wherever, should have a park just for the kids, like us. . . ." Previously, 'Hall,' 47, likewise told the *Arizona Republic* (Hermann 1999) that "he would rather stay in parks than live in a shelter. 'I've heard horror stories about those shelters,' he said" (cf. Arnold 1998:220: "A temporary solution – the shelter – represents the characteristics of discipline. Like a penal institution, a shelter can be the ultimate representation of the means [by] which the marginalized can be controlled, documented, observed, and molded"). As a *State Press* column (Rosenfeld 2000) plaintively inquired: "Why not just let them camp in the parks? They're not hurting anyone by sleeping. This area is blessed with at least some open space, which is depleting fast, so let them be."

On the political front, after the city council approved the funds for the homeless study, things seemed to grow quiet for a while – so quiet that the *State Press* ran an editorial in April 2000 entitled 'Tempe Ignores Its Homeless Population,' which argued that "with no functioning public shelter, or even a place where the shelterless can take a shower and wash clothes, Tempe would probably get a [low] rating" from its homeless. The silence finally broke in September of 2000, when the Tempe Community Council released Volume I of its 'Homeless Task Force Report,' which observed that "Tempe has no emergency shelters within its boundaries," that "many youth are fearful or reluctant to go into shelter programs," and that "the sum total of all the help being provided does not meet the current needs." The Task Force – which arose following then-Mayor Giuliano's State of the City address on February 11, 1999, calling for the appointment of a community task force in response to a public battle over the city's adoption of an ordinance that criminalized sitting on the sidewalks – concluded that the establishment of a Day Resource Center (complete with showers, bathrooms, laundry, and food pantry) was of paramount importance. The Task Force report also included a summary of the 'needs study' that had been commissioned and conducted in the interim. Among the more interesting findings:

- Over 90% report they live in Tempe. The length of time living in Tempe ranged from 15 days to 37 years with the average length of time being 4.5 years and the median being 2 years.
- Almost 80% have spent most of their time sleeping outside at campsites in town or on the outskirts of town or in the streets/alleys.
- The responses for type of work in the past two weeks include day labor, odd jobs, cleaning up litter, yard work, and selling plasma.
- The barriers to work include: "no ID, no home, not enough work in the area, alcoholic, going blind, don't fit in, staying clean, teeth problems, stroke, transportation, lack of clean clothes, pregnant, tools were stolen, people don't like homeless people, sleep patterns, looking after girlfriend, too hot, not enough work."
- Over 50% reported they are currently seeking work. Thirty percent reported trading and swapping as a source of income. 11% reported receiving gifts.

- Approximately 65% of respondents reported spending some time in a city or county jail.
- Over 80% believe shelters are needed in Tempe.
- A number of those expressing a need for shelter in Tempe said, for various reasons, they themselves would not wish to go into a shelter.
- When asked what they most needed right now the most common responses were shelter, job assistance, and medical assistance. Other responses were transportation and food.

The public release of the Task Force's findings generated a number of articles praising the report and its recommendations (e.g., Diaz 2000; Zawicki 2000a), including a column entitled 'Tempe Takes Positive Step in Dealing with Homelessness' (Rosenfeld 2000). Somewhat prophetically, however, the column also noted with typical *State Press* irony: "My question is, why has this taken so long? Look how quick it took for the entire Brickyard {a high-end development project} to be constructed on Mill [Avenue]. For the day resource center, no one has made plans for even a single brick, let alone a yard of them."

A Spike Out is Not a Hand Up

For a moment, it seemed as if progress was indeed being made, even including the street peoples' self-described needs in the formulation of alternatives and responses. And then, just two weeks before the city council was to decide whether to adopt the Homeless Task Force's recommendations, an atrocity happened that changed everything. As reported by Neil Zawicki (2000b) in the *State Press* on October 16th:

> "The Downtown Tempe Community, an association formed to promote business and quality of life in Tempe, put up spiked fences around the Salvation Army last week to prevent homeless people camping out, a move that has Salvation Army officials crying foul. The action stems from pressure by nearby businesses, which are frustrated by the presence of transients in and around their shops, said Rod Keeling, executive director of the DTC. . . . The spiked fences were installed on sitting areas that surround planters in front of the

> Salvation Army center. It is normally crowded with homeless people but was completely deserted Sunday. . . . 'If we're going to have a homeless service center, we need one that is well managed,' Keeling said. 'The Salvation Army has not managed the population, and to give them an environment where they are enabled to be there, I think, is wrong.'"

Were the spectacle of wrought iron spikes aimed directly at the homeless not so graphically poignant in itself (see Davis 1991, on "vicious out-turned spikes;" and Wachholz 2005 on 'prickly space' that is designed to "make people feel unwelcome"), it might be thought cynical to suggest that the timing here was equally revealing, in that the DTC asserted its corporate might *vis-a-vis* the 'homeless problem' just as the city council was poised to consider approval of a downtown day resource center, which by far would have been the most significant non-punitive step Tempe had taken in response to the homelessness issue. And indeed, in short order, a matter of mere days in fact, the spikes were removed, to headlines proclaiming 'Homeless Gripe, City Fences Fall' (Navarro 2000) and 'Tempe Takes Down Spiked Fences' (Zawicki 2000d). Apparently, the 'point' (pun intended) had sufficiently been made. And in the coming months, the DTC would in fact install spiked, rounded, horned, and otherwise discomfiting architectural amendments to most of the places (e.g., planters, benches) available for sitting anywhere in the downtown area (except of course restaurant sidewalk patios). Fittingly, a website called 'The Anti-Sit Archives' has documented in a comprehensive visual manner the range of creative architectural disincentives employed across the country.

At least the 'spike' issue in Tempe was in play long enough for DTC then-Executive Director Rod Keeling to state that "the canned goods the Salvation Army hands out 'enable' the homeless lifestyle" (Navarro 2000). To which Bill (2000) retorted, "You try living off that food!" But sentiments similar to Keeling's are not altogether uncommon, as an *Arizona Republic* article (Hermann 2000) noted: "Many valley residents not only wouldn't join [the church people feeding the homeless in a park], but resent what she and others like her are doing. They believe the many church groups that feed the homeless in Valley parks and neighborhoods do more harm than good. They say church outreach programs attract thousands of homeless people to areas they'd never frequented before." In this light, both Kress (1995:90) and the National Coalition for the Homeless (NCH 1997) describe how homeless service providers including 'the religious community' have been targeted by municipalities. Secular groups such as 'Food Not Bombs' that also feed the homeless free food in public places are similarly disdained, with the added dimension that such groups are often confronted by law enforcement and even arrested in pursuit of their efforts, as Wright (1997:193) describes: "Over 350 Food Not Bombs volunteers were arrested for distributing free food in San Francisco between September 1993 and September 1994." All of this antagonism to food providers led to a comprehensive report released in November 2007 by the National Law Center on Homelessness & Poverty (NLCHP) and the NCH, entitled 'Feeding Intolerance: Prohibitions on Sharing Food with People Experiencing Homelessness,' where it is poignantly asserted that: "Framing sharing food as a factor in enabling people to remain homeless is misleading. Food is not an addiction; food is necessary for survival. Depriving a person of food means that she must put all of her energy into obtaining food and less energy on improving other aspects of her life. Food sharing programs that reach out to those in public spaces may be the only way some homeless individuals can obtain healthy and safe food."

Despite the frequent antagonism and even criminalization of food providers, many remain undeterred, as the aforementioned *Arizona Republic* article (Navarro 2000) concluded: "'I've heard the criticisms of the 'experts' who say we're enabling the homeless to continue being homeless,' said Gary Bartlett, service ministries director for the Tempe Church of Christ. Bartlett was helping serve food Sunday at Moeur Park. 'Well, the experts have their opinions, but Christian churches must act as the Bible teaches, and it says to help the needy and suffering,' he said." As two of my informants concurred:

> Jocko: I'll never understand those Christians who celebrate the resurrection of their savior – who fed the poor – and now they decline food for the poor?
> Piper: They could at least give us respect as human beings . . . we still deserve love –

'Katy' (2000), 37, was philosophical about the little that she did receive to sustain her: "There are churches that'll come out here and help us, like with bedrolls, clothing. We're not asking for a whole lot, we're just asking that we're blessed every day that we can wake up every morning and smell a nice cool breath of air. Life is life, take it or leave it – so I pray over my food every day and I say thank you or whatever."

One informant felt the taint of the 'enabling' charge firsthand. Leon (2000) was the manager of the 'Daily Grind' coffee shop on Mill Avenue when I interviewed him. The shop was in a small courtyard with a few benches, near a piercing parlor and a vegetarian restaurant. 'The Grind' was known as a friendly space to many of the street kids I spoke with, and Leon in particular had a reputation for generosity and kindness, including letting kids 'slide' sometimes on purchases, giving them the bathroom key once in a while, or speaking on their behalf in conversations with other local merchants. For his efforts, Leon was harassed by the business community, to such a degree that he finally was forced to abandon his business: "I have been called an 'undesirable sympathizer' by some of the other business people, because when they say 'we gotta run those bums out,' I say, 'now just a minute.' . . . You know, this is such a newfangled clean city, they don't want this 'blight' aspect – the business people think if they provide services for the homeless it's only gonna attract more . . . ." Unlike Leon, as a full-time street person 'Nona' (2001) often experienced a more direct form of official dissuasion, lamenting that "once again, the police burned my tent and blankets and money from home – it's all gone, and I'm fucked." Likewise Katy (2000): "We've had different threats – like the cops'll go out and find our squats and burn all our clothing, our IDs, and then – at least the Salvation Army is nice enough to help us get new IDs." And in Prescott, Arizona nine officers were suspended for acts of harassment including pepper spraying and urinating on homeless camps over a period of months (Buric-Adam 2004).

Against these harsh realities, a brief word about the DTC's version of 'homeless outreach' is in order. As part of its program, the DTC hired an "ambassador to the homeless" whose function was to inform transients of local laws and rules, distribute cards entitled 'A HANDOUT IS NOT A HAND UP,' and provide phone numbers for some service providers (see Jones 1999; Prendergast 1999; DTC 1999). The text of the cards read: "In the long run, giving food to the homeless may hurt more than help. 'Street Resources' encourage life on the street and discourage the recipient from seeking real help" (DTC 1998). The Downtown Phoenix Partnership (DPP) oversaw a similar effort, distributing cards titled, 'Real Change . . . NOT Spare Change,' and noting that, "Your spare change may actually be hurting the person, by enabling him or her to delay seeking help" (Flashes 1998). Along these lines, the DTC's web page (circa 1999) stated that its 'Homeless Outreach Program' consisted of "a 5-part approach to dealing with both the truly homeless and the 'slackers,' or homeless youth":

- Contact and document each individual.
- Direct each individual to services and transport them.
- Consistently notify the individuals of the laws of Tempe and the Code of Conduct for downtown patrons.
- Act as the eyes and ears of the Tempe Police Department.
- Educate the public, local businesses, and other givers of the ramifications of providing 'street resources' to panhandlers, beggars, and unauthorized street vendors.

The DTC literature, again circa 1999, went on to note:

> "Through this program, we have been able to contact and document 86 people living on the streets of downtown Tempe, direct 20 people to various social services, transport 20 people to . . . other cities, arrange for the return of 5 runaways to their families, directly affect the arrest of 8 individuals engaged in illegal activity and provide information on criminal activity to the police officers assigned to the downtown. We also affected the removal of 15 individuals from private property through 'trespassing agreements' with private property owners."

With programs like this passing for 'outreach' (cf. Mitchell & Staeheli 2006:163, on similar efforts in San Diego), it's little wonder that street people are ambivalent and even disdainful of social service opportunities, as noted by Kurt, a homeless man in Phoenix (in Pela 2004): "You're not a human being to them, you're just a number that they use to get their funding." What happened with the Day Resource Center in Tempe wasn't likely to make them feel any more sanguine. Following the fence-spiking debacle, the mood around downtown took a bit of a surly turn. Suddenly, the idea of 'coddling' or 'enabling' the homeless didn't seem quite as appealing to the political elite in terms of the possible outcomes that a resource center might yield. My own frustrations and concerns led to an open letter to the Mayor and City Council before the crucial deliberations, where I asserted:

"The recommendation to establish a Day Resource Center is indeed a good start – but it is only a start. The needs of the homeless don't suddenly end at night; in fact, this is when their plight often grows most perilous. The Report omits any discussion of a 24-hour center or overnight shelter that is desperately needed in Tempe, and is lacking as to matters of health care, restrooms, and water. Despite being anxious to interpret the City's possible adoption of the Task Force recommendations as a sign of a 'spirit of assistance' and not one of persecution, it is hard not to question the sincerity of such efforts when the only true service provider in town (the Salvation Army) has been repeatedly harassed by the DTC, evidenced most recently by the spiked fences erected there last week. Is the City concerned about helping the homeless, or just helping businesses by removing the homeless from view?

The Task Force Report also does not mention the continued enforcement of anti-homeless ordinances such as 'aggressive panhandling' and especially 'urban camping.' I have witnessed and been informed about numerous arrests for urban camping, some of which occurred where homeless individuals were not actually sleeping but merely resting against a backpack while sitting in a public space. In addition to the apparent unconstitutionality of the 'no sitting on the sidewalk' ordinance, it should be understood that many courts have ruled that it is unconstitutional to arrest someone for urban camping when there are no alternatives provided.

In the end, it appears the City has forgotten that diversity includes the homeless; that 'public space' is essential and carries rights of access for all; and that 'compassion' is not equivalent to enabling but is about treating people with respect and helping to restore their dignity. Too often in the Report and in City Hall dialogues, homelessness is referred to as a problem and compared to things like 'fixing broken windows.' Certainly there are aspects of the issue that are problematic, but when we view the homeless as inanimate objects and not as human beings, then we are a long way from finding a workable solution that promotes self-reliance and respects the rights of all citizens – especially those who are among the least politically powerful or economically dominant."

Finally, after years of wrangling and months of debate, the city council on October 26, 2000, "accepted the report and its recommendations and asked staff to move the recommendations through the budget process," with some council members expressing hope that "from this day forward [Tempe] will do right" by its homeless residents. This eventually led to the hiring of a 'coordinator' and the establishment of more local services, as noted above. Still, despite the *Republic* opining that "a day resource center for the homeless likely will be built in Tempe" (Nelson 2006) and the city laying out five site options, the project was effectively scuttled and remains a non-starter (James 2008).

Communities of Coping: Mutual Aid and Homeless Heterotopias

For the homeless, faced with micro-level struggles for basic survival, as well as macro-level pressures of ostracism and regulation, the construct of 'community' becomes a necessity. Contrary to prevailing dogma, when confronted with hardship and a sense of struggle, the outcome is more often solidarity than brutality (cf. Kropotkin 1972). Despite desperate struggles for subsistence – or perhaps because of them – street people often evolve "complex social organizations" (Duneier 1999:162) based on "the desire to help each other" (VanderStaay 1992:185). Sometimes street communities develop reactively, as a response to the lack of and mistrust for service and outreach programs, while other aspects reflect greater proactivity in their evolution (see Stein & McCall 1994) – but in either case the aim appears to be "the formation of a homeless community free of institutional shelter restraints" (Wright 1997:297). Studying young homeless people in Hollywood, Susan Ruddick (1990:188) observed: "The homeless gather together, develop networks which often confound the objectives of service providers." In a study of homeless park dwellers in Orange County, California, Wright & Vermund (1996:130) noted that, "when asked why they clustered together, residents responded that they needed mutual protection. It was this mutual support provided by the network that constituted one form of local resistance to the authoritative attempt to exclude and separate the homeless. Informal social networks, developed out of survival needs, provided a means of socializing and passing the time for park residents."

Homeless communities have been described as "intricate and cohesive," made up of "considerable social networks" (Wagner

1993:19), and premised upon "collective sharing and mutual aid" (Wagner 1995:141). In his study of the 'Checkerboard Square' homeless community in 'North City,' David Wagner (1993:148) specifically identifies three foundational community attributes: (1) *sociability*: "street people actively seek each other out to spend time together and to participate in various primary groups;" (2) *mutual aid*: "norms of sharing food, cigarettes, alcohol, drugs, information about social services and benefits, money, and housing (if and when available) existed in all subcultures of this community;" and (3) *solidarity*: "the community saw itself as an oppressed group and under certain circumstances was capable of uniting for joint action." Similarly, among 'hippie tramps,' Snow & Anderson (1993:188) noted a "coherent subcultural group" premised upon self-sufficiency, mobility, sociability, countercultural values, and a "sense of solidarity."

An analysis of Tempe's homeless community is similarly revealing. At the outset, Tempe's homeless population is a diverse lot that in many ways mirrors homeless populations elsewhere (in particular, in the western United States), but is nonetheless unique in some respects. The Tempe Homeless Task Force Report, for instance, observes that the city has a "homeless youth population" (ages 18-23), comprising almost 40% of its total homeless population, possessing a high degree of "visibility on downtown streets" that renders it distinct from other homeless youth populations generally perceived as being characterized by "invisibility" (e.g., Harter, et al. 2005). Sometimes this homeless youth population is referred to colloquially as 'crusties,' 'gutter punks,' 'street kids,' or the more localized label, Mill Rats (see Holthouse 1998a). My own interviews and conversations with this youth segment of Tempe's homeless population indicate that they are primarily white, largely male, and often from middle-class backgrounds – although many claim to have disavowed any benefits attendant to their race, class, and gender locations, including having 'broken off' relations with their families (e.g., Dante 2000; Melee 2000; Nona 2001; Piper 2000; 'Yogi' 1999; 'Half-pint' 2000). Beyond this youth contingent, Tempe's overall homeless population includes many people of color, families, middle-aged women, and the elderly (e.g., Katy 2000; Bill 2000; 'Blossom' 1998; cf. Leon 2000). Thus, while Tempe's homeless youths are often taken by the media, city officials, and the business community as representative of the whole population, it cannot be overstated that whenever 'the homeless' are referred to categorically in this text, it should be understood that this is simply a linguistic convenience and not an attempt to portray them as a monolithic entity lacking demographic diversity.

Taken together, Tempe's homeless residents may accurately be described as "a complex geography of informational networks" that work to "ensure access to resources for members of a community stretched across space" (cf. May 2000:754). Such a definition includes as 'resources' both tangible items such as food or shelter as well as information about where to secure these basics of survival. In terms of the tangibles, it has been said of some Tempe homeless that "they do look out for each other and make sure 'everyone gets.' This includes placing any unneeded items on top of a cement pedestal that serves as the community Goodwill" (MacDonald 2001). Other studies note the practices of homeless teens, "who band together in groups or pool belongings to squat an abandoned building" (VanderStaay 1992:82). Interestingly, such mutual aid practices often extend across sub-subcultural boundaries, as Kevin (1999) described to me: "We all stick together out here, we hang together pretty tight – even though there's lots of different groups, like goths and slackers and hippie kids, and there's devil worshipping kids, and there's gutter punks – but we all get along . . . yeah, we all stick together, we all get along, it's pretty much all good." Spending time on Mill Avenue, one immediately sees the results of such expressions of solidarity, as meager supplies of food, water, blankets, drugs, and clothing are routinely shared.

Information is especially important in communities that are transient and ever-changing. A wealth of secrets, scams, and service insights are core components of the community, being passed on to new arrivals who invariably pass the same along to the next wave of newcomers. In this way, by evolving an organic oral history of local knowledge and lore, the community is able to sustain itself across time, throughout space, and during the many upheavals among its members. As Piper, 20, explained: "When I first got on the streets I know the only reason I survived is because I shut up. The [older homeless] have been here so long you kinda look up to them, they're the ones who are gonna show you the ropes. It's only because I shut up and listened that I'm still here. There's almost like an initiation thing" (see also Harter, et al. 2006:319, discussing "street smarts" and quoting homeless informants who note how important it is "to know how to keep your mouth shut" and "how to bite your tongue in certain situations"). Crucial in such initiation scenarios is the presence of the "home guard tramp . . . who stayed around town year in and year out. When a man arrived in a new town, it was the home guard tramp he looked for to find out about police practices or to seek other helpful information" (Spradley 1970:77). Among my informants in Tempe, Prem (1999) seemed to serve this function, having been on the streets for over 15 years. He says that he "chooses his lifestyle," and often refuses offers of assistance. Perhaps due to his notoriety in the community, his passive demeanor, and his articulate ruminations, law enforcement agents seem to 'tolerate' Prem and let him do his 'thing' – which includes ongoing research on street life and health care for the homeless. Kevin, 34, is another likely candidate: "I'm one of the originals, been here four years – I'm probably the most popular homeless person out here now!"

In this regard, studies and journalistic accounts of homeless community life often depict a strong sense of kindredness among street people. Homeless teens in particular "often report finding more love and family in each other than they have ever known" (VanderStaay 1992:82). As Piper (2000) observed: "Jeez, you know, I got more love now, I got more of a family type of thing than with my own family." Likewise, a *State Press* article (Beaver 2000b) describes Tempe's homeless kids as "an extended family [who] love each other." The article goes on to quote 'Rudie,' 15, who notes that "Tempe kids are good at taking care of each other. . . . These people here are my family. These guys take care of me – they give me affection, and some of them are like my brothers." As the article concludes, "The Mill family has members filling nearly every role – little sisters, protective fathers, and concerned mothers." As 'Kat' notes (in Ferrell 2001a:171): "[My friends on Mill] are nicer than all the Babylon people, more about brotherly love than in their material world. It's all about friendship, that's what counts." Such views are apparent in other fluid 'communities' like the Rainbow Family (see Niman 1997) – and in fact Snow & Anderson (1993:188) note that there is a definite sense of overlap between homeless communities and the Rainbow Family, recalling that "many of them spent hours discussing 'Rainbows.'"

This raises the further point that every community, even the most transient, has some sense of a moral code at work among its members. Homeless enclaves, which generally lack any institutional, bureaucratic system for enforcing norms, tend to rely on informal standards such as "what goes around, comes around" (Snow & Anderson 1993:189), basically comprising what has been termed a "karmic code" involving a "norm of reciprocity" (Snow & Anderson 1993:107). More bluntly, as Tempe's Katy (2000) describes it, "shit on me, shit on somebody else, god'll getcha for it." Reliance on such loose norms can often be tenuous, especially in circumstances that are already difficult and fraught with danger. Nonetheless, as 'Jocko' (2000) maintains: "We can police ourselves – we got our own community." Leon (2000), however, waxed more nostalgic about how changes in Tempe have impacted the homeless community's sense of self-governance:

> L: It used to be that the kids were self-policing, like "chill out man, you're gonna ruin it for us all," but now it's like this "don't judge me" attitude that they actually get from society.
> RA: So the evolution is away from community on the streets?
> L: A little, like in society itself nowadays, and every time the city displaces whatever community does exist, new people come in with even less a sense of community, not like when it was more of a mom-and-pop feeling down here – they've destroyed a sense of community.

In this sense of 'destroying community' on the streets, it must not be overlooked that in many cases "the police, relentlessly lobbied by downtown merchants and developers, have foiled every attempt by the homeless and their allies to create safe havens or self-governed encampments," such as with 'Justiceville' in Los Angeles, which was characterized by its maintenance of a "pacific social order" and even a "rudimentary 'government'" (Davis 1991; Ropers 1988; see also Norse 2001 and Norse & Johnson 2002, reporting from Santa Cruz that "Camp Paradise, the homeless-run, self-help encampment sheltering 50-70 people," has been under constant attack from the city council and law enforcement, and generally "faces exile" at every turn). During the brief period of its existence, the 63 individuals comprising Justiceville attempted to create a "self-sufficient homeless community based on food sharing, an affirmation of dignity, and personal empowerment" (see Glaser 1987; cf. Ropers 1988). Before its unofficial 'leaders' were arrested, its makeshift houses and other structures mercilessly bulldozed, and its homeless residents forcibly "returned to the streets," Justiceville represented a model for a "workable society" that provided for its members a brief "chance to be human again" (Glaser 1987; cf. Davis 1990; see generally Ropers 1988).

Another significant part of homeless communities is the expansive and inclusive definition of *community* that is often applied: "Homeless people usually have a much more inclusive definition of community, which includes those with homes and those without" (VanderStaay 1992:186). My interview with Piper (2000) made this clear:

> "People around here, you just try to speak to them like a 'normal' person, a person-to-person thing, not as like a homeless person to a yuppie thing, just to stop 'em and say 'hey, how's it going' – and they have to have the type of attitude like you're a piece of shit. But there's some beautiful people – I try to be about love, I try not to be like 'that fucking yuppie,' I try to give love to everyone – it just doesn't seem to work sometimes cuz I don't get it back. I love people – these city council members, and all them, they treat us like we're pieces of shit, not with respect – you have to have respect for EVERYBODY, just for them being human beings . . . ."

More confrontational feelings are to be found as well. As Kevin (2000) asserts: "I wanna see one of these rich snobby yuppies lose everything for a week, not even a fuckin' comb on you or a wallet or money, nothing, and just go out and see what the fuck we've got to deal with, see how you're gonna get your shitters, get your food, get yourself cleaned up, how you're gonna survive. That's one of my dreams, to see one of these rich snobby – I mean, I'm not discriminating against them personally – they're just not kind to us." Likewise Katy (2000):

> "A lot of times they'll harass us, because a lot of the yuppie students don't want us here, and I think 'that's a joke' – I mean, where is the homeless gonna go? They don't want us here, they think we're crowding their town; the locals are really a pain in the ass, cuz they haven't been in our shoes, they don't know, they ain't been there – why don't they trade places with me? Just to see how bad it is, just to see how you guys like living in the gutter the way we are. I look at it this way, when you start living out here, where we're at, then you put your fuckin' money where your mouth is."

Yet Kevin (1999), who had been arrested 43 separate times in a three-year period, still maintained his communitarian spirit toward the police: "Hey man, cops are human beings like we are." 'Wolf', 50, a homeless man in Santa Cruz, California, similarly notes (in Herman 1997): "I respect these business owners. They are watching out for themselves because they are being taken advantage of sometimes." The article goes on to note that Wolf "speaks of the police with similar equanimity": "They ticket people sometimes. It's their job. I understand that. They don't make the rules, they just enforce them." A recent study of homeless males reflects similarly nuanced views of law enforcement, noting that some see the police as "decent" and "alright," whereas others experienced interactions that were "hurtful" and "degrading" (Phipps 2007:58-60). Still, a sense of inclusivity seems to pervade, as 'Cosmo' told the *Arizona Republic* (in Navarro 2000), "People need to look at us like human beings – like they are." Journalist Don Henninger (2000) and a party of public officials noticed this same spirit during their brief sojourn with the Mill Avenue enclave: "From the moment we arrived we were among friends."

What's surprising isn't that the homeless develop strong bonds among themselves, although such are indeed mildly miraculous when due consideration is given to the circumstances under which they are often formed. What really intrigues is how so many homeless people maintain positive, even loving views toward many of the individuals who are essentially their oppressors, or at least their antagonists. Despite all the degradations and depravations, the overt animus and official hostility, the homeless still recognize that everyone concerned constitutes a member of the community. Of course, merchants' groups and political lobbies (such as the DTC in Tempe) explicitly construct street people as *not* part of the community, and therefore as subject to displacement and exclusion. Unquestionably – so much so that it is a bit awkward to have to argue the point – there is no going forward in any positive way absent a firm understanding that the homeless "are members of the community too" (Waldron 2000). Perhaps even more so, as Tempe's Leon once noted: "A homeless transient living on the same strip of beach for years is more a part of the community than the just-moved-in yuppies telling the police to get rid of him. If you are part of a community, you are always at home" (quoted in Bolig 1995).

As the foregoing implies, a central feature of homeless communities is that they are not only concerned with subsistence, but with resistance as well (cf. Snow & Mulcahy 2001). As Susan

Ruddick's (1996:57-60,194) research suggests, "ethnographic studies reveal the creativity in the range of place-making tactics that the homeless deploy to survive," representing a "tactical use of space" in which their "mere presence" works to "subvert the meaning of structures that were not intended for them" (cf. Mitchell 2003:182). This is the macro-level of resistance, although it plainly arises from and is interconnected with the micro-level realization that, for the homeless, "the body emerges as the stake and the site of the contest over public space" (Kawash 1998:323). In this regard, Wagner (1993:148) observes that "the [homeless] community can be characterized as a culture of resistance whose adaptations to mistreatment in the family, in the workplace, and by the state are structured around its insights into societal hostility and its rejection of the conventional wisdom about the family, the work ethic, and the 'American Dream' generally." The pervasive reality of these "cultures of resistance on the streets" (Wagner 1995) stands in stark contrast with dominant definitions of the homeless as pathological or as victims of 'dislocation' and 'disaffiliation' (e.g., Grunberg 1998), and often appears as a form of "collective action" (Snow & Mulcahy 2001:163) comprising a nascent "loosely organized social movement" that "may overlap with other social movements and currents in American society not directly related to poverty and homelessness" (Wagner 1995:141).

A particularly evocative image of homeless communities derives from Foucault's invocation of the concept of *heterotopias* as sites of identity construction and the creative contestation of power relations in society (see Wright 1997:51; Ruddick 1996:54-6). In her early work on homeless teens, Ruddick (1990:188) observes that "[homeless] gathering places share several qualities with Foucault's heterotopias. They are at once spaces of deviation, often obscured from view literally or ontologically, and they contain within them, in an 'impossible space,' a large number of 'fragmentary possible worlds.'" In more general terms, heterotopias have been analyzed and explained as sites that are incongruous, paradoxical, transgressive, ambivalent, uncertain, multiple, mysterious, dangerous, marginal, perfect, and impossible (see Hetherington 1997:41). Applying such frameworks to homeless communities in particular, Talmadge Wright (1997:52) concludes that "when the very poor begin to move, organize, or demonstrate, such spaces cease being simple heterotopias of 'difference' and instead become what I would term 'resistant heterotopias.'" In other words, when the homeless embrace the values of *agency* and *community* and organize themselves accordingly, such moments are inherently resistant and subversive – a fact apparently not lost on authorities and officials.

Concentrating (on) Space

One of the most common, and perhaps even predominant, methods for dealing with the 'homeless problem' is the enclosure and designation of some forlorn and forgotten section of the city as a kind of 'Skid Row' redux, where the homeless and other social 'detritus' can pass their days mostly out of proximity to the gentry class (e.g., Ellickson 1996, advocating the establishment of 'red zones' to manage and segregate homeless and deviant populations). As Snow & Anderson (1993:103) explain, "Marginal space is ceded both intentionally and unwittingly to the powerless and propertyless. It is ceded intentionally for the purpose of containment and control, as was the case with the traditional skid row." Likewise Wright (1997:193), who perceives: "One set of strategic practices pushes the homeless out of areas of concern for redevelopers and local government officials while another set of practices concentrates them into controllable areas where they may be assimilated, or at the very least controlled." Richard Ropers (1988:207) quotes sources describing one such locale in Los Angeles as "a concentration camp for segregating the poor" and as "a camp gulag for the homeless." Wachholz refers to similar efforts as attempts at "legal segregation" that seek to "ghettoize the homeless."

In direct opposition to the spirit of homeless resistance, officials thus have often sought to create and impose 'concentrated' spaces that essentially constitute "a homogeneous terrain of surveillance and discipline" (Wright 1997:53). Both Wright (1997:53) and Ruddick (1996:54) invoke the graphic phrase 'service dependent ghetto' to describe such spaces, and specifically counterpose the positive notion of heterotopia as a remedy to the stigmatization of the ghetto. But this issue of 'ghetto versus heterotopia' is not merely a semantic one, since the 'services' available in the ghetto are, as Wagner (1995:141) indicates, "not an answer. Rather these very institutions are at the heart of the problem." As Ruddick (1990:188) likewise observes, "the new homeless bring with them different sets of survival tactics, coping mechanisms, including intermittent employment, ties to community, friends, lovers, and preferences for a range of different sites within the city, better suited to their survival than Skid Row." All of this begins to suggest why homeless people are often suspicious of and reluctant to accept officially-sanctioned, institutional services (cf. James 2008).

Despite the overt taint of 'concentration' and 'ghettoization,' a regional 'homeless campus' has been constructed in downtown Phoenix. As the *Arizona Republic* reported (Hermann 2000b) when the concept was still in its infancy: "An unusual alliance of business leaders, public officials and homeless advocates is considering relocating the homeless to a new 'campus'. . . . The ambitious plan would have two goals: remove the homeless from the path of downtown redevelopment and provide them a cluster of services." A supporting editorial one week later (Arizona Republic 2000) similarly speculated that "removing about 900 homeless men clears the way for downtown redevelopment and revitalization." Other cities have floated similar 'push-pull' plans, including one in Austin, Texas, that would "provide a place to take the 'homeless by choice' out of downtown and into a heated concrete pavilion in an area where tourists and taxpayers never have to venture" (see Duff 1999), and another in Key West, Florida, where downtown tourism has led to local homeless camps being *pushed* out of existence, while the individual homeless are simultaneously being *pulled* into a new city-sponsored 'safe zone' that is "about 1½ miles from downtown, behind the jail and near a landfill dubbed Mount Trashmore" (Carlson 2004). Academic studies of the "geography of homelessness" have likewise observed forces of both 'dispersion' and 'concentration' (e.g., Lee & Price-Spratlen 2004).

Still, underscored by an *ASU State Press* editorial expressly stating that "we won't speculate about Phoenix's intentions in moving the homeless" (2000a), the local media in Arizona largely promoted the campus concept (e.g., Diaz 2001a). Aside from predictably unfriendly responses from some residents in the neighborhood (e.g., McCloy 2001, quoting residents lamenting 'infestation;' Diaz 2001b, noting residents said it would "further undermine their neighborhood"), only a few dissenting opinions to the 'campus' plan appeared in the media, including a letter to the *Arizona Republic* (April 29, 2000) from a representative of a church that sometimes feeds the homeless noting that the plan "places profit ahead of human compassion;" and a quote from a former County Supervisor observing that, "if placed there, the homeless will only be out of sight and out of mind. It would be unfair to the residents in the area and to the homeless" (in Hermann 2000b).

Much like the battle over the Tempe day resource center, the implementation of the Phoenix campus plan didn't entirely proceed as originally conceived. In addition to increasing neighborhood hostility toward both the project and the homeless themselves (see Zoellner & Diaz 2001, describing one family who have taken to using "water sprinklers to douse the loiterers"), political wrangling over funding and precise location stalled the project for years. One important step had been to move the proposed campus to a site "which has been Phoenix's unofficial nucleus for the homeless for the past quarter of a century . . . it has been a homeless haven since the early 1980s, when 800 urban refugees settled in a lot that came to be known as 'Tent City'" (Zoellner & Diaz 2001). "In every city, this is the area where the homeless congregate," one the project's architects told the Republic (in McCloy 2001). The same former County Supervisor, described as "one of the leaders of the effort" in an apparent political and philosophical about-face, concurred: "We're not going to bring in anything that's not already there. We're just going to make it cleaner and more modern" (in Zoellner & Diaz 2001). As the project moved toward implementation, a *Republic* editorial (2002) touted the campus concept since "it would clean up the eyesore that extends for blocks." A letter to the editor from the same time frame by the project's ostensible coordinator more bluntly observed that "the campus will provide an environment that will centralize services for people away from the downtown business and events areas." Finally, in announcing the groundbreaking in late 2003, another *Republic* editorial (2003) reemphasized its positive spin on the project, calling it a "campus for dignity" and noting that it is a step meant to help "solve" homelessness.

But as it stood when initially proposed, the area designated for the campus – reminiscent of the 'skid row' idea throughout history – was observed to be "infested, unsafe, and uncontrollable," according to a county human services director (in McCloy 2001; see also NCH/NLCHP 2002:95, noting that in Phoenix "city officials attempt to displace homeless individuals from downtown or tourist areas using many tactics. They have attempted to relocate all of the homeless services to a 'campus' that will provide medical care, food, shelter and employment programs for homeless individuals. Homeless people are relocated to an undesirable area of town surrounded by a dog pound, the county jail and a rendering plant"). Of course, the whole point of the 'concentration campus' is to control the uncontrollable through surveillance and sedation (Arnold 1998; 2004); thus, the Phoenix plan for the campus included "specific entrances and exits, with a shaded area where the homeless could watch television," as well as an on-site police substation so that "anybody on the campus would know there is the potential for police to be there" (McCloy 2001; see also Arizona Republic 2002, lauding the campus concept and its "police presence"). The dystopian implications of such efforts were not lost on Tempe's street denizens, including the perceptive and colorful Kevin (2000):

> K: I heard they were fucking building some – homeless campus, some shit like that – that's bullshit, it's gonna be *Escape from New York*, I can already see it –
> RA: It's like they're building a homeless ghetto?
> K: Yeah, it's fuckin' right there, next to all the jails – they're gonna have it fenced in, and I heard they're just gonna pick people up who are homeless, and you can't leave that place –
> RA: You check in, but you don't check out?
> K: Yeah, you can check out, but you can never leave . . . .

A recent article (Cohn 2007) likewise quotes a local homeless woman noting that official offers "to buy bus tickets" to the campus are merely attempts by the city "to rid itself of the homeless." Kathleen Arnold (1998:201,210-11) views such projects as "internment camps" bent on achieving the "erasure" of the homeless by "encouraging their obscurity." Tempe's Bill (2000) believes that "the homeless campus is basically a concentration camp," and that "it's becoming like Gestapo Germany in Tempe," a point echoed by Stoner (1995:161): "Homeless sweeps are reminiscent of holocaust roundups in Nazi Germany."

Public Space Perils: Living in the Open . . . Living in Oblivion

The prospect of a 'concentration campus' is a stark reminder that the homeless are generally and repeatedly subjected to "violent processes of containment, constriction, and compression that seek not simply to exclude or control the homeless but rather to efface their presence altogether" (Kawash 1998:330). Indeed, a sense of routine pain and flagrant violence often pervades the homeless experience, as Waldron (1991) notes: "Lack of freedom is not all there is to the nightmare of homelessness. There is also the cold, the hunger, the disease and lack of medical treatment, the danger, the beatings, the loneliness, the shame, and the despair." Some have even "been burned alive while sleeping on park benches" (VanderStaay 1992:4), while others recall being "spit in my face" (Katy 2000) and having "the shit beat out of me" (Piper 2000). In a recent study, Wachholz (2005) documents frequent episodes of "hate crime victimization" against the homeless, including being "hit in the face" and called "sluts" and "pieces of shit." And then there are the episodes that are nearly too brutal to describe:

> RA: Do you see a lot of people out here selling their bodies?
> Katy: Yeah, male and female. I seen some young girls out here gettin' pregnant; some places will even pay for your abortions. I've seen girls give babies up for adoption too.
> RA: What's the worst thing you've ever seen out on the street in the time you've been homeless?
> K: I've seen, okay, this child was 12 years old, her father gave her AIDS, she turned around and hung herself on the Mill Avenue bridge, she slit her own throat, put the rope 'round her neck and just hung herself –
> RA: Was she a street kid?
> K: Yeah, she was a runaway and stuff, her father'd been sexually molesting her since she was a baby. . . . So I buried her on the north side of the mountain, in an unmarked grave – she was 12 years old when she died, nobody really cared –

"An unmarked grave. . . ." In many ways this is a succinct metaphor for the dark side of life as a homeless person, a logical permutation of the simple fact that "little in the lives of homeless men and women takes place behind closed doors" (Passaro 1996:85), yielding a condition of having "no place to perform elementary human activities like urinating, washing, sleeping, cooking, eating, and standing around" (Waldron 1991). In analyzing 'stigma management strategies' of the homeless, Anderson & Snow (1994:138) conclude: "Lacking the resources to secure and maintain their own shelter, they are forced to conduct much of their daily lives in public, where they find themselves subject to pervasive stigmatization." Constrained to exist in public places, the homeless, once stigmatized, are constant targets of regulation, criminalization, expulsion, and annihilation (see Mitchell 2003:167). They are at once exceedingly obvious, and yet ghost-like in their transparency; "both visible and invisible at the same

time" (Miller 1991:164). In the end, "their private use of public space tests democracy's promise of universal access in a very literal fashion" (Crawford 1995:8), a promise that remains largely unrealized.

The implications of this are clear: to be homeless is to be confronted with the reality of having, quite literally, "nowhere else to go" (Waldron 2000; cf. Simon 1995:727), "no place to be" (Mitchell 2003:171), "of no longer having the right to occupy the earth" (Arnold 1998:171), of having "lost entitlement to any existential ground whatsoever" (Davis 1991) – of being, in essence, '*lost in space*.' An *ASU State Press* editorial (2004) noted that Tempe "needs to realize that it can't round up all its homeless and send them whimpering into the sunset;" as Katy (2000) muses: "What're they gonna do, put us on a rocket ship and send us to Mars? I mean, where the heck is the homeless gonna go, besides Tempe, Arizona?" Likewise 'Judy,' sitting on a Mill Avenue sidewalk, from an interview with the *Student Press* (McIntyre 1999): "Millions of us people sit here. Where else are we supposed to go?" Like another 'homeless resident' of Mill Avenue laments (in Reed & Venable 2001), "They kick us out of everywhere we go and then they tell us we can't even sit on the sidewalks. No matter where we're at, we're not supposed to be there. Where are we supposed to stay if we're homeless?" As one of Wachholz's (2005) informants opined, "I feel like I'm losing my place on the planet."

Extending the point further, Kawash (1998:326) similarly reflects that "there is no place in the contemporary urban landscape for the homeless to be," since "to be without a home is to be without that domain of the private into which the public subject is supposed to be able to withdraw; to be homeless is thus to be thrust into the public without recourse. The question of homelessness is therefore necessarily always also a question of public space – of who the public is, of who may inhabit public space, and of how such space will be constituted and controlled" (Kawash 1998:325; see also Arnold 1998:114-5). Waldron (2000) likewise observes that homeless people are those who "have no private space" and are thus left with "no alternative but to be and remain and live all their lives in public," a pointed echoed by Baron (2004:284): "The homeless live in a legal status that might be called 'no property.'" As Kawash (1998:320) explains, "People who are homeless – without private homes and therefore by definition residents of public space – [are subject to] increasingly violent forms of exclusion from public spaces," as Blomley (2004:4) concurs: "Their world . . . is an intrinsically vulnerable and negative one, premised on the ever-present logic of exclusion." Viewed against this backdrop of the rampant preclusion of basic survival acts in public such as sleeping, eliminating, sitting, begging, and eating (see Blomley 1994:55; Mitchell 2003), the dilemma becomes apparent: "The homeless are excluded from all of the places governed by private property. . . . Since private places and public places between them exhaust all the places that there are, there is nowhere that these actions may be performed by the homeless person" (Waldron 1991). In this light, as Waldron concludes, "such a person would not be permitted to exist."

Non-existence. This is the apocalyptic horizon of the homeless experience. A 2001 *Arizona Republic* editorial entitled 'Give Hope to the Homeless' almost reads like an epitaph, or at least a post-mortem description: "Without purpose in a world ever rushing headlong to do everything at once, the homeless serve only to provide the occasional twinge of guilt or remorse. They too had places to go . . . once. They too had people to see when they populated the real world." Such ruminations conjure up dystopian images of wraith-like beings, forced into ever shrinking spaces, confronted with extinction at every turn – "apocalyptic visions of a deterritorialized homeless people on a forced march to nowhere" (Ruddick 1996:42). In Samira Kawash's words (1998:327), "The homeless are forced into constant motion not because they are going somewhere, but because they have nowhere to go. Going nowhere is simultaneously being nowhere; homelessness is not only being without home, but more generally without place."

How might we evaluate the import of such stark and moving images? For a moment, picture the canary in the coal mine, being the first to feel the chill of death from the gases in the shaft. In a sense that makes for an unfortunate simile, the homeless, forced to occupy and perform myriad essential functions in public space, appear as the first to feel the deleterious effects of forces that work to exert control over those spaces through privatization, regulation, and policing. In many ways, the nature of the spaces themselves – public, open, unclaimed, unconquered, anarchic – represent features likewise associated with the homeless as well. Thus, in a feat of suspicious synergy, both the spaces and the people who occupy them are subject to constant attack (cf. Mitchell 2003), intended to result in the elimination and erasure of the perceived threat. The next two chapters explore these related themes, beginning with the erosion of public space and continuing with the attempt to criminalize the 'social problem' of homelessness.

CHAPTER TWO

Urban Ecology and Public Space

Disney, Development, and Dystopia

In this chapter the discussion turns from a focus on 'the homeless' themselves to the spaces they are often constrained to occupy. Due to their visibility in 'public space' and the shrinking nature of that realm, homeless people frequently find themselves literally on the front lines of the struggle to preserve spaces that are open equally to everyone regardless of status. Urban spaces in particular manifest a complex and dynamic 'ecology' that is comprised of people, culture, architecture, technology, and the natural environment. Taken together, these spheres interact in the city to create both opportunities and challenges, often cohering around processes including gentrification, redevelopment, and privatization.

Public Space: The Final Frontier?

"Not all city life is modern; but all modern life is city life, [which] contains always an element of risk and adventure. City life is carried on by strangers among strangers" (Bauman 1995:126). Accordingly, as alluded to in the opening of the previous chapter, "the experiential ambiguity of the postmodern city rebounds in the postmodern ambivalence of the stranger" (Bauman 1995:138). Lyn Lofland similarly characterizes city life as 'A World of Strangers,' and specifically notes that "the city's *public space* is the locus of the world of strangers" (1973:20), positing that public space is comprised of "those areas of a city to which, in the main, all persons have *legal access*" (1973:19). In particular, such areas include *streets* (Lofland 1973:19; Lofland 1998:186-7), *parks* (Lofland 1973:19), and especially *sidewalks* (e.g., Duneier 1999), as well as places of "public accommodation" (Lofland 1973:19) (see generally Carr, et al. 1992:79-84). Jeremy Waldron (1991) similarly describes the concept of *common property* as "places where anyone may be," including "streets, sidewalks, subways, city parks, national parks, and wilderness areas," closely paralleling the "traditional public fora" recognized in First Amendment jurisprudence as foundational spaces for expressive activities (see McCarthy & McPhail 2006; cf. Mitchell 1996b).

In light of their historically open and egalitarian quality (Waldron 1991), public spaces have often been important sites for communication, contestation, and community building (Mitchell 1995; 2003). Nonetheless, Mitchell (1995:116, 1996b:155-6) also contends that "public space has long been a place of exclusion, no matter how much democratic ideology would like to argue otherwise." Similarly, Koskela (2000:261 n.2) asserts that "there is a need to be critical about the extent to which public spaces were ever public and the extent to which 'the death of public space' might be a largely rhetorical change." Therefore, to the extent that 'public space' is invoked herein as a paragon of inclusion and access, it must be noted that such visions mainly concern the *ideal* of public space and the *principles* embedded in its formation, and not necessarily the realities of historical action and availability – although the aim of *resistance* of course is to challenge current and historical alignments and availabilities, and thus to help move 'reality' closer to its 'ideal' form by uniting practice with principle. And indeed, as a matter of principle "public spaces are vital to the personal and political life of a society, offering sites of significant communication, and serving as sources for news, information, and dialogue" (Drucker & Gumpert 1997:2). Likewise Lofland (1998:124), noting that "public space is a natural stage and a powerful medium of communication," especially for "those who cannot command significant private space," including "the outcasts, the proletariat, the underclass;" and Kohn (2004:70), observing that "public spaces are the last domains where the opportunity to communicate is not something bought and sold." Along these lines, Doreen Massey (1994; 1999) characterizes such spaces as sites of possibility, plurality, nomadism, chaos, spontaneity, openness, potentiality, and "progressive politics." *Public space*, then, as the sole site of guaranteed access in the city, stands materially and metaphorically as the essence of pluralism, political participation, and personal freedom.

As such, it becomes clear that public space is integral to conceptions of *resistance* and the appearance of *social movements*. As Don Mitchell (1995:115 & 123-4) cogently describes it:

> "Public spaces are also, and very importantly, *spaces for representation*. That is, public space is a place within which a political movement can stake out the space that allows it to be *seen*. By claiming space in public, social groups themselves become public. *Only* in public spaces can the homeless, for example, represent themselves as a legitimate part of 'the public.' And in this sense, public spaces are absolutely essential to the functioning of democratic politics. . . . Social movements must, and do, occupy and reconfigure material public spaces in the city. Indeed, these movements are premised on the notion that democratic (and certainly revolutionary) politics are impossible without the simultaneous creation and control of *material* space. . . . Whether challenged from the left or the right, the established power of the state and capital are threatened by the exercise of public rights within public spaces."

Thus, we come to see public space as both a site of contestation as well as its product (cf. Mitchell 1997a:327). "Definitions of public space and 'the public' are not universal and enduring; they are produced rather through constant struggle in the past and in the present" (Mitchell 1995:121). In short, "public space is always and inescapably a product of social negotiation and contest" (Mitchell 1996a:131).

Unfortunately, it is by now apparent that "a gradual but steady decline of public space has occurred" (Drucker & Gumpert 1997:1; Lloyd & Auld 2003:344), to such an extent that we are close to witnessing the "shrinkage and disappearance of public spaces" (Bauman 2000:221; see also Mitchell 1995; McCarthy & McPhail 2006; but see Crawford 1995:9, arguing for "a new discourse of public space" that is not based on "loss, but filled with possibilities"). Initially spurred on by the quest to construct "defensible space" (Carr, et al. 1992:150) and to keep out strangers and "unfamiliar people" (Bauman

1995:135-6), cities have employed a variety of tactics of control over their public spaces, including the presence of surveillance cameras and security guards (Lofland 1998:213; Carr, et al. 1992:15,149-50; Koskela 2000), the adoption of municipal ordinances regulating behavior or access (e.g., Simon 1996; Smith 1996; Stoner 1995), and the reliance on increased policing (Lofland 1973:90-1; Jones & Newburn 1999; Berkley & Thayer 2000). Perhaps the most significant trend in this regard has been the *privatization* of public spaces (Lofland 1998:210), whereby rights of access are "severely limited" (Carr, et al. 1992:16,139) to the point that the "dream of the private city" is not far from reality (cf. Lofland 1998:196; see also Sorkin 1992; Hannigan 1998). In the process, as Lloyd & Auld (2003:344) contend,

> "the venues of public space – the marketplace, the park, the city sidewalk – that for thousands of years nurtured community and political communion, have been transformed into commodified public places [that through] a process of privatization . . . are socially sanitized, homogenized spaces, legally capable of excluding socially stigmatized and disruptive elements. Although the public is encouraged to enter and enjoy a form of urban ambience in such spaces, they are not truly public spaces because they are owned and controlled as commercial businesses. . . . These spaces allow for personal self-expression only within the constraint of consumer identity."

The idea that at all of this is intimately tied to processes of *gentrification* and *redevelopment* is certainly not a revelation, nor is the notion that such mechanisms reflect the desire of business entities to have control over determining "the type of people who are desired" in the spaces of the city (see Carr et al. 1992:149), "thus protecting the inalienable right of the well-to-do to spend their money without having to rub shoulders with the 'dangerous classes'" (Lofland 1973:76). Mitchell (1997a:322-4) similarly expounds on the 'aesthetics' of public space as a "landscape in which the propertied classes express 'possession' of the land, and their control over the social relations within it." In this sense, and as the foregoing will amplify, we begin to perceive the reflexive, ideological nature of space and the manner in which it simultaneously is: (i) a *reflection* of social processes, (ii) the *location* of their occurrence, and (iii) a primary factor in the *production* of such relations as well (see Soja 1989; Smith 1984; Harvey 1973; Lefebvre 1996). As Lloyd & Auld (2003:345) succinctly observe, "space possesses the dual characteristic of being both a product of social relations and a producer of social relations."

Exploring the practical implications of all of this requires a deepening of the concept of *urban ecology* – namely the interplay of people and place, of cultural and material policies and practices (cf. Ferrell 2006:172-8) – through an analysis of the eminently spatial processes of redevelopment, gentrification, privatization, and what has come to be known as 'Disneyfication,' always bearing in mind the reality that, "ultimately, capital shapes and controls the urban ecology" (Lloyd & Auld 2003:344). Thus, it is without a trace of shame or irony that the headline of the November 2000 issue of *The Downtowner* blared: 'Downtown Tempe *IS* Fantasy Land!' (DTC 2000c). Intended as a celebration and not a critique, the headline inadvertently captures the unfortunate reality that redevelopment has wrought on the city. Drawing upon events in Tempe as the basis for a grounded case study, this chapter describes and documents how economic changes in the city (and cities in general) have contributed to processes of exclusion and containment, both materially in terms of spatial control and homeless bodies, as well as ideologically in terms of 'theming' and elitism. Along the way, we'll encounter yuppies, BIDs, and the panopticon – skipping merrily toward that magical kingdom where none need confront the horrors of poverty while out consuming conspicuously, both on Tempe's Mill Avenue and on city streets the world over.

Redevelopment and Its Discontents

Trumpeting the attractiveness of Tempe for businesses and investors, the Chamber of Commerce web site (circa 2001) observed: "Tempe has the highest concentration of high technology firms in Arizona. In addition, Tempe has the densest industrial area in Arizona, and two [of its] zip codes represent the highest concentration of businesses in Arizona. . . . Tempe's favorable tax structure and proactive approach to business development combined with its prime location creates the ideal climate for businesses to grow and prosper." Up to the time of this writing, Tempe has continued its push to attract commercial interests, even sponsoring a retailing showcase in 2003 called

'Romancing the Store' bent on filling downtown business spaces (Rau 2003b). Extending these points further, a local columnist noted that "the approach Tempe has taken is highly governmentally driven and subsidized redevelopment. It has subsidized the retail transformation of Mill Avenue and various other commercial and residential developments in its downtown area" (Robb 2004) – leading him to conclude that "there is a certain coziness that has settled in among a few Tempe developers, city political leaders and staff." By way of contrast, consider Loretta Lees' (2003:621) description of redevelopment trends in Portland, Maine: "Urban redevelopment in Portland has largely been market-led and dependent upon individual entrepreneurial energy rather than large-scale government initiatives. . . . Rather than directing the redevelopment of downtown Portland, the City has been in the position of trying to steer, through the planning process, and capitalize on, through its place marketing efforts, a commercially-led and substantially grassroots process of entertainment-led reinvestment." Still, despite (or perhaps due to) its rampant pro-business 'coziness,' Tempe was named an 'All American City' in 2003 by the National Civic League (Rau 2003d).

Fig. 1: Downtown Tempe, Arizona (circa 2004)

Less than a decade earlier, before the current cycle of commercialization had begun in earnest, the *Republic* (Porter 1997b) heralded: 'Tempe on Brink of Redevelopment Explosion.' "This is a very exciting time to be in Tempe," mused Ross Robb, then-president of the Downtown Tempe Community, Inc. (DTC), a business development and lobbying organization noted in the previous chapter that will also figure prominently in the ensuing discussion. As a partner in a local development firm, "Robb has a personal stake in the matter," and the article quotes him predicting that "Tempe residents are going to see a physical transformation of the downtown's northern end that to date has been merely a dream and a set of artists' renderings."

In the same time frame (early 1997) other predictions were beginning to surface as well. Gayle Shanks, former owner of the independent Changing Hands bookstore on Mill Avenue (which is long gone by now, having been supplanted by Borders Books), told the *Republic* (in Porter 1997a): "If downtown doesn't remain distinctive from other shopping areas in the Valley, then it becomes just another homogenized shopping experience that people will at first find trendy, then become bored with in a couple of years." In trying to set the record straight a year later, Vic Linoff (1998), former president of the Mill Avenue Merchants Association (MAMA) – a kinder, gentler DTC precursor made up mostly of smaller local businesses – challenged former Mayor Neil Giuliano's interpretation of the recent history of redevelopment in Tempe: "The early years of the downtown redevelopment debate were not focused on city incentives to developers. The concerns, rather, were centered on the alarmingly increased speed of the process, lack of any historic preservation plan and an indiscriminate use of eminent domain to acquire and assemble individual private properties for the purpose of making them someone else's private property. Though technically legal, there were strong, valid questions raised about morality and ethics."

Interestingly, by the time of this writing, it is apparent that both camps' predictions have largely proven true. Downtown Tempe has indeed undergone a 'physical transformation' of startling proportions, pushing upward vertically, increasing density, and through the addition of the $200 million man-made Town Lake (see Petrie 2003). This wave of redevelopment included the Brickyard, a massive commercial and condominium project dubbed 'Tempe's Lap of Luxury' by the *East Valley Tribune* (Gately 2000), offering "ritzy lofts and penthouses overlooking Tempe Town Lake" at prices of up to $660,000. The *Republic* (Fiscus 2000), in an article entitled 'Upscale Living Coming to Downtown Tempe,' noted that Brickyard residents "will live in a project that will bring a different kind of home – and a different kind of tax bracket – to Mill Avenue" (see also Rau 2003c). "There's probably room for three more Brickyards," Rod Keeling, then-Executive Director of the DTC, happily told the *Tribune* (Gately 2000). "The community's vision is the Brickyard at Mill would be a prototype project for the new, vertically mixed-use, pedestrian-oriented projects."

Unfortunately, it appears that 'the community' – or at least Keeling's version of it, the DTC – was right on this one: the Brickyard was only the beginning. A year later, the *Tribune* ran a front page feature called 'Things Looking Up These Days for Tempe Builders' (Templar 2001a), which reported that "a rising wave of development in downtown Tempe will be the tallest, most dense and most expensive the city has ever seen, causing excitement and fear among residents." The article does note that "critics have repeatedly protested the evolving nature of downtown businesses from local single-location owners to chain stores and nationally recognized brand names." The then-mayor, however, deflected such concerns by maintaining his frequent stance of inevitability that "Tempe can't stop such growth." "You can continue to be the leader of the Valley or you can become an inner-city slum," city Development Services Coordinator Dave Fackler warned. Indeed, as a front-page inset box titled 'The future of Tempe's urban core' made clear, Fackler's slum scenario (at least as he intended the term) is not a likely prospect in the near future. Depicting eighteen separate development projects "for downtown Tempe that are under construction, proposed or in concept stages," the inset text detailed the looming 'next wave' in Tempe's rampant and ongoing redevelopment:

> "Tempe faces an enormous wave of redevelopment and construction in the downtown area, pushing it toward a true urban core. In the next 10 years, the amount of residential, retail and commercial space could jump from 3 million square feet to more than 5 million square feet. Including all the land around Tempe Town Lake . . . the total could surpass 11 million square feet, nearly four times what exists today."

Aside from propagandist accounts of such changes as bringing Tempe closer to an 'urban nirvana' (e.g., Durrenberger 2000), many of the statements reported in the media were explicitly or inadvertently critical of the breakneck pace and massive footprint of the changes, collectively wondering whether, "far from creating a nirvana, many of these changes seem destined to bring nothing but bad karma" (Amster 2000a). For example, an April 2000 *Republic* article dubbed 'Mall Avenue Tied Up in Chains' (Rose 2000) observed that, "now that space once occupied by the independent Changing Hands Bookstore is to become a food court, some folks say the corporate chain takeover of the area once celebrated for its quirks is nearly complete. Many of the independent stores have closed on Mill Avenue in the last few years, and many chain stores such as Abercrombie & Fitch and The Gap have moved in." Other critical voices at this time included the *ASU State Press* warning of "impending rampant commercialism" on Mill Avenue (Wolf 1999) and pointing out that, "in the past there's been a small-town charm to this little strip of street. But in the years to come, we might not even recognize it." My own similar concerns voiced at this time included wondering about "the ways in which 'development' transforms civic space, both structurally and ideologically [through] the rapid corporate colonization of the physical landscape and the concomitant imposition of a mindset of disposability, artificiality, and order" (Amster 1999c), and advising against "letting crass commercial interests dominate the dialogue and impose their sterile vision of 'order' in the obsessive pursuit of 'development'" (Amster 1999f).

The voices of criticism grew even stronger in succeeding years. By way of inadvertent critique, a front page *Tribune* article entitled 'Corporate World Invades Mill Avenue' (Stern 2000) noted that "quirky independent shops and retail businesses are suffering;" quoted Dave Fackler proclaiming matter-of-factly that "there is sterilization, but it's not just downtown Tempe;" and concluded with Vice Mayor Leonard Copple warmly predicting that "there's going to be a high-income population living there that would support high-end stores." The *State Press* took a more direct approach with a front page headline noting that 'Mill Avenue Development Sends Mom and Pop Shops Packing, Creates Upscale Urban Flavor' (Beaver 2000a), and ran a subsequent story ('Residents Concerned About Changes on Mill,' Zawicki 2000a) which quoted the owner of the last independent coffee shop on Mill lamenting that "the city planners wanted their 'outdoor mall' and they got it." One of the most scathing critiques came from an ASU senior in a *State Press* opinion column (Galindo 2000): "Mill was once a small, quaint, local business-oriented college avenue, as opposed to the pretentious, ultra-capitalist, revolting California carbon copy it is now. Mill Avenue has died and a sick golden calf has been erected in its place. It has been mutated into an evil avenue run on greed and money, and every last inch of small, local ideals that happen to remain are being systematically crushed under the fist of the almighty dollar." A subsequent *Arizona Republic* guest column (Bachler 2000, 'Downtown Plan for Tempe Caters to Corporate Greed') similarly argued that "Tempe has got its sights set on one type of customer, one kind of resident, one kind of person . . . the young, hip, rich urban professional." As recently as 2003, articles appearing under headlines such as 'They just don't want kids on Mill' (e.g., Rau 2003a) continued to document these ongoing trends.

Nonetheless, the propagandist perspective would still find voice in articles such as one from March 2005 (Durrenberger) proclaiming 'Tempe on Way to Its Potential,' touting the approval of the 'Centerpoint Condominiums' comprising four 20-plus story towers made possible by significant zoning variances being granted by the city – built in "one of the most distinctive urban environments in North America," according to Centerpoint's website, in the heart of the "Mill District: Your Playground," brimming with "untold luxury appointments . . . and a stunning array of amenities all set amidst Tempe's rich, vibrant Mill District." The newspaper piece went on to note that there were several more 'high-end' condominium projects in the works, and that the presence of over 1000 new upscale condos "should improve the general ambience of Tempe's downtown. It will no longer be the exclusive franchise of homeless teenagers. . . ." At prices ranging from almost $400,000 to nearly $1 million, this will **not** yield 'affordable housing' for a wider range of people than just the homeless. Interestingly, despite a purported nationwide housing 'slowdown,' other cities have recently undergone almost identical development booms, as noted in a *Real Change* article (Harris 2008):

> "Seattle is changing much more rapidly than most of us realize. . . . [F]our new towers are under construction that will, within two years, contain 505 new luxury condos with an average value of $2 million each. This is but a tenth of the downtown condo boom that was unleashed by recent zoning changes. Seattle's visible poor are not a good advertisement for downtown living, and the carrot of more housing for the

> chronically homeless has been joined by the stick of heightened repression. This has happened, with variations on the theme, in cities across the nation."

Indeed, as many residents perceived through their objections to and warnings about the direction of development in Tempe, academic treatments of the subject make clear how high the stakes really are in terms of what such changes portend. In their classic tome *Gentrification of the City*, Neil Smith and Peter Williams (1986:211-17) observe that, in addition to an "architectural Manhattanization" of skyscrapers and vertical growth, such scenarios also bring "a social Manhattanization whereby the agglomeration of corporate and corporate-related activities at the center leads to a further agglomeration of upper-income residential neighborhoods and of lavish recreation and entertainment facilities," constituting a nascent "bourgeois playground." Many scholars note the inevitable "relationship between gentrification and displacement" (Williams 1996:147; see also Hetzler, et al. 2006), including Samira Kawash (1998:320): "Renewal has most often meant a two-pronged attack on the most economically and socially marginal members of the urban community via a combined gentrification of residential areas and privatization of previously public spaces." More recently, Loretta Lees (2003:613-14) notes that "over the last three decades schemes to attract the wealthy middle class back to the inner city have become central to urban redevelopment strategies," yielding urban spaces that "are in practice socially exclusive and insulated from the poor and other so-called 'deviants,'" – constituting what some have referred to as a "modern urban apartheid" (Hetzler, et al. 2006).

Homeless people are often thus among the first to feel the effects of redevelopment and gentrification. Susan Ruddick (1996:40-2) notes that such processes "necessarily exclude the homeless," and points out that there is a "connection between the development of postindustrial city space and the stigmatization of the homeless." As Talmadge Wright (1997:81,92) likewise observes: "It is no secret that the redevelopment of a city's central business district often leads to gentrification of the immediate and surrounding area, displacing poor, often minority, populations and local industries. . . . Gentrification is the vehicle through which displacement and concentration are accomplished; it is about who is allowed 'in,' who is to be accepted and who is to be excluded." Wright (1997:89) concludes that "the consequence of city redevelopment for the very poor and homeless is dispersion to the city periphery or to the interstices between developed city locations. [S]uch redevelopments *necessarily* demand the removal of very poor and homeless populations" (cf. Mitchell 2001). And Sarah Brinegar (2000:509-11) similarly concluded her recent study of the 'Response to Homelessness in Tempe' by noting that "Tempe officials have conducted a de facto policy of homeless displacement, [reflecting] the social exclusionary forces at work in Tempe, [and] preserving public space for 'ideal' public activities by appropriate groups."

Variations on a Scheme: The Mechanisms of Privatization

> "The first man who, having enclosed a piece of ground, bethought himself of saying 'This is mine,' and found some people simple enough to believe him, was the real founder of civil society. From how many crimes, wars, and murders, from how many horrors and misfortunes might not any one have saved mankind, by pulling up the stakes, or filling up the ditch, and crying to his fellows: 'Beware of listening to this impostor; you are undone if you once forget that the fruits of the earth belong to us all, and the earth itself to nobody.'"
>
> -- Rousseau (1973:84), *Discourse on Inequality*

"Move over, Disneyland. The world's newest theme park is right here in Tempe. We call it Yuppieland," sardonically lamented a *State Press* editorial (2000b). As Jeff Ferrell (2001a:169) notes, "in Tempe, it is a Disneyland and increasingly so, as officials and developers invite tourists and local consumers to see Mill Avenue gradually be remade into a commercial wonderworld, transforming Tempe's 'decrepit central core' into a uniformly appealing location for shopping and nightlife, 'creating a sort-of theme-park downtown.'" Call it what you will – Yuppieland, Disneyland, Mall Avenue, Unpleasantville – but there is no mistaking the fact that Tempe has undergone significant changes in the past decade. An analysis of these trends and forces reveals that the Kingdom presently under construction in downtown Tempe, and elsewhere, may in fact be more Tragic than Magic.

In his influential edited volume *Variations on a Theme Park: The New American City and the End of Public Space*, Michael Sorkin (1992:xiii-xv) divines four salient characteristics of the new theme park city: (a) "the dissipation of all stable relations to local physical and cultural geography [and the imposition of] a generic urbanism;" (b) an "obsession with 'security,' with rising levels of manipulation and surveillance over its citizenry and with a proliferation of new modes of segregation;" (c) the creation of a "new realm of simulations, television city, the city as theme park;" and (d) a condition in which "speech is restricted: there are no demonstrations in Disneyland." Amplifying his point further, Sorkin (1992:208,222) notes that "the highly regulated, completely synthetic vision provides a simplified, sanitized experience that stands in for the more undisciplined complexities of the city. . . . The security checks, the certifying credit cards and passports, the disciplined, carefully segmented movements, the ersatz geography, the grafted cachet – this is Disneyville." In analyzing the *Fantasy City*, John Hannigan (1998:81,129) similarly equates "the theme park city" with a process of "McDonaldization" that is premised on "efficiency, calculability, predictability, and control." As Lyn Lofland (1998:216) further observes, "Disney environments are tightly controlled and highly sanitized." Likewise Talmadge Wright (1997:105), concluding that "the world is becoming Disneyfied as consumption is increasingly organized within well-controlled pleasure spaces that are selective about who is admitted and what kind of behavior can occur in them."

Another image that resonates with and embodies these themes is that of the 'private city,' as described by Lofland (1998:196): "It is quite possible to build environments that have almost no public space – and thus have no areas available for the creation of a public realm – or that have public space that is of such a character that public realm formation is discouraged. It is quite possible to build, that is, a 'private city.'" As Hannigan (1998:6) explains, the 'private city' is one "in which the disorganized reality of older streets and cities is replaced by a measured, controlled and organized kind of urban experience which is intimately linked to a fusion of consumerism, entertainment and popular culture." Referring to such spaces as "quasi-urban environments," Hannigan (1998:7) wonders portentously: "Are fantasy cities the culmination of a long-term trend in which private space replaces public space?" Perhaps in partial response to his own question, Hannigan (1998:193) subsequently notes how the "differences between private and public space soon became apparent. . . . [In private space], groups which espoused a social or political cause were excluded. Political demonstrations were banned. Small vendors were kept out in favor of large, chain-store tenants. Curfews were imposed on those suspected of bringing trouble with them, notably teenagers. In the spirit of Disneyland, dress rules were declared."

By contrast, "public spaces are the places where we are all equal and where we are all 'home.' They are the places where our freedoms of speech and assembly are protected, where we can exercise the precious right of criticizing the government" (Kressel 2000). The same article laments, however, that "governments are shifting oversight of the public realm to private corporations unconstrained by legal mandates regarding such things as union labor, universal access, free speech, and free assembly." Continuing with what turns out to be a devastating critique of privatization, the author opines:

> "Privatization of public space enables large-scale property owners to exclude 'undesirables,' the homeless, the non-shoppers, from places of investment and privilege intended to attract up-scale suburbanites, the urban elite, and tourists with disposable income. But privatization of public space also represents a more fundamental elite agenda. Privatization of the public realm substitutes the private corporation for public institutions as the repository of trust, legitimacy, and communal identity in our society. The private sector subverts the idea of democracy and the public good and makes all of America a 'company town' to which we are coming to owe our soul. Democracy cannot survive when we have no place to gather where there is 'no purchase necessary.'"

As Lyn Lofland (1998:212) concurs, "many municipalities have entered into 'faustian bargains' with developers." Likewise Steve Galindo (2000): "The city of Tempe received an offer from Satan." Picking up on these demonic themes, a loose collective of artists, pagans, anarchists, greens, and the homeless staged an action in December 2002 to "confront, curse, and celebrate the demise of yuppie and rich developers' business establishments (especially the Brickyard) on Mill Avenue." Having become aware of a severe mold problem in the upscale Brickyard, the group declared their opposition to Tempe's "'if you build it they will come' method of gentrification," and vowed their "solidarity with the dreaded Black Mold," by calling upon the aid of "other Nature Spirits and Elementals in cursing with bad luck the individuals responsible, as long as they continue to 'develop' Tempe based on their own greedy and prejudiced desires, instead of the needs of the actual residents and workers of the area."

In the belief that Tempe has accepted the dark prince's offer – or at least is involved in intensive negotiations – many residents have railed against "the mechanism of privatization," which Lofland (1998:210) describes as the process of "bringing ever more publicly accessible space under the control of private ownership" (see also Zukin 1995; and Lees 2003, discussing "the virtual privatization of public space"). An *Arizona Republic* guest column (Cox 2000), for example, urged that "the citizens of Tempe should never let it change into private land. With privatization, the city would be exempt from legal ramifications of shunning away specific segments of the population. Months of prior public discourse have demonstrated and foretold of these trends. Don't let downtown Tempe develop a Disney-like atmosphere. Aren't we already a little too familiar with how that goes anyway? You know, 'fun for all,' if you have enough money and get past the 'reserve the right to deny service to anyone' clause" (see also Foscarinis, et al. 1999, noting how "cities have proposed or implemented plans to privatize public property as a way of restricting homeless people's access to certain areas"). In a subsequent 'open letter' that the *Republic* titled 'Tempe Destroying its Public Spaces,' I (2000b) challenged the then-mayor's spatial policy as "one in which public spaces can readily be turned into private ones whenever a developer wants to build." The letter to the editor continued: "If you want your legacy to be the complete eradication of open/public space in downtown Tempe, then you are well on your way to that unfortunate end. Meanwhile, the citizens are being reduced to mere onlookers as you push Tempe along the fast track to Disneyfication and Manhattanization."

A recent article from the *Phoenix New Times* lays bare many of these themes, even including its titular invocation of the demonic nature of redevelopment and all that it implies: 'The Devil Went Down to Phoenix: Will it be Any Better than Downtown Tempe?' (Irwin 2006). Wondering at the outset whether Phoenix will "wind up as a cross between Disneyland and Mill Avenue," the piece reviews some of the key moments in Tempe's downtown chronology, including the chasing off of independent bookseller Changing Hands and the moral lamentations of Vic Linoff about Mill Avenue's locally-owned, not-too-distant past and how it was replaced by a generic chain-store monoculture. In so doing, however, the city and business community may have gone too far in undermining the very things that made downtown Tempe attractive in the first place, and is trying to correct it:

> "This is the only stretch of several blocks in the entire [Phoenix metropolitan area] that's even remotely urban, but something is missing. Or too well-planned. One of the most depressing things about Mill Avenue is its self-awareness – it knows it's not big city. And efforts to mask that are embarrassing. As it turns out, even the homeless street kids selling their hemp jewelry are here by design. The city of Tempe actually has an agreement with the police department not to kick homeless people, street vendors or street performers off Mill. Not because they have a right to be there, but because in a downtown as planned and controlled by the city as Mill Avenue is, even the homeless serve a purpose – to make the street feel more 'authentic'" (Irwin 2006).

Well, if you can't 'beat them,' I guess exploiting them is the next best thing. Still, despite this journalistic insight, the homeless as a class are not generally welcome in downtown Tempe. But the author's point is well-taken and the city's dilemma understandable: if people want absolute control and Disney-like sterility, there are plenty of indoor shopping malls to choose from; but when they frequent the area's only real quasi-urban center, they actually desire some of the character and unpredictability of street life. Letting a few of the more presentable street people mill about on Mill – including some street performers, who are allowed to "put out a container for tips" but will be "escorted off the property" if they solicit people (Yara 2007) – during busy weekend hours could actually be good for business, and helps avoid the logical result of hyper-regulating this 'master-planned' downtown in which "there's no room to explore, no way to get lost. Every single experience has been engineered by a group of people in love with new-urbanism, with the same idea of what is cool and interesting. The final product? Downtown Disney, from sea to shining sea" (Irwin 2006).

Looking back to the earlier days in this ongoing Disneyfication process, it turns out that there were good reasons to issue rhetorical challenges to the city's nascent policies. In 2001, commenting on the impending completion of the Brickyard, Rod Keeling ominously noted that "the residential is important because *you want a certain group of people to have ownership of downtown*" (in Steckner 2001c). The Brickyard, however, went bankrupt and was taken over by Arizona State University, so the downtown area instead added 'The Lofts at Orchidhouse' as an "upscale development" project oriented toward the residential, which had the minor misfortune of being located too close to a weekly musical gathering (Pela 2006): "Residents there recently put the smackdown on hippies and street kids who've been performing drum circles at the neighboring Sixth Street Park into the night." Having both observed and participated in these drum circles over the years, it is apparent that they are not particularly useful for commercial purposes, often attracting an eclectic and raucous crowd that doesn't quite embody the same atmospheric potential of a street vendor or solo busker. This is a more boisterous, spontaneous, and voluminous experience, which one might think has some utility or even desirability in an urban setting – but the quest for 'authentic' urban experiences apparently has its limits to that "certain group of people" that have taken ownership of downtown Tempe, as a recent *New Times* article (Pela 2006) quite bluntly concludes: "'If you're going to live in a condominium within 200 yards of Mill Avenue, you should be expecting some background noise,' grumped Gelatinous Groove guitarist Steve Allen. 'Close your fucking patio door, turn up your TV, and shut the fuck up.' Or move back to suburbia, where you belong."

In addition to a blatant form of elitism that would give a certain class of people ownership of and entitlement to the city, another disturbing and related trend that had begun to take form in the earlier stages is the concept of *shadow privatization*, described by Lofland (1998:211) as: "public-private partnerships [and] numerous odd arrangements whereby (1) publicly owned space is transferred to private or semiprivate control with the understanding that the space is 'sort of' public or (2) in exchange for one or another consideration from government, privately owned space is declared to be 'sort of' public." One example of this is a 1995 licensing agreement in which Tempe merchants ceded to the DTC the power of "modification of pedestrian walkways in order to preserve a clean and pleasant environment" (Zawicki 2000c) – a power that was invoked most starkly with the installation of fence spikes at the Salvation Army described in the previous chapter, which Keeling claimed was done "to create more public space for pedestrians" (in Zawicki 2000c). The groundwork for such agreements was laid the year before when Development Services director Dave Fackler was quoted (in Petrie 1994a) as saying that "the City is interested in having the DTC take over sidewalk activities" – to which a *Republic* editorial (1998a) belatedly responded, "The sidewalks belong to the public, and the last time we checked, the First Amendment was still in effect." Under similarly dubious authority, in May 2001 the DTC endorsed many of the planters on Mill Avenue being made 'homeless-proof' with an arched concrete ridge that makes sitting for any length of time extremely uncomfortable. Mike Davis (1990:233) likewise describes "bumproof benches" as offering "a minimal surface for uncomfortable sitting, while making sleeping utterly impossible," and Wright (1997:108) similarly notes the use of "homeless-proof benches or uninviting wall alcoves," constituting what one scholar has referred to as "prickly space" (Wachholz 2005).

Perhaps the most striking example of *shadow privatization* in Tempe has been the seeming one-brick-at-a-time conversion of the sidewalks in and around the 'Centerpoint' development in the heart of downtown – some four square city blocks of terrain – to private property. As reported by local ABC affiliate KNXV in January 2000, in a 'bonus report' segment entitled 'Tempe's Sidewalks Sold' (Ley 2000), the effect is that "the developers control the sidewalks" – a fact echoed by Rod Keeling, who noted that "on one side of that invisible line is Centerpoint's property. When you pass on to their private property, you give up certain rights." Scholars have likewise noted that "such a patchwork of public and private ownership of public space is almost guaranteed to make these places problematic as ones where citizens may expect to freely congregate in" (McCarthy & McPhail 2006:233). Keeling had previously expounded on such troubling processes in a *New Times* article (Holthouse 1998a): "'The whole Centerpoint area is what's known as a super block,' says Rod Keeling, executive director of Downtown Tempe Community, Inc. 'It's a public space, but it's not public property. It was turned over to the developer by the city.' Which means Centerpoint can make and enforce a different set of rules. No panhandling, for one . . . and no hanging around unless you buy something. . . ." This is precisely what Lofland (1998:211) meant by her observation that once inside such spaces, "the individual is fully in privately owned space and, to whatever degree the owners wish it and the law allows, fully under the control of those owners." In their analysis of agency and public space, Hil & Bessant

(1999:41) similarly describe "the regulation and exclusion of young people from increasingly privatised and commodified urban spaces." And in nearby Tucson, "City Council members proposed looking into a plan to privatize the sidewalks which would allow business owners to regulate homeless people's access to those areas" (Foscarinis, et al. 1999; NLCHP 1999; see also Romano 1998; Snow & Mulcahy 2001).

In January 2000, two incidents I was involved in illustrate these points graphically. The first occurred the day of the 'bonus report' noted above, when I was waiting to be interviewed by the reporter (who was occupied with Rod Keeling at the moment). Standing near the Coffee Plantation on Mill Avenue, one of Centerpoint's corporate centerpieces, I observed two TEAM (Total Events and Management) security guards confronting a slacker-like group of kids at one of the wrought-iron tables on the open concourse behind the coffee house. When the kids protested that they were paying customers, the TEAM 'officer' got the word over his radio that all the 'slackers' in the area were to be removed immediately. One of the supposed 'ne'er-do-wells' removed that day turned out to be the manager of a local video store who, when I pointed the situation out to the TV reporter, was interviewed for the 'sidewalks sold' segment. The whole episode caused me to write a short online piece called 'Privatizing Public Spaces: The Selling of Your Sidewalks,' in which I criticized "the privatization of historically and functionally 'public spaces,' hiring private security guards to police these suddenly private areas, and discriminating based on appearance and physical characteristics against persons that the DTC, et al., deem 'undesirable.' Like a theme park, Tempe now apparently reserves the right to refuse service to anyone for any reason it wants – especially the crime of being 'diverse' in a non-commercial sort of way." Melee (2000), one of Tempe's street kids, likewise told me that the private security force known as TEAM "goes way overboard in kicking people out based on appearance."

The second episode took place one week later, when I was out collecting petition signatures to save Tempe Butte (also known as 'A' Mountain), an important cultural and historical feature of the city and one of its last remaining natural open spaces. Upon arriving, I was told by a group of street kids that they had been removed from Coffee Plantation earlier that day, even though they had made purchases. Removed along with them was a young man who appeared slacker-like enough in his day-off attire to warrant removal, even though he was actually a Coffee Plantation employee who just happened to be sitting with the street kids that day! As my friends and I began collecting signatures on the sidewalk, we were approached by TEAM aegnts who informed us of the 'rules' that apply on their property. Curiously, the TEAM guard in charge that day was wearing an official-looking Tempe Police Department T-shirt, which he said was given to him by the police in order to increase his "authority and effectiveness." In substance, the rules related to me that day were as follows:

- The sidewalks from University Drive to 6th Street and over to Ash Avenue are the 'private property' of Centerpoint and DMB developers.
- By the developers' 'good graces,' a narrow portion of the sidewalks (i.e., the walking corridor) have essentially been deemed 'public' space, although the developers reserve the right to revoke that designation at any time.
- Even the so-called 'public' parts of the sidewalks still have rules attached (which we were warned to obey or else be cited for trespassing), including that a person cannot remain in one location for more than 2 hours, after which time they must move at least 50 feet away.
- Centerpoint and DMB reserve the right to refuse services to anyone for any reason, including the right to enforce their own 'code of conduct' in any manner they choose.

The trend here is disturbing, allowing developers to control spaces that historically and traditionally have been sites of public discourse. This means that developers can unilaterally decide who has rights of access, expression, and association in the most central parts of town – effectively abolishing the First Amendment rights that attach to public spaces, and creating a scenario that is "verging on the totalitarian" (Blomley 2004:4). The net result is a sanitizing of the downtown area, with a not-so-subtle tinge of elitism driving the exclusionary agenda. As Rod Keeling noted back in a 1998 article appropriately titled 'Time to Sweep Slackers Off Mill': "To allow a small number of misbehaving individuals to 'run off' the citizens of this community from our finest public space, space that was paid for by those very citizens, is wrong. We abdicated the sidewalks of our finest avenue." Of course, Keeling was referring to the slackers as those who have 'run off' the good people of Tempe, but his sense for unintentional irony is amazing:

think of the developers and TEAM as the 'misbehaving individuals,' and consider that the sidewalks have indeed been abdicated – to Centerpoint, the DTC, and in effect Keeling himself.

The full import of these exclusionary forces crystallized for me in a series of e-mail exchanges I had with Keeling and Mick Hirko (owner and operator of TEAM) in May 2001, which was triggered when myself and friends were confronted by a TEAM guard while sitting on the sidewalk near Coffee Plantation (tellingly, my contemporaneous notes quote the guard as saying, "Don't get too comfortable – soon the benches and planters will be removed altogether. Hey, the almighty dollar rules down here – that's just the way it is, business dominates"):

> **MH**: The guard was fully within his rights to ask you and your compatriots to move, as you were not on a public sidewalk, but rather on private property. Sixth Street, west of Mill Avenue, is owned by Centerpoint, not the City of Tempe. We enforce the rules of private property, and one of them is that people do not sit on the ground. As Mr. Keeling explained, we do not work for the DTC or the City of Tempe in this regard, and are responsible for private property issues only.
>
> **RA**: There is some confusion here. I was told previously that Centerpoint's private ownership excludes the actual public rights-of-way themselves – in other words, the walking corridors between the building facings and the street. If Tempe's sidewalks have in fact been sold – so that people on those sidewalks have no First Amendment rights, and no right to be there without the owner's approval – then I think the citizens of Tempe deserve to know where those boundaries are and how it came to be so. Simply put: are the sidewalks along Mill Avenue between University and Sixth Street public or private spaces?
>
> **MH**: You bring up some valid concerns. I cannot speak for the property owners or the City designers, but I believe that the reason the delineation between private and public property is not more clearly pronounced, is to prevent the visual appearance or perception of deterrence of use. Obviously, Centerpoint exists for the use and pleasure of the public, to

shop, eat, and enjoy the shops. Since it is private, it does allow a more broad enforcement of what is desired or not. Specifically, no one wants signs every 20 feet, stating: 'Entering Private Property.' I see how you would think that we discriminate against certain people because of their appearance. It is not true. There are a lot more factors at play here. I cannot say that what you allege, that a well-dressed person might not be removed, and a slacker may, never happens, but it is not policy. It should be based on consumer factors. Let us also keep in mind that many of the people whose rights you so vehemently are protecting are dealing drugs, stealing property and committing crimes of violence against others.

RA: I appreciate your candor in stating that the delineation between public and private space is left intentionally vague so as not to deter shoppers and consumers. Frankly, I find this scary as hell. As I've said, the distinction is crucial in terms of individual and associative rights, and also raises the all-important point that private property rights are rights of exclusion (i.e., the right of the owner to determine who it will allow to enter the property), whereas public spaces are characterized by inclusion and equal rights of access for all. Here, we have Centerpoint not only taking over public space in a legal sense, but hiring a private security squad to enforce its rights of exclusion. This is a city, not a theme park or a shopping mall, and rights of access should never be "based on consumer factors" (your words) nor limited to those who can afford to pay the price of admission. Finally, your statement that I am 'protecting' the rights of people who deal drugs, steal property, or commit violence against others is intended to be ironic, right? I mean, you run a SECURITY company and are therefore paid to protect the property rights of your employers. As far as the ethics of who is being protected are concerned, you might consider that the class of people you are protecting (i.e., wealthy, influential developers and businessmen) are also at times drug dealers, thieves, and perpetrators of violence. Indeed, some would argue that the very essence of their business is all about 'drugs' (caffeine, nicotine, and alcohol), 'theft' (profit and privatization), and

> 'violence' (exclusion and enforcement). I'd rather be accused of defending the rights of those marginalized by society than those who are the current incarnation of historical processes built around slavery, genocide, theft of land, and the destruction of the natural environment.

The Ecology of Good Intentions . . . and Vice-Versa?

These sorts of episodes and discussions illuminate a number of critical points about the nature and consequences of privatization. It is all too easy to idealize 'public space' as the 'great equalizer' and locus of 'democratic activity,' just as it is tempting to paint all 'developers' and 'yuppies' with the broad brush of 'authoritarianism' and 'elitism.' Still, the parameters of a society are defined through practices and relationships, and as the vignettes described here indicate, there is an inherently exclusionary power dynamic at work in many ostensibly public places that in reality have become private property. Some of the rights lost in this transformation are foundational in a democratic society, as delineated by Marina Peterson (2006:363) in her analysis of privatization in Los Angeles' California Plaza and its attendant 'rules and regulations': "No person, without the written consent of the Operator, shall do any of the following in or on any part of the Common Area: (b) Exhibit any sign, placard, banner, notice or other written material; (c) Distribute any circular, booklet, handbill, placard or other material; (e) Parade, rally, patrol, picket, demonstrate, or engage in any conduct that might tend to interfere with or impede the use of the Common Area by any Permittees, create a disturbance, attract attention or harass, annoy, disparage or be detrimental to the interest of any of the establishments within the Center." In essence, the property owner ('Operator') has literally abolished the First Amendment in what to all appearances is a very public place, effectively immunizing its constituent commercial 'establishments' from any sort of overt contestation and, more generally, denying access to a wide audience for any message at all.

This all begins to demarcate the boundaries not only of spatial control but social control as well, indicating the efficacy of an ecological perspective that explores the relationship between the environment (both in its 'built' and 'natural' forms) and human culture (including social, political, and economic spheres, among others). Jeff Ferrell (2006) suggests a discursive rubric of 'urban ecologies' to describe these types of phenomena, and almost two decades earlier Richard Ropers (1988) framed his investigation of homelessness in America around the sub-titular theme of "a new urban ecology." Sometimes scholars and/or organizations adopting the 'urban ecology' label will tend to emphasize either the sociological or the environmental aspects depending on their particular interests and intentions. Ropers, for example, did not focus very much on architectural, spatial, or environmental issues in his landmark study of homelessness in America, whereas the Wikipedia entry (circa 2007) for 'urban ecology' is framed almost exclusively in environmental terms. Taking a more balanced approach, in a chapter entitled 'The Ecology of Everyday Urban Life,' Fitzpatrick & LaGory (2000) look at hazards in urban settings, and in a subsequent chapter further consider health risks to the homeless from both social and environmental factors, concluding (2000:150) that homelessness is "a unique ecological circumstance."

For me as well, these spheres are always already interconnected in a manner analogous to the inherent nexus between social and spatial processes. A planter lining a city street, to take a small example, is usually a concrete edifice of some sort that contains a tree or other form of shrubbery, and is often sat or leaned upon by people as they go about their business in the city; when that planter is altered with spikes or arches meant to deter people from sitting there, it keeps certain types of people from frequenting the area (e.g., the homeless) but it also creates a distance between all people and the plant life contained therein. On a larger scale, when a new building or some other commercially-intended feature such as an artificial lake is under construction, homeless people will often be displaced in the process but so will animals, birds, and plants that previously occupied the area; also during construction of big projects, health risks to workers and the larger community increase. When a neighborhood near a downtown is gentrified and grass lawns start to replace the native vegetation that previously existed there, the ecology of the area (e.g., water use, temperature gradient) is altered even as low-wage workers suddenly find employment as landscapers. When businesses create copious amounts of trash and homeless people survive by picking through the garbage dumpsters, there is an explicit social-material loop created in the process. The removal of public restrooms will cause people with no other options to eliminate elsewhere, sometimes fouling riverbeds or parks. And so on. It is this reflexive nexus of social processes and environmental practices that an *urban ecology* seeks to illuminate, as Ferrell (2006:172-3) suggests:

> "'Consumption oriented societies are not sustainable, for environmental or social reasons.' Along with noting the profound environmental harms proffered by this world culture of spiraling consumption, criminologists and scholars of the city have begun to notice some of these unsustainable 'social reasons.' In fact, as trajectories of increasing urban consumption collide with growing intensities of urban inequality, all manner of deformities are now emerging in the practice of everyday life."

In the end, urban forces such as those embodied in the rubric of 'privatization' constitute a pervasive and expanding set of socio-economic policies that have vast implications, including environmental ones, as suggested by Rousseau (1973:84) in the famous quote that opens this section, reminding us quite forcefully that "you are undone if you once forget that the fruits of the earth belong to us all, and the earth itself to nobody." In this light, the impetus to privatize is also the impetus to control and dominate. On a macroscopic level, cities themselves often represent the human desire to control the natural environment, and in turn those same cities can wind up controlling us. If the sum total of these efforts is injurious on some level – whether economically, emotionally, socially, or environmentally – then it cannot be gainsaid that it is a self-inflicted wound. Still, if we can cause injury we can also create health, since, as Fitzpatrick & LaGory (2000:48) observe, "those who manipulate the environment . . . have great capacity for good or ill." The reflexive nature of space is, quite literally, a two-way street, meaning that what we shape also shapes us in ways that can be either liberatory or repressive depending on the values we ascribe and cultivate. In order for the positive side to manifest, however, some of those longed-for values of democratic participation that are believed to adhere in public space will need to be more deeply actualized. In other words, to realize the positive potential of spatial ecology – the 'capacity for good' in shaping the environment – we cannot rely on the developer or the elected official to have sole authority. Unfortunately, privatization and the like allow just that.

BID-ing for Dollar$!

Any analysis of processes such as privatization in the city must account for the growing presence of BIDs ('business improvement districts') and CBDs ('central business districts'), which Lofland (1998:212) notes "also give control of publicly owned space to private interests." In many municipalities with BIDs or CBDs, "the most influential nexus of interests is often the 'downtown business elite': directors of real estate companies, department stores and banks, together with retail merchants and directors of local newspapers who rely heavily on central city business fortunes" (Knox 1995:94). As Hannigan (1998:139) further notes, BIDs "have legal status which allows merchants and property owners in commercial districts to tax themselves in order to provide an expanded repertoire of services." More critically, Christian Parenti (2000:96) describes BIDs as "private, self-taxing, urban micro-states that do everything from cleaning streets and guiding tourists to floating bonds and arresting beggars. BIDs embody all the power and privileges of the state yet bear none of the responsibilities and limitations of democratic government." Likewise Talmadge Wright (1997:86), who observes that "more than a thousand BIDs have expanded across the United States, creating special districts where taxes are raised or lowered independent of the majority of the population within a given city. This raises a key issue in the preservation of public democratic city spaces. The privatization of public space promoted by such schemes means that political and economic decisions will be made by those who own the most property." Margaret Kohn (2004:82) adds that BIDs are essentially "publicly regulated, private governments" that "have been at the forefront of the attempt to apply the logic of the shopping mall to downtown centers." One recent study further notes that "there are BIDs in cities as far apart as Kingston, Jamaica and Wellington, New Zealand," and that "the number of BIDs in the USA is increasing so rapidly it is hard to find a definite number" (Steel & Symes 2005:322).

In terms of what the decisions carried out by BIDs will actually look like, Hannigan (1998:14) offers a now-familiar scenario:

> "In their new role as developers, BIDs have begun to embrace urban entertainment in various ways. They are increasingly prone to follow Disney's lead in identifying theme and style with public order. This means both securing consumption

> space by limiting public access and controlling visual design, key elements in the success of Disney theme parks."

Others observe that, through BIDs, "private control of public space has been extended to the public realm of the sidewalk," and that features such as 'surveillance' and 'private security' are frequently found within their confines (Loukaitou-Sideris, et al. 2005). This has again yielded some familiar outcomes, as noted by McCarthy & McPhail (2006:233):

> "The creation of these districts in conjunction with laws aimed at restricting the access of homeless individuals to public space has the serious potential to discourage speech access to public space. . . . This has resulted in controlled access, security guards, and surveillance effectively taking these traditional commons out of the public forum. . . . Attempting to control access and behaviors in traditional public fora at best discourages the use of these places for speech and at worst denies it."

Kohn (2004:85-6) further asserts that "BIDs, as private, non-profit organizations, may be able to circumvent the constitutional provisions that require local governments to protect the civil liberties of their citizens," and relates an episode where "four former [BID] outreach workers claimed that they were told by supervisors to use all means necessary in order to remove homeless people from the district. They admitted to beating homeless people and destroying their belongings. These statements corroborated the stories of homeless people who claimed they had been beaten and threatened by [BID] employees."

As you might already have guessed, Tempe has its very own BID for our critical pleasure: the Downtown Tempe Community, Inc., or simply the DTC, that has frequently appeared in this case study. Created in late 1993 with a $250,000 interest-free loan from the city of Tempe, early reports described the entity as being "funded by an assessment on downtown businesses, [which] is paid by the business as part of its property tax" (Petrie 1994b). Rod Keeling was hired as the organization's Executive Director in January 1994 (and served in that capacity for over a decade), and in addition to touting accomplishments such as "starting an ambassadors program" and "spearheading the effort toward building public restrooms," he predicted that "there's going to be some serious marketing in this district." By mid-1997, it had become apparent that in creating the DTC – described then as "a quasi-governmental policymaker" – the city had "passed the redevelopment baton to the private sector" (Porter 1997a). Shortly thereafter, the DTC's contract with the city of Tempe was up for renewal; with the area being "poised for tremendous growth," then-Mayor Neil Giuliano touted the DTC's accomplishments (in Petrie 1997): "Things are positive. Crime is down, development is up, new business starts are up, the number of people coming to town is up."

Despite the mayor's endorsement, however, critical voices were beginning to emerge. Longtime city watchdog Art Jacobs (1997) noted in the *Arizona Republic* that the city council had actually 'lent' the DTC $750,000 (not $250,000 as had been reported), and that "the DTC has been built upon the 'blood, sweat, and tears' of the Tempe citizen taxpayer." Amplifying his point further in another *Republic* column early the following year, Jacobs (1998) lamented that "the Tempe taxpayers have graciously given millions to the merchants of the Downtown Tempe Community," pointing out again that the city had advanced "$750,000 ($250,000 interest-free) in loans to the DTC. These loans are being 'paid for' by the coins inserted (about $400,000 annually) into the parking meters by the Tempe taxpayers. The merchants pay nothing for the loans." And in fact, the DTC web site in 2001 did note that "the City start up advance is repaid on a 10 year schedule from parking revenues, beginning in 1998."

Jacobs' column elicited a defensive response from Ross Robb (1998), then-President, who argued that the DTC was "not the enemy of the community [since] more than 83 percent of our funding comes from a special assessment on commercial property in downtown Tempe, paid for by property owners." In particular, Robb asserted: "Let us not confuse the DTC as an organization and the downtown as a 'place.' The DTC is not a consumer of city services, it is a complement to such services. It is a private, non-profit, downtown management organization created by city ordinance and made up of all downtown stakeholders, including business and property owners, residents, employees and the city itself." Robb's column then drew a pointed response from fifth-generation Tempean Robert Enright (1998), the first elected president of the Tempe Historical Society: "The DTC resulted from a process that isolated the downtown area from the larger community. It was instigated by a few individuals, with assistance from a few members of the city staff. Our City Council acquiesced.

The DTC now controls a vital element of our city. With legalized borders, and practically its own codified government, the DTC has set itself apart. The core of our city represents our values. That representation is now controlled by a few. Downtown began as a place for all of us. That is not the case today. Those who now make decisions about the most visible representation we have are not responsive to the electorate. We *all* have stakes here, Mr. Robb."

Despite such criticisms, the DTC web site (downtowntempe.com) still (circa 2008) overtly touts its 'strategic plan' for downtown Tempe as one that represents a "consensus of ideas" among the "commercial and civic stakeholders of downtown Tempe," including the intentions to "create and market an image for the [district]," and to "encourage higher density and vertical development." As of mid-2001, the DTC reported over $1.6 million in revenues, and boasted board members including Ross Robb, Rod Keeling, Ted Claasen (a prominent downtown developer on many of the highest-profile projects), Dave Fackler (Development Services director for the city of Tempe), and former Mayor Giuliano. Today, in 2008, board members include Robb, former city council member Pam Goronkin (now President and Executive Director of the DTC), Michael Crow (President of Arizona State University), Grady Gammage (a leading attorney for developers), and "Permanent Seat" representatives from both Centerpoint and the Brickyard. With so many friends in high places, the DTC's 'stakeholders' have consistently been among the most vocal proponents of redevelopment and gentrification, and the organization itself has been the leading advocate for ordinances and police practices aimed at restricting and/or removing street kids and the homeless from the "downtown commercial district," the micro-state that constitutes the exclusive domain of the DTC. As Kohn (2004:88) appropriately concludes: "It is not surprising that the wealthy and powerful would prefer to govern themselves without interference from everyone else. What is surprising is that a democracy is willing the let them."

Eyes in the Skies: Public Space Surveillance

As noted above, one of the dominant features of this emerging and exclusive terrain is the omnipresence of security and surveillance. As one writer (Passaro 1996:82) explains, "public space has come to be seen not as the last frontier of freedom, but rather as a frontline in battles over social control. Since Foucault redeployed Jeremy Bentham's notion of the panopticon to describe a multivalent and mutlipurpose surveillance mechanism that could be incorporated into the design of built environments, recognition of the powers inherent in spatial representations has led to a reexamination of the relationship of social and spatial arrangements" (see also Arnold 2004:106-16). In this regard, Tempe's socio-spatial policies are starkly memorialized in the CPTED program (Crime Prevention Through Environmental Design), which seeks to yield "an improvement in the quality of life [through] the design of physical space so that it enhances the needs of *bona fide* users." The program is implemented through five stated principles (with a not-so-subtle nod to Oscar Newman's controversial 1973 volume, *Defensible Space*) as follows:

(1) **Territoriality**, which "clearly delineates private space from semi-public and public spaces, and creates a sense of *ownership*, [which] thereby creates an environment where the appearance of *strangers* and intruders stands out."
(2) **Natural Surveillance**, which is "a design concept directed primarily at keeping *intruders* under observation."
(3) **Access Control**, which "limits access and increases natural surveillance to *restrict criminal intrusion*," creating an environment in which "intruders are more readily recognized."
(4) **Activity Support**, which entails the promotion of "safe activities" to increase both "the perception of safety for *normal users*, and the perception of risk for offenders."
(5) **Maintenance**, which includes the use of "landscaping, lighting treatment and other features [to] facilitate the principles of CPTED, *territorial reinforcement*, natural surveillance and natural access control."

This five-point program is at least notable for its brute honesty, but is also profoundly disturbing in its full implications. At the outset, by attempting to ferret out 'strangers' and conflating them with 'intruders,' a key attribute of city life – namely diversity of interactions – is undermined; still, this confirms the notion raised in the preceding chapter that 'strangers' are historical cousins of today's 'homeless' and are thus equally subject to regulation and exclusion. More troubling are the invocations of 'bona fide users' and 'normal users' as the intended beneficiaries of these policies and practices; unquestionably the implication is that such preferred users (i.e., consumers) are superior to 'intruders' and deserving of special protection from undesirable elements. Phrases such as 'a sense of ownership' and 'territorial reinforcement' are wholly revealing of a property-based perspective that connotes a rightful assertion of authority but smacks more of an attempt to convince oneself of something that is known to be false or violative of another's rights (cf. Mitchell & Staeheli 2006:153, on "pseudo-private spaces"). And finally, concepts such as 'natural surveillance' and 'access control' are apparent nods to architectural and environmental features that accomplish the dual aims of social and spatial control, validating the central premise of an *urban ecology* perspective, as Peterson (2006:377-9) suggests:

> "The built environment, often designed to produce and support particular forms of public and private, provides the terrain on which concerns of access, security, surveillance and use are played out. . . . While the 'general' user of the space is consenting and harmonious, the markedness of the excluded (homeless or protestor) facilitates rupture of the seeming seamlessness of privatized public space. The exclusion of the homeless from public space reflects an exclusion on the basis of class as well as the exclusion of class as a category of diversity. The homeless, recognizable as such by virtue of being unbathed or poorly clothed, make class differences visible, and thus cannot be part of a consenting, harmonious public. . . . For reasons such as these, it is important to take privatized public space seriously, examining what kind of space it provides for the formation of citizenship both in itself and in relation to its other."

One significant feature of these types of surveillance schemes is the pervasive presence of security cameras in public places. Tempe presently has at least two cameras mounted along Mill Avenue, which it actively promotes on its web site as 'Sneaky Peak,' offering visitors real-time images of downtown Tempe that update regularly, with a catchy slogan urging that "the next time you're strolling down Mill . . .

look up . . . smile . . . and wave!" (tempe.gov/millcam). However, an *ASU State Press* article titled 'Cameras Have Locals Saying Cheese on Mill' (Prendergast 1998b), written when the cameras were first installed, indicates that not all of the views in town were quite as celebratory as the city's, noting that "some Tempe visitors and residents feel their privacy is being invaded." By 2001, ongoing concerns and dissent had spawned a counter-surveillance movement in Tempe, led by a group calling itself the Arizona Surveillance Camera Players (AZSCP). By positioning themselves strategically before the camera's gaze and holding up signs with text such as 'Don't Worry – You'll Still Be Allowed to Shop,' the group sought to expose and interrupt "the kinds of intrusions that are altering the meaning of urban anonymity and security," and also to provide "a commentary on the no skateboarding, no sitting attitude down there, and on the fact that all they really want to encourage is shopping" (Lebow 2001). Interestingly, the same *New Times* article highlighting the exploits of the AZSCP concluded by describing a familiar-sounding episode that illuminates the public/private tensions in downtown Tempe:

> "A few times, a befuddled-looking security guard moved in to remind the troupe to stay off of Centerpoint property and keep their signs on the public fringe of the sidewalk. Yet to no avail; the protest signs kept spilling across the invisible line separating private from public. With the performance winding down, Centerpoint's chief bouncer emerged from the shade and demanded, 'Who's in charge here? I'm Centerpoint security. I work for this property. Get your signs off of here or I'm going to throw them in the trash.' 'So you're telling me that a government-owned Web cam is broadcasting images in a privately owned space?' bellowed [Charles Banaszewski, AZSCP founder]. 'I don't know anything about a government Web cam on a private space,' said [the TEAM guard]. 'All I know is you need to get your signs out of here.'"

Occasional outbreaks of open resistance notwithstanding, it is plain that the use of surveillance strategies in public places is sharply increasing. As Lyn Lofland (1998:213) describes it, this "panopticon approach" often entails "indoor and outdoor surveillance cameras, closed-circuit TVs, two-way mirrors, hidden microphones – all the paraphernalia we associate with the modern police state." In their study of youths in public spaces, Hil & Bessant (1999:46) likewise note that "the gaze of the security officer, the sweep of the video camera, the sideways glances by anxious shoppers are continual reminders of the omnipresence of surveillance." More recently, Peterson (2006:370-3) discusses the 'Panoptical Plaza,' a space in which "the security mechanisms are similar to those of Disneyworld," where guards monitoring pervasive camera feeds will "'follow' an individual who has visible traits that mark him or her as homeless," and where "the camera reflects a wider social control [on] the marginal citizen . . . who bears the weight of the camera's control over space and bodies . . . and whose practices are curtailed;" most chillingly, a person spotted by the cameras as being "unkempt but not disturbing anyone" will inevitably find a guard standing "about three feet away from the person, following until he or she feels uncomfortable enough to leave the Plaza." In analyzing the effects of "making our cities like enormous panopticons," Koskela (2000:243-7) appropriately concludes:

> "Surveillance is easy to use to exclude groups that are marginal. [Security] guards' routine work is to use surveillance cameras to look for 'undesirables.' The reason for excluding someone is that person's appearance. A person's appearance is considered as reflecting that person's ability to consume: one must always look as if one has bought something or is about to buy, because presumed noncustomers (such as bag ladies, the homeless, or teenagers) 'will be asked to move on or will be thrown out.' The spaces of consumption become 'aestheticized' by exclusion, and the urban experience is 'purified.' Thus, ostensibly public spaces are not public for everyone; public space can be seen as if it refers to places under public scrutiny. The erosion of public space will increasingly spread to open publicly owned urban space. The controlled spaces which signal exclusion will no longer be restricted to particular private premises. Public space – or at least spontaneous social behavior in it – will be forced to die."

Next Stop, Dystopia

And so, welcome to the "apocalypse theme park" (Davis 1998), the even darker underbelly of these trends toward over-development and Disneyfication. In ruminating on such themes of "urban eschatology," Mike Davis (1998:397) observes that a Disneyfied space "is 'not a mall' but a 'revolution in urban design,' a monumental exercise in sociological hygiene. [It is] the architectural equivalent of the neutron bomb: the city emptied of all lived experience." As Michael Sorkin (1992:230) envisions, the dark side of Disney "inevitably conjures up other, more dystopian images, most notably the underworld in Fritz Lang's *Metropolis*, its workers trapped in carceral caverns dancing their robotic ballet. . . ." Talmadge Wright (1997:97) sees the homeless as the unwitting inhabitants of this underworld: "The dystopic images from *Blade Runner, Brazil, Escape from New York*, and the *Mad Max* films constitute the socially imagined 'other half,' the homeless and the poor, segregated from glittering shopping/entertainment malls and theme parks." Tempe's homeless 'Mill Rats' presage this apocalyptic edge as well, forced to "sleep anywhere they can, caves and the *Road Warrior*-esque camps on the edge of Papago Park" (Holthouse 1998a). Even the DTC's Rod Serling, I mean Keeling (1998b), master of the ironic twist, sees it – although in him it inspires antipathy rather than compassion: "We turned our most historic community park into a *Mad Max*, post-apocalyptic-looking campground."

The emerging "dystopian dream" that Jeff Ferrell (1998a:30) identifies is all-too-real in its full implications, constituting "a dream of sanitized communities mirroring visions of consensual conformity; of streets swept free of young, marginalized populations, of urban trash, and the uncomfortable reminders of social decay that they present; and of an urban environment made safe for suburban excursions and endless, effortless consumption, for the discovery of urban charm and prepackaged urban adventure." Unfortunately, as Lyn Lofland (1998:218-20) notes, "Orwellian surveillance may be firmly in place in America's counterlocales, but the inhabitants are apparently too busy enjoying the delights of Huxley's *Brave New World* to be even the slightest bit alarmed." But who can really blame them, after all, living a dystopian nightmare that's so pervasive as to be imperceptible, moving through *film noir* spaces right out of *Blade Runner*, *Dark City*, and *Memento* – spaces where ceaseless changes render 'memory' problematic, where all that once was is repeatedly wiped away in favor of the new – the proverbial hypermodern dystopia of simulacra and artifice. If only this were all relegated to the realm of speculative fiction, celebratory comments such as the following from the DTC's *Downtowner* (2001b) might be received as more comedic than chilling, more asinine than apocalyptic:

> "The downtown has been developing at an increasingly frantic rate. A person who hasn't visited the area in the last decade wouldn't recognize a lot of the buildings along Mill Avenue. Most of them have been restored and, in some cases, are newly built. In the past five years, the lake has been filled in and Tempe Beach Park has been rebuilt. It's completely possible that in another five years the downtown will be unrecognizable to those who inhabit it now. The Brickyard's construction should be completed any time now, but following close on its heels are an army of construction projects that will only serve to enhance the current beauty of the downtown."

Indeed, life sometimes does imitate art, but the result here is not particularly beautiful. Such dystopian geographies are relentlessly exclusionary, forcing out independent local retailers, marginalizing the undesirable and non-commodifiable, replacing the openness of the public sphere with admissions standards developed at the whim of private property owners, imposing homogeneity and predictability on spaces prized for their diversity and spontaneity, and manipulating the environment to eradicate any orienting sense of history or place. This, indeed, may well be a form of *urban ecology*, although of a perverse sort that is ultimately self-defeating: a city space so obsessively managed and hyper-regulated that it is "emptied of all lived experience" – even as it touts itself as being a place for 'night life,' 'the good life,' or (as on Mill Avenue) a 'place to live, work, and play.' As Ferrell (2006:181) observes, "these strategies build bad urban policy on a foundation of inadequate urban understanding; they ignore the ambiguous interplay of identities, the informal transgressing of spatial and cultural borders, essential to the life of the contemporary city." A recent *New Times* article (Irwin 2006) noted that "Mill Avenue is all but a ghost town," and that "tonight, as on many nights, there's almost no one on the street." Is this the result of almost a decade of sanitizing spaces and Disneyfying experiences in the downtown area? Calling someplace a 'hot spot' or the 'place to be' simply does not make it so.

What else would we expect? Consistent with the values of dystopia and the simulacra of the 'artificial natural environment,' it is essentially as if a carefully-chosen marketing phrase replaces the actual thing that has been destroyed. And perhaps this is why people go to Disneyland or the shopping mall in the first place, to have a pseudo-experience of diversity or excitement that carries no risk of having to get one's hands 'dirty' in the process. Come to think of it, all of this is reminiscent of the way in which 'master-planned' communities (often located just outside the city limits) are named, after the very thing they have eradicated: 'Quail Run' – 'Pronghorn Ranch' – 'Juniper Heights' – 'Hawk's Nest.' Perhaps we need a *suburban ecology* to explain this, although I suspect that similar principles would hold both here and there. By this logic, back in the city perhaps we'll soon see 'Vagabond Villas,' 'Transient Towers,' or a 'Homeless Hi-Rise.' In the meantime, welcome to AnyTown . . . coming soon to an everywhere near you.

CHAPTER THREE

Patterns of Exclusion

The Perversity of Homelessness Criminalization

What is it really about the homeless that seems to inspire such overt antipathy from mainstream society? What is so special about their particular variety of 'deviance' that it often elicits so vehement and violent a response to their presence? Why would cities risk undermining their distinctiveness and desirability over so vulnerable a group as the homeless? After all, homeless people lack almost any indicia of societal power, posing no viable political or military threat to the dominant culture. Of course, it is often the case that a society's response to deviant elements is rarely linked directly to an actual threat (see, e.g., Lauderdale 2003). Rather, the threat generally is more one of perception than reality, more of a societal preemptive strike against an as-yet-unborn threat – a threat that often originates within the dominant culture itself but finds concrete expression in some abject, powerless element of society. As the literature reviewed in this chapter indicates, depictions of 'deviant subcultures 'are likely to feed into stereotypes of danger, disorder, disease, and criminality, helping to construct the 'other' as inferior, inhuman, and perhaps even requiring punitive measures. That all of this arises more from perception than fact becomes eminently clear, suggesting that it is, after all, a short journey from diversity to deviance, from deification to demonization, and from sanctification to stigmatization.

Perceptions of Demonization and Disease

Before proceeding further, it is important to understand the genesis of societal misgivings about homeless people. As Henry Miller (1991) observes, there have been times in history where the image of the homeless beggar was one of sacrificial piety and mendicant holiness. But by and large such characterizations have been the exception and, at least since the enclosure of the common lands in sixteenth-century England, almost nonexistent. Once domains of private property began to dominate the cultural and physical landscape, "vagrancy began to be seen as a threat to the order of things;" later, as urban centers began to develop and market economies took hold, "vagrancy was to be perceived as a threat to capitalism" (Miller 1991:9). This would become particularly true in the developing United States, where a version of the Protestant Work Ethic is intimately connected to the national mythos of open opportunity and free-market meritocracy (cf. Weber 1958). Fast forwarding to the present, it is apparent that the dominant culture heavily stigmatizes poverty as an 'individual pathology' more than a structural phenomenon, and that the homeless – because of their inescapably public presence and frequent juxtaposition to centers of leisure – invariably inspire the most virulent derogation and overt animus. Poor people with homes are at least 'out of sight' for the dominant culture, if not 'out of mind;' lacking private spaces, however, the homeless are often in plain view, and therefore are subject to the most direct forms of official exclusion and public persecution.

In mainstream publications, both academic and journalistic, even depictions intended to be sympathetic to the homeless often contribute to a mindset of *demonization*. One of the most enduring signs of this is the association of homelessness with images of dirt, filth, decay, disease, disgust, pests, and vermin (see Gowan 2000:98; Mitchell 2003:196-7; cf. Lees 2003:625-6). In what is ostensibly an empathetic rendering of the health risks inherent in homelessness, Fitzpatrick & LaGory (2000:145) nonetheless reify this pervasive view by noting the prevalence of infections, ailments, numerous "chronic physical disorders," and diseases such as "AIDS and tuberculosis." Miller (1991:22) likewise observes that historically the vagrant was seen as a person of "many vices and debilities; was sickly and suffered from the ravages of tuberculosis, typhus, cholera, scrofula, rickets, and other disorders too numerous to mention; was apt to be a member of the despised races; [and whose] life was characterized by all the usual depravities: sexual license, bastardy, prostitution, theft." Miller's analysis suggests two related but distinct strands contributing to homeless stigmatization. The first arises out of invocations of disorder, illegality, and immorality, and leads to processes of regulation, criminalization, and enforcement. The second is the disease and decay image, which leads to processes of sanitization, sterilization, and quarantine. In a sense, these two spheres are undoubtedly inseparable, both leading to the same ends of *exclusion*, *eradication*, and *erasure*. On a deeper level, both spheres also converge around the homeless, who occupy spaces that (like themselves) are often viewed as dirty and disorderly, and therefore require both regulation and sterilization. As Mike Davis (1990:260) observes, public spaces, like the homeless, are imbued with "democratic intoxications, risks and unscented odors."

For purposes of the analysis here, I believe it will be illustrative to consider the *disease* image as conceptually distinct from the *disorder* characterization. This arises primarily out of the Disneyfication of space in general (and downtown Tempe in particular) that has been indicated thus far, since the Disney metaphor (and reality) is one of antiseptic sterility and disinfected experience, of shiny surfaces and squeaky-clean images. It is the apotheosis of what Herman Hesse described in *Steppenwolf* (1972:16) as "bourgeois cleanliness," representing "the very essence of neatness and meticulousness, of duty and devotion . . . a paradise of cleanliness and spotless mediocrity, of ordered ways." Disney is above all the 'sterilized' environment, a place stripped of any outward signs of filth, decay, spoliation, or despair. Underneath that facade, however, is an interior dystopian world of darkness, brutal efficiency, neurosis, rigid control, and emptiness. As Hesse (1972:23-4) describes the plight of his protagonist, trapped in a place not unlike the Disney-dystopia (or 'Dis-topia' for short), the disease he suffers from "is not the eccentricity of a single individual, but the sickness of the times themselves, the neurosis of that generation . . . a sickness, it seems, that by no means attacks the weak and worthless only but, rather, precisely those who are strongest in spirit and richest in gifts." Dis-topia, then, comes to be seen not as a place for the 'clean' to gather and play, but as an antiseptic retreat for the diseased of spirit to be temporarily distracted from the depredations of their existence. When that temporary distraction is made permanent, control is complete and the inevitability of dystopia is realized.

This is an important caveat and merits amplification. The assertion is that the condition of *disease* and the fears it engenders primarily originate within the dominant culture, and are only secondarily projected onto the homeless. As Lees (2003:626) notes, "the persistent rhetoric of filth, disgust, and abjection associated with youth downtown might be read in psychoanalytic terms as indicative of underlying psycho-social anxieties about individual and collective identity and the wider symbolic order on which they depend." As Fitzpatrick & LaGory (2000:137) intuit, homelessness is "a vivid reminder of . . . our own vulnerability," a point suggested by Ropers (1988:28) as well: "We are afraid to face them, because we may recognize our own vulnerability to economic and social insecurity." Kohn (2004:14) also considers the impetus to avoid "sources of discomfort for [consumers], including panhandlers and homeless people," and reflects on "the widely shared expectation that one should not be forced to view the unpleasant consequences of our social system." And Snow & Mulcahy (2001:151,159) evaluate encounters with homeless people as "a rupture of the urban order that engenders a sense of unease and discomfort among many citizens," bringing to mind "the image of Third World cities teeming with highly visible unhoused beggars," and constituting "a blunt rupture of the idealized American dream."

The fact that so much of this antipathy toward homeless people arises out of the perceptions and anxieties of merchants, consumers, and politicians is well documented (e.g., Mitchell 1997a:328, noting that the "public sphere" is modeled on "the palpable fears of the bourgeoisie;" and Harvey 2006:29-30, observing that "bourgeois anxiety" often manifests in the drive to attain "total control over public spaces and the public sphere"). As Talmadge Wright (1997:69) further infers, "the homeless body in the public imagination represents the body of decay, the degenerate body, a body that is constantly rejected by the public as 'sick,' 'scary,' 'dirty,' and 'smelly,' and a host of other pejoratives used to create social distance between housed and unhoused persons." This sense of *social distancing* reflects "the desire of those who feel threatened to distance themselves from defiled people and defiled places . . . places associated with ethnic and racial minorities, like the inner city, [that] are still tainted and perceived as polluting in racist discourses, and place-related phobias [that] are similarly evident in response to other minorities, like gays and the homeless" (Sibley 1995:49). Analyzing 'new urban spaces,' Wright (2000:27) concludes:

> "In effect street people, camping in parks, who exhibit appearances at odds with middle class comportment, evoke fears of 'contamination' and disgust, a reminder of the power

> of abjection. Homeless persons embody the social fear of privileged consumers, fear for their families, for their children, fear that 'those' people will harm them and therefore must be placed as far away as possible from safe neighborhoods. The subsequent social death which homeless persons endure is all too often accompanied by real death and injury as social exclusion moves from criminalization of poverty to social isolation and incarceration in institutional systems of control – shelters and prisons."

Likewise Samira Kawash (1998:329): "The public view of the homeless as 'filth' marks the danger of this body *as body* to the homogeneity and wholeness of the public. . . . The solution to this impasse appears as the ultimate aim of the 'homeless wars': to exert such pressures against this body that will reduce it to nothing, to squeeze it until it is so small that it disappears, such that the circle of the social will again appear closed."

Many of those in favor of regulating, containing, and/or criminalizing the homeless readily embrace such disease metaphors and their potentially ethnocidal implications. Robert Ellickson (1996) implicitly affirms the image through his "revulsion at body odors and the stink of urine and feces" (Waldron 2000); as Kohn (2004:169) adds in her critique of Ellickson's vision of 'homeless free zones,' it is often the perception of policymakers that "the smell or appearance of street people may discourage others from sharing public space." A recent piece advocating for the utility of policing practices in Los Angeles' Skid Row (MacDonald 2007) invokes images of "feces, urine, and drug-resistant bacteria coating the ground," as well as "filth and disease." On the other side of the ideological coin, a homeless advocate in Seattle recently observed that there would be a "smear campaign" in advance of new city policies regarding homeless encampments that would focus upon "trash, feces, drug use, and criminality" (Harris 2008). Further confirming this perspective, it has been observed that "others, including many city officials, celebrate gentrification for reversing urban decay and boosting the tax base. They often refer to it as 'revitalization,' drawing on the metaphors of disease, deterioration, death, and rebirth" (Williams 1996:147). As Jeff Ferrell (2001a:175) contends, "drawing on evocative images of filth, disease, and decay, economic and political authorities engage in an ideological alchemy through which unwanted individuals become [a] sort of 'street trash' [and which] demonizes economic outsiders, stigmatizes cultural trespassers, and thereby justifies the symbolic cleansing of the cultural spaces they occupy." Countless newspaper editorials, including political cartoons (cf. Wright 1997:209), contribute to these trends by depicting the homeless as vile, malodorous, and dangerous – starkly evident in this *Arizona Republic* editorial image from February 2002 of Tempe's Mill Avenue:

Fig. 2: Editorial cartoon re: homeless people on Mill Avenue, 2/02

In political terms, the pervasiveness of the disease image in connection with the homeless serves simultaneously to empower officials and merchants to assume the mantle of speaking for 'the health and safety of the community' in devising and implementing schemes to remove the perceived threat, and to disempower the homeless themselves from having effective domains of self-presentation and resistance. As Wright (1997:39) concludes, "living with 'spoiled identities,' the very poor are categorized, inspected, dissected, and rendered mute in the public discourse about their future by those who have the power to enforce [such] categorical distinctions." Tempe's Piper (2000) waxes philosophically about the whole state of affairs:

"They think their lives would be so much better if they didn't have to see the 'slime' and the 'scum' that lives on the street, but you know what? This is fucking real life, this is *here*, a diverse amount of things – in this world you never know what you're gonna see, so why try to hide it? Their kids are gonna find out about it anyway. . . ." Lyn Lofland (1998:190) also acknowledges this sense of the eventual permeation of homeless identity, despite attempts at regulation: "If regulation alone could achieve the purification of the public realm, we would all currently live in a world from which . . . the homeless . . . had completely disappeared." Nonetheless, despite their lack of full realization in the present, it is apparent, as Jeff Ferrell (2001a:175) explains, that such regulatory efforts serve to

> "reinforce patterns of power and privilege, as they spawn new aggressions and indignities against the disadvantaged, enforce new forms of spatial exclusion within urban areas, and promote a type of spatial cleansing whereby unwanted populations are removed, by the force of law and money, from particular locations and situations. But this spatial cleansing is at the same time a cultural cleansing; as economic, political, and legal authorities work to recapture and redesign the public spaces of the city, they work to control public identity and public perception as well, to remove from new spaces of consumption and development images of alternative identity. Forces of economic development and corporate control, of legal and political domination, of symbolic erasure and perceptual policing all intersect and intertwine in the cultural spaces of the city."

Here, then, is the upshot of an ecological perspective on homeless demonization: a geography of 'cleansing' put into the service of regimes of control that construct the 'other' as vile and diseased. It is a classic twist borrowed from the sociology of deviance, to fan the flames of public perception around the 'danger' presented by some abject class of people, and then to use this burgeoning public fear to justify a spate of policies and practices aimed at attaining greater degrees of political and economic control. From the so-called 'war on terror' to the implicit 'war on the homeless,' the cultural arithmetic is the same: fear, demonization, regulation, authoritarianism. It is an old story, perhaps new only in its areas of application, and comprises a framework that might come to be called 'the ecology of social control.'

Disorderly Conduct: The Absurdity of Anti-Homeless Legislation

Following this line of reasoning, it doesn't take much of a stretch to segue from Jeff Ferrell's (2001a:169) sense of 'spatial cleansing' and 'cultural sanitization' to patterns of criminalization and enforcement. As one writer notes, "increasingly, communities are using the criminal law to cleanse their streets of homeless survivors" (Smith 1994). Whereas the *disease* metaphor is predicated upon a view of the homeless as physical pestilence, the *disorder* image upon which criminalization often is based arises out of a view of the homeless as a "moral pestilence" (Simon 1992; cf. McConkey 1996) and a "threat to the social order" (Simon 1992). As Ferrell (1993:142) likewise observes in connection with anti-graffiti campaigns, it is the fear of "anarchy and chaos . . . disorder and decay" that comprise the ostensible reasons for the laws and crackdowns, a point echoed in a recent valorization of policing efforts purportedly designed to achieve "a reduction of Skid Row's anarchy" (MacDonald 2007). This tack apparently wasn't lost on Rod Keeling (1998b) (then-Director of Tempe's BID, the DTC) who, in urging passage of a no-sitting ordinance, warned that we cannot "allow anarchy in downtown." Thus, whereas the depiction of disease leads to the imposition of regimes of sterility and sanitization, images of moral decay and being 'out of order' set the stage for legislative efforts aimed at regulating street people and criminalizing homelessness. Where the former results in a type of 'cultural cleansing' (cf. Noonan 1996), the latter begins to approach ethnocidal proportions in its use of overt force, imprisonment, and concentration – constituting what Don Mitchell (1997a) has likened to a 'pogrom.' Where Disney is the 'friendly' face of fascism, Criminal Justice can often represent its blatant, casual brutality.

For at least six centuries there has been an association of homelessness with disorder (e.g., Simon 1996:159; Farrell 2005:1034) and criminality (e.g., Snow & Anderson 1993:11; Wright 1997:212), patterns which contemporary "official efforts to harass, punish, or restrict transient people who use public space are repeating" (Stoner 1995:151). Mitchell (1997a:312) thus suggests, quite appropriately, that we ought to be talking about "*recriminalizing* homelessness."

Obviously, constructing the 'other' as disorderly and criminal throughout history has required the construction and maintenance of a dominant culture that embodies order and lawfulness (cf. Smith 1996 on 'revanchism;' see also Mitchell 1997a:317). Equally apparent is that standards of civility and legality are generally determined by those in positions of power and advantage who can manipulate such standards to suit their interests and protect their domains of property and authority. In this manner, any construction of 'otherness' as lawlessness necessarily becomes a self-fulfilling prophecy, since in theory one can only be guilty of violating a law *after* someone else passes it – a point made excruciatingly clear by former Tempe Mayor Neil Giuliano in an interview about 'homeless transients' with the *Phoenix New Times* (Gilstrap 1995): "I asked him, in this transient issue, what is the law that's being broken? . . . I said they're not breaking any laws, and he said, 'We can change that.'" In other words, it is the law itself that creates the crime – or, in Kropotkin-esque terms (1968), "the greatest source of crime is law," since without laws there could be no crime. These base tautologies are all illustrated in an article written soon after the passage of Seattle's sidewalk sitting ordinance:

> "'This is not aimed at the homeless, it is aimed at the lawless,' says Seattle City Attorney Mark Sidran. By 'the lawless' Sidran and other city officials mean people who, lacking anywhere else to go, sit down on the sidewalk. Jim Jackson, an Atlanta businessman, confidently declares that his city's new laws will 'not punish anyone but the criminal.' San Francisco's Mayor Frank Jordan assures us that 'homelessness is not a crime. It is not a crime to be out there looking like an unmade bed. But if criminal behavior begins . . . then we will step in and enforce the law'" (Howland 1994:33).

Despite such stated intentions, Barak (1991:80) has observed that "business owners can be heard complaining about the physical presence of the homeless vagrants panhandling on virtually every city block where commerce and services exist. In Atlanta, a group of business executives and civic leaders have proposed a 'safeguard zone' to enforce 'quality of life' crime ordinances in order to 'provide significant control of the movement of street persons, transients, hangers-on, loiterers, and street vendors.'"

The logical flaw in the 'official' position is all too apparent. "If criminal behavior begins . . ." "We punish only the criminal." "It is aimed at the lawless." All of these statements were made in reference to conduct such as sitting on sidewalks or sleeping in public that, before passage of the most recent spate of anti-homeless laws, had heretofore been perfectly legal and generally seen as innocent acts. Along these lines, in a telling summary of recent efforts to regulate and manage Skid Row in Los Angeles, Gary Blasi (2007:29) documents how the official deliberations focused on crafting a message indicating that "the problem is 'lawlessness,' not 'homelessness,'" and yet how "there was *no* discussion at the meetings about lawlessness other than violations that inevitably accompany homelessness in the absence of adequate shelter or other facilities: sleeping or sitting on the sidewalk, conducting biological functions in locations other than bathrooms." The report further observes that "there was in the minutes of these meetings not a single mention of 'crime' that does not necessarily accompany homelessness when there is a lack of shelter or other facilities: nothing about drug sales, nothing about violence perpetrated against homeless people. Nothing."

Now, by virtue of laws prohibiting conduct such as sitting or sleeping, an entire category of people is made 'criminal' for acts committed *before* the law existed. The lesson? If you want to eliminate a particular social class or subculture or deviant group, locate some behavior that is largely unique to that group and make it illegal. Or, pass laws under the guise of universal applicability that plainly impact only the target community: "The law in its majestic equality forbids the rich as well as the poor to sleep under the bridges" (Anatole France, in Waldron 1991). As Mitchell (1996b:166,171) observes, in "asserting the primacy of property rights," the lawgivers "often struggled to couch those rights in a universal language that masked the class-based nature of their rulings. This universal language typically was a language of civility and order. . . . Orderliness can thus quite easily serve power." Hence, as Waldron (1991) points out, "everyone is perfectly aware of the point of passing these ordinances, and any attempt to defend them on the basis of their generality is quite disingenuous." Still, such rationales are repeatedly offered, invoking the same well-worn and thinly-disguised logic in a manner that is often unintentionally self-revealing: "the 'criminalization of homelessness' [is] a ubiquitous slogan used to discredit any effort to apply rules and laws evenhandedly in areas colonized by vagrants" (MacDonald 2007).

As to the first of the strategies sarcastically suggested above, in which "the targeted 'behaviors' are those which characterize certain social classes" (IWW 1994), the idea is to simply locate a behavior particular to the target group and criminalize it. With the homeless, it is only too apparent: panhandling, sleeping in public, sidewalk sitting, etc. Despite frequent assertions that only 'conduct' is being targeted and not 'status' (e.g., Kelling & Coles 1996:40; cf. MacDonald 2007: "[it] is about not poverty but behavior"), it is clear that certain conduct attaches to specific groups, and that proscribing the conduct is equivalent to criminalizing the category. In some cases, as with teen curfews or 'car cruising' laws, the prohibited conduct impacts the targets' identities and liberties – but does not necessarily undermine their basic ability to survive. Neil Smith (1996:225), however, discerns that "the criminalization of more and more aspects of the everyday life of homeless people is increasingly pervasive." Likewise Ferrell (2001a:164), noting that the homeless' "daily lives are all but outlawed through a plethora of new statutes and enforcement strategies regarding sitting, sleeping, begging, loitering, and 'urban camping.'" Indeed, legal scholars such as McConkey (1996) and Baker (1990) assert that prohibitions against conduct associated with basic survival come dangerously close to violating the Supreme Court's proscription against 'status crimes,' and suggest the interposition of a 'necessity defense' when there is no other choice presented to people charged with crimes regarding acts such as sleeping and eliminating. As Mitchell (1998a:10) emphasizes, "If homeless people can only live in public, and if the things one must do to live are not allowed in public space, then homelessness is not just criminalized; life for homeless people is made impossible." The implications and intentions are all too apparent:

> "By in effect annihilating the spaces in which the homeless *must* live, these laws seek simply to annihilate homeless people themselves. . . . The intent is clear: to control behavior and space such that homeless people simply cannot do what they must do in order to survive without breaking laws. Survival itself is criminalized. . . . In other words, we are creating a world in which a whole class of people simply cannot be, entirely because they have no place to be" (Mitchell 1997a:305-311; see also Howland 1994: "If sleeping in public places – under freeways, in parks, or on heating grates – is illegal, that means at least 325,000 people are faced with the nightly choice of breaking the law or staying awake").

As Smith (1996:230) thus concludes, "in the revanchist city, homeless people suffer a symbolic extermination and erasure." As in a recurring nightmare, dystopian images of annihilation and non-existence keep reappearing, like an evil evening edition of *News from Nowhere*.

An impressive and detailed body of work that illustrates and amplifies all of these points has been generated by Maria Foscarinis and various associates affiliated with the National Law Center on Homelessness & Poverty (NLCHP). In a series of scholarly articles (e.g., Foscarinis, et al. 1999; Foscarinis 1996; Foscarinis & Herz 1995; Brown 1999), it is demonstrated beyond doubt that there has been and still is an ongoing and pervasive national trend toward the criminalization of homelessness, evidenced by the mounting number of cities and towns with laws prohibiting behaviors including 'aggressive panhandling,' 'urban camping,' and 'sitting or lying on sidewalks.' Numerous studies confirm the growing appearance and application of 'anti-homeless legislation' over the past two decades, including Baker (1990); Barak (1991); Smith (1994); Millich (1994); Stoner (1995); NCH (1997); Munzer (1997); Mitchell (1998a; 1998b; 2003); and Mitchell & Staeheli (2006). A series of reports issued by two leading national homelessness organizations (NCH/NLCHP 2002, 2006; NCH 2004) focusing specifically on 'The Criminalization of Homelessness in the United States,' are particularly illuminating in this regard, demonstrating through exhaustive documentation "the widespread trend of the violations of the basic human rights of people experiencing homelessness." In assessing the purpose of these anti-homeless laws, Foscarinis (1996:22) observes: "Some cities state expressly that their intention is to drive their homeless residents out of the city. . . . In other cases, the stated purpose is to remove homeless people from particular places, such as parks, streets or downtown areas. . . . Some target the 'visible' homeless with the goal of making them 'invisible.'" Noting certain negative effects of such laws in terms of public policy – including poor use of fiscal resources, divisiveness, and a deepening of political and social tensions – Foscarinis (1996:63) concludes that "criminalization responses to homelessness are inhumane, do not solve the problem, and are subject to constitutional challenge."

In 1999, the NLCHP published an influential report (*Out of Sight – Out of Mind? Anti-Homeless Laws, Litigation, and Alternatives in 50 United States Cities*) that expanded on some of these important points. The report found that, in the cross-section of cities surveyed, 86% had anti-begging ordinances, while 73% had anti-sleeping laws. The presence of such laws and accompanying enforcement strategies was also found to constitute "poor public policy" by: acting as barriers to self-sufficiency; unduly burdening the criminal justice system; wasting scarce municipal resources; and subjecting cities to legal liabilities and expenses. The report concluded that "criminalization is ineffective, counterproductive, and inhumane," and suggested various "alternatives to criminalization" including: expanded services, places to perform necessary functions, transitional housing, public housing, more employment opportunities, and greater cooperation among city officials, business people, and the homeless themselves (see generally NLCHP 1999; Foscarinis, et al. 1999; Brown 1999). By the time that the 2004 report was released (NCH), the sample size of cities embodying "the widespread trend" of criminalization had grown to 179, and the analysis had concomitantly become more systematic in terms of the depth and breadth of its reporting from each locale, and more subtle in its consideration of 'social consequences' including how criminalization both creates and legitimizes public fear of homeless people. Tempe and Phoenix both appeared in the 2004 report, the former as possessing "no shelter facilities" yet still arresting people for urban camping, and the latter as having broken ground on a new 'homeless campus' that would centralize services but "can also be viewed as paving the way for downtown development." The 2006 report (NCH/NLCHP) included 224 cities in its sample and concluded that, by all accounts, "criminalization measures have increased;" the report also cited "constructive alternatives to criminalization" being explored in various places, including homeless outreach and healthcare programs, the creation of resource centers to assist with food and hygiene, and homeless court programs that have the potential to assist homeless people in clearing warrants and avoiding incarceration.

Additional positive alternatives were depicted in an article analyzing the 1999 NLCHP report (Fabyankovic 2000), encompassing alliances formed between police officers and homeless advocates and outreach workers; programs that help the homeless move toward self-sufficiency; compassionate approaches rather than law enforcement approaches; the development of police sensitivity training programs; the creation of a day labor center; and the mediation of disputes between property owners and the homeless. Some of these possibilities have begun to take shape in Palo Alto, California, where "the community lets [the homeless] stay," the police chief reminds his officers that "it's not a crime to be poor," public benches and restrooms have been installed, "merchants know many of the regulars who hang out by name," and in general the public "respects their right to be here" (Khanh 2002). In other locales, the possibilities are evident but remain problematic, as in New York City where police officer Eduardo Delacruz "was suspended for 30 days without pay after he refused a sergeant's order to arrest a homeless man found sleeping in a parking garage. In gratitude, organizations for the homeless put together a fund for the officer, his wife, and five children. Homeless people also contributed change scrounged from passersby, money earned from recycling cans and bottles, even a portion of their welfare checks. According to police, Delacruz told his superiors in the department's Homeless Outreach Unit that he would not arrest a homeless man for trespassing because the man had nowhere else to go" (Williams, 2002).

Despite the overwhelming evidence offered that criminalization is an untenable and inhumane approach – summed up in the insight that "no amount of criminalization or harassment can prevent people from performing activities intrinsic to life itself" (Kohn 2004:167) – it is apparent that the trend is increasing, as indicated by the scores of articles on the subject in recent years (e.g., Moss 1999: 'Increasingly, Homeless Seen as Blight;' Lydersen 2000: 'In Many Cities, Being Homeless is Against the Law;' NCH 2003: 'As Homelessness Increases, Number of Laws Targeting Homeless People Rise;' Street Sheet 2007a: 'Lock 'em All Up!: Are Policing and Prisons the Solution to Homelessness?'). A *Denver Post* column (Kulp 2000) further observed that "many local governments have responded [to a growing number of homeless people] by empowering police to basically 'run them out of town' through sweeps of homeless campgrounds, liberalized stop-and-search procedures and laws against behaviors characteristic of the homeless. Known as the criminalization of homelessness, this response is seen in a spate of new laws passed in U.S. cities." An earlier *London Guardian* piece dubbed 'Homeless Are Run Out of Town' (Pressley 1996) likewise noted that "in more than 40 cities across the United States, the homeless are facing a determined push of new laws aimed at banishing them from the streets. What is notable now is the forcefulness with which these communities are attacking the problem – using the police as their main weapon. Even more striking is that many of the cities in the vanguard of the get-tough approach are among the country's most liberal," including Seattle, New Orleans, and San Francisco (see O'Brien 2001; Nieves 2002); other cities in this vanguard include: Denver, CO (Rocky Mountain News

2000); Asheville, NC (Barber 1998); Chapel Hill, NC (Blythe 1998); Santa Cruz, CA (Herman 1997); Austin, TX (Duff 1999); Tucson, AZ (Tobin 2000); and of course Tempe (e.g., Riordan 1999b, subtitled 'Tempe follows college towns' trend of tougher restrictions,' and noting that "the Valley's liberal college town has attacked personal liberties with a slew of restrictive laws").

As Harry Simon (1996:148) confirms: "In city after city, municipal decisions to use criminal sanctions to protect public spaces have come into conflict with efforts by civil rights advocates to prevent the criminalization of homelessness. Ironically, cities traditionally identified as liberal or progressive have seen some of the most bitter struggles." While there is no obvious single reason for this trend, some possible explanations include: (1) so-called 'liberal cities' have often been viewed by the homeless as more tolerant and welcoming, thereby increasing the number of homeless in such cities; (2) many of these liberal cities are in the 'new West,' where development schemes are fast being implemented, causing immediate spatial conflicts with homeless populations; and (3) liberalism as a socio-economic philosophy often devolves upon corporate hegemony and managerial values, which can contribute to homeless persecution and/or exclusion. Seattle is known as a liberal city, but a recent article (Harris 2008) documents a new campaign based on "campsite clearances," the removal of personal belongings, and "a zero-tolerance policy." San Francisco is well-known in the public perception as a liberal city, and yet "has spent nearly $8 million [over the last four years] in enforcing an array of 'crimes that include sleeping on the sidewalk and urinating in public. Over 56,000 citations have been issued, most of them to people who cannot pay and thus end up with warrants" (Street Sheet 2007b); moreover, "giving folks citations doesn't solve homelessness. It doesn't get people off the streets and into stable housing. And it doesn't keep Golden Gate Park Disneyland clean" (Street Sheet 2007c). And an in-depth report on the first year of a new homeless initiative in Los Angeles (Blasi 2007) found that approximately 12,000 citations had been issued for minor 'pedestrian' offenses that often resulted in fines that "lead to arrest warrants," and that the city had spent around $6 million on enforcement while the percentage of its homeless residents that were 'sheltered' (21%) was among the nation's lowest.

One of the most notable 'liberal cities' to resort to criminalization is Berkeley, California, exemplified by articles including the *New York*

Times' 'Fed Up, Berkeley Takes Aim at Homeless Youths' (Nieves 1998). The story's brief summary of events there is instructive:

> "Whether they are scared or just plain fed up, plenty of people in the nation's most famously liberal city want the youths, panhandlers, drug addicts, drinkers, and mentally ill homeless swept off Telegraph Avenue, the shopping district here mentioned in every tourist guide. Last week, the all-Democratic City Council, which is dominated by a progressive faction, unanimously passed an emergency measure authorizing police overtime to . . . disperse the entrenched camps of the homeless. The police have been all over Telegraph Avenue, in squad cars, on bicycles and in front of businesses. . . . Homeless people have congregated here for 30 years, but many locals say the more recent newcomers have more than tested the limits of tolerance with their drinking, drug dealing, defecating, urinating, and aggressive panhandling. . . . The mayor said she is proposing a plan that involves both increased social services for the homeless youths and 'tough love.' That includes pushing them off the streets with an anti-encampment ordinance."

Recent articles out of San Francisco (Street Sheet 2007c) also cite evidence of city officials attempting to "solve homelessness with a little 'tough love,'" and have noted Los Angeles' efforts to "employ a tough-love approach, and illegally pack homeless people into already over-crowded jails" (Street Sheet 2007a). Events in Cleveland illustrate similar strategies that are plainly more 'tough' than 'love':

> "In a move to attract holiday shoppers downtown, Mayor Michael R. White has ordered stepped-up police patrols. The mayor said the patrols are aimed at keeping the city's streets safer and will focus not only on shoplifters, muggers and other criminals but also on panhandlers and homeless people sleeping on sidewalks" (O'Malley 1999).

> "White said this 'crackdown' is designed to 'move poverty out of sight so they (shoppers) will have a peaceful shopping season'" (Faith 1999).

> "'It's not an issue of being anti-homeless,' said the mayor. 'It's an issue of balancing everyone's rights'" (O'Malley 1999).

Even while touting the humane nature of its new 'homeless campus,' known officially as the Human Services Center, Phoenix still earned the distinction of being named one of the top 20 'meanest cities' in the 2006 NCH/NLHCP report due to its adoption of a ban on camping in "all city parks in order to preserve the parks as 'family places.'" Interestingly, despite these sorts of 'tough love' approaches that are often framed in terms of protecting "everyone's rights" by keeping homeless people out of sight of domiciled people, an important line of recent research found that "exposure to homeless people . . . actually improves public attitudes toward homelessness" (ASA 2004), a point implicitly echoed in the NCH report from 2004: "Sympathy for homeless people depends in large measure on understanding the economic causes of homelessness and the oppressive conditions of living without a private space. Legislating against the behavior and circumstances of people who have no place to go is a giant step backward in the effort to end homelessness." The study that first illuminated this connection between exposure and empathy involved a reexamination of the 'contact hypothesis' through an analysis of over 1300 interviews, and concluded that, "Respondents exposed to homelessness are more willing to support the rights of homeless people and to make sacrifices to help them" (Lee, et al. 2004:50-1).

Building upon these somewhat surprising insights about the potential for public empathy, it is equally surprising that many of the articles and columns detailing ongoing patterns of criminalization also present various alternatives to criminalization that accord with but also surpass those promulgated by the NCH and the NLCHP. An article from Chapel Hill (Blythe 1998), for example, quotes a local civil rights lawyer asserting that "the town needs to think comprehensively and have a comprehensive strategy for eliminating the poverty and racism that's at the root of a lot of these problems." In Berkeley, "homeless advocates said the city would be wiser to address the problems of homelessness, rather than criminalize the behavior of the people on the street" (Nieves 1998). A *Denver Post* column (Kulp 2000) inquires:

> "When will governments realize they cannot solve the problem of homelessness through new laws, police action and

> incarceration? The causes are more complex. Furthermore, the cost of enforcing these laws can be greater than the problem they are supposed to fix. . . . Pretty soon jails will be full with 'homeless criminals,' and then more jails have to be built to house the growing non-violent criminal population. Sound familiar? . . . It is a never-ending road to nowhere. If governments are sincerely concerned about reducing the visibility of the homeless, then a more rational and cost-effective strategy involves affordable housing, medical care, public transportation, decent-paying jobs and patching up the holes in public benefit systems. . . ."

A telephone survey of 500 residents conducted by the Coalition on Homelessness and Housing in Ohio (in Faith 1999) similarly reflects

> "the public's strong belief that homelessness primarily is caused by external factors such as unemployment rather than internal factors such as mental illness or drug use. . . . Those surveyed overwhelmingly rejected proposals to 'make life on the street more difficult and unpleasant until the homeless decide to leave town' as a possible remedy for homelessness. They strongly endorsed a fundamental shift in overall policy, and a move from large emergency shelters to smaller, geographically scattered permanent housing and programs that include job training and supportive services. . . . The poll seems to indicate that residents may understand better than our political leaders that the remedy for homelessness depends on jobs, affordable housing and services – not criminalization."

Even though it has had something of a checkered past regarding its treatment of homeless residents, the city of Tempe has actually taken some positive steps in recent years that mirror these sorts of suggestions. In 2006, the city authorized $50,000 for a pilot program called HOPE (Homeless Outreach Program Effort), made up primarily of two outreach workers who comb the city in a van offering various service and referral options including help securing identification, substance-abuse counseling, medications, temporary shelter, and in some cases even federally subsidized housing (Hermann 2007a, James 2008). After almost 6 months, the program reported "significant contact with 97 homeless people," including several who had been "moved into housing," "taken for medical care," or who had "found work" (Hermann 2007a). Program director and Tempe Homeless Coordinator Theresa James noted that "the program's outreach specialists go out of their way to make sure individuals get the help they need," and that by the end of the first year of its existence the program had "worked with about 250 homeless [people]" (Hermann 2007b), a number that had grown to over 425 by the next year (James 2008). The United States Interagency Council on Homelessness (2007) further reports on some of the strides that have been made in the city:

> "Tempe became the first Arizona community to host a Project Homeless Connect, providing hospitality and assistance to more than 105 homeless adults and youth with the help of 35 community volunteers and representatives of 21 service providers . . . City leaders and community volunteers followed up that successful first effort with a second Homeless Connect held again at the Tempe First United Methodist Church, with 49 volunteers on hand to welcome and act as guest guides for the 135 homeless guests to connect them to a variety of service providers offering housing screening, medical care, IDs, legal and benefit application assistance, domestic violence intervention, behavioral health assistance including transportation to detox programs, clothing vouchers, showers, haircuts, and massages. Tempe Mayor Hugh Hallman, who helped serve lunch to the homeless guests . . . thanked the many businesses and community organizations supporting the Homeless Connect effort. 'Your willingness to collaborate and break down barriers to service has made today possible. I look forward to continuing to support and expand community participation in Project Homeless Connect because it is a proven strategy to help end homelessness in Tempe. . . .'"

Picking up on these themes, some of the more interesting specific alternatives have been suggested by the homeless themselves. In Berkeley, it was reported (Nieves 1998) as follows:

> "Some of the young people have come up with their own plan, which they presented to the City Council last week. They promise that they will stop urinating and sleeping on Telegraph Avenue, panhandle in smaller groups, keep their

> dogs on leashes and pick up their trash. In return, they have asked the city to provide more trash cans, create a dog run, clean the public bathrooms more often and open Berkeley's first shelter for young people. The mayor called the plan 'interesting.' But on Telegraph, there were grumblings that the city would never take the plan seriously. 'They're making us out to be devils,' [one homeless youth] said."

Cleveland's Lynn Key, one of the "first homeless targets" of crackdowns there, was equally pragmatic in his suggestion, as described in the *Plain Dealer* (O'Malley 1999): "[Key] was sleeping on a warm steam pipe cover outside the county welfare building. Police told Key he had to move, but the homeless man refused, saying that he had been banned from downtown emergency shelters for a month for being drunk and that he had no place to go. Police arrested him, charged him with disorderly conduct and took him to jail, where he spent the night. . . . 'If you can't sleep in front of the welfare building at night, there's nowhere else in the world,' Key said. 'If the city doesn't want them on the streets, they should open City Hall and let them sleep in there.'" Back in Tempe, even with the current mayor taking less draconian steps than the previous one, there still isn't an overnight shelter in the city – but there is in fact a modern and spacious City Hall!

Apology Rejected: The Incivility of 'Civility'

With anti-homeless ordinances rapidly proliferating, their proponents and apologists have worked hard to construct justifications for laws restricting conduct in public places. Standard justifications have included public health and safety, economics, and aesthetics (see NLCHP 1999; Foscarinis 1996), typified recently by city officials in Los Angeles preparing to roll out a new 'Homeless Reduction Strategy' (later changed to the 'Safer City Initiative') by reminding proponents that "moral arguments need to be developed from every point of view: health concerns, child safety, etc." (in Blasi 2007:28). Concerns of the *health and safety* variety essentially employ the 'disease' image discussed above to depict the homeless as "unsanitary" and responsible for the "attraction of vermin" (Foscarinis 1996:57). Factors cited in terms of *economic* considerations include: maintaining "commercial vitality" and preventing "urban decay" (NLCHP 1999); merchants' fears of losing clients and consumers' fears of encountering homeless people; and promoting tourism and shopping (Foscarinis 1996:56). *Aesthetic* concerns are generally expressed in terms of preserving and protecting the "quality of life" of the community, and often include overt desires to "remove 'unsightly people' from public view . . . and to make downtown areas 'welcoming to all'" (Foscarinis 1996:55). In evaluating such "aesthetic and pecuniary" justifications, one writer (Smith 1994) notes that even if effective, "it is deeply troubling to find a community valuing these interests more than the survival of street people." Even the editorial board of the *Arizona Republic* (2004) – not exactly bleeding hearts, to be sure – have argued in favor of more services aimed at "improving each homeless person's quality of life." As the NLCHP report from 1999 observed, when it comes to health and safety concerns, "in most cases the presence of people sleeping, sitting, or lying down in public places, or peacefully soliciting alms, cannot reasonably be deemed a direct threat to public health or safety." The report further noted that aesthetic concerns are often merely "a pretext for rationalizing biases against a certain group of people, or as an excuse for excluding certain people from public spaces based on stereotypes and stigmas." And finally, with regard to economic concerns that the homeless are bad for business, I hope that it has sufficiently been demonstrated herein that such concerns are inverted, and that, indeed, it is business that's bad for the homeless.

Another justification for *quality of life* campaigns, one that has become something of a mantra for its proponents, is the notion of 'civility.' As Robert Ellickson (1996:1246) predicted, "cities, merchants, and pedestrians will increasingly reassert traditional norms of street civility." One of the staunchest proponents of the concept has been Rob Teir, who begins from a premise that public spaces are primarily spaces of commerce, shopping, and recreation (1998:256). Teir (1996) laments that "homeless people have taken over parks, depriving everyone else of once-beautiful places," but believes that through "fair-minded law enforcement and 'tough love' . . . urban communities can reclaim their public spaces." Another proponent similarly notes that a "perception grew that [the homeless], and not the community as a whole, 'owned' the areas they occupied," and concludes that efforts ought to be undertaken toward "reclaiming public spaces from 'the homeless'" (Conner 1999). Likewise Chuck Jackson (1998), director of a BID in downtown Houston, who claims that the homeless have "colonized public areas." As Neil Smith (1996:211) points out, however, a more accurate description than 'civility' of such views would be 'revanchism,' namely the establishment of a vengeful policy bent on regaining original areas lost in war:

> "This revanchist urbanism represents a reaction against the supposed 'theft' of the city, a desperate defense of a challenged phalanx of privileges, cloaked in the populist language of civic morality, family values, and neighborhood security. . . . It portends a vicious reaction against minorities, the working class, homeless people, the unemployed, women, gays and lesbians, immigrants."

Nonetheless, proponents such as Teir (1996) continue to argue that "measures aimed at maintaining street order help mostly the poor and the middle class [since] the well off can leave an area when it gets intolerable. It is the rest of us who depend on the safety and civility of public spaces." The problem of course, as detailed in the previous chapter's discussion of privatization, is that it is precisely the 'well-off' who have 'stolen' and 'colonized' the public places of the city, literally and legally converting supposedly prized havens of public space into exclusionary domains of private property. Thus, as Don Mitchell (1996b:164) observes, the concept of civility often has been invoked throughout history "to assure that the free trade in ideas in no way threatened property rights." The very essence of such civility, then, is to protect and reinforce private property claims (many of which include previously public spaces now converted to private ownership) advanced by "urban stakeholders" including "central business district property owners, small business owners, real estate developers, and elected officials" (Conner 1999). The DTC's literature (circa 2000), for example, emphasized that "we seek ordinances that advance our strategy of order and civility in the public space. Working with our private property owners, we seek cooperation on interdependent security issues." The DTC further claimed that such efforts have "made the downtown a safer place." It must be noted that images of 'public safety,' as with similar invocations of 'community standards,' specifically exclude the homeless and the poor from participation, since these groups are constructed as **not** part of the community, the public, or those with a stake in political decisions and city affairs.

Civility proponents, including former DTC Director Rod Keeling (see Petrie 1999), also emphasize that public behavior laws "apply to everyone equally" (Teir 1998) and simply "ask all residents to observe minimum standards of public life" that will "put a stop to much of the anti-social conduct that is destroying property values and the quality of downtown life" (Teir 1996). Further, it is argued that "civility ordinances demand that all citizens adhere to a reasonable level of behavior while operating in public space" (Jackson 1998); in response to these assertions, however, a Houston alternative paper (Liskow 1999) said that "in reality, civility ordinances would primarily target street people." For the homeless, of course, there are no private spaces available in which to perform 'anti-social' and 'uncivil' functions such as eliminating and sleeping – reminding us once again of the words of Anatole France that "the law in its majestic equality forbids the rich as well as the poor to sleep under the bridges." As John Hannigan (1998:9) opines, "it is easy to equate civility with a certain lifestyle."

It is thus apparent that claims such as Teir's (1998:290), that the effect of ordinances prohibiting sleeping, begging, and sitting on sidewalks is "preserving welcoming, attractive, and safe public spaces for all of us to use and enjoy," amount to little more than "cynical hucksterism" (cf. Hannigan 1998:9). Plainly, 'all are welcome' – except the homeless and others who would threaten to undermine bourgeois consumerist values. It is also clear that civility proponents have no interest in 'preserving public spaces,' but in fact are the chief advocates and direct beneficiaries of processes of privatization that are eroding the public spaces of the city. Ironically, it is the homeless themselves who function to preserve public spaces as democratic, spontaneous, and inclusive. They are not the colonizers of public space, but rather, like the proverbial canaries in the coal mines, the most immediate victims of its colonization.

Breaking Down 'Broken Windows'

Another significant justification for anti-homeless laws, one that has received widespread attention and critical treatment, is the 'broken windows' theory. Originating in a landmark *Atlantic Monthly* article, the theory's chief proponents, James Wilson and George Kelling (1982), in accord with 'order and civility' principles, argue that

> "disorder and crime are usually inextricably linked, in a kind of developmental sequence. Social psychologists and police

> officers tend to agree that if a window in a building is broken and left unrepaired, all the rest of the windows will soon be broken. . . . [S]erious street crime flourishes in areas in which disorderly behavior goes unchecked. The unchecked panhandler is, in effect, the first broken window. . . . [S]o the police – and the rest of us – ought to recognize the importance of maintaining, intact, communities without broken windows."

In other words, the aim ought to be the maintenance of communities without 'broken people,' since such represent the source and origin of the entire crime problem, the first step on the slippery slope from 'untended property' to 'untended behavior' to 'serious street crime.' Robert Ellickson (1996:1171,1182) attempts to describe the link from one step to the next in this suspect syllogism: "A regular beggar is like an unrepaired broken window – a sign of the absence of effective social-control mechanisms in that public space. . . . Passersby, sensing this diminished control, become prone to committing additional, perhaps more serious, criminal acts." Wilson & Kelling (1982) attempt to support the progression from 'disorder' to 'serious crime' by citing studies in which 'untended property' (such as a parked car with a its hood up or with no license plates) was found to lead eventually to the complete vandalization of that property, suggesting that "untended behavior [exemplified by the 'unchecked panhandler'] also leads to the breakdown of community controls," and that in short order, "such a neighborhood [becomes] vulnerable to criminal invasion."

The broken windows theory has become a cornerstone of *community policing* programs premised upon "aggressive order maintenance" and a proactive, "interventionist police strategy" (e.g., Kelling & Coles 1996; Kelling 1999). Given its widespread implementation and the obvious implications for the proper function of police in society, the theory has been roundly criticized from a number of fronts. The first wave of critical questions, in fact, were raised by Wilson & Kelling (1982) themselves, who, upon noting that "society wants an officer to have the legal tools to remove undesirable persons," ask: "How do we ensure that the police do not become the agents of neighborhood bigotry?" Disturbingly, Wilson & Kelling respond to this crucial concern of equity by stating: "We can offer no wholly satisfactory answer to this important question . . . except to hope that by their selection, training, and supervision, the police will be inculcated with a clear sense of the outer limit of their discretionary authority."

Thus, in terms of deciding who is deemed 'undesirable' and subject to intervention or removal, the sole check on police harassment, abuse, or discrimination is to be the discretion of the police themselves. A subsequent study called *Fixing Broken Windows* (Kelling & Coles 1996:256) even asks, "Can citizens go too far? Will there be injustices? Yes, at times." In a more recent work, Kelling (1999) admits that "order maintenance has the potential for abuse, [since] police have used vagrancy, loitering, and panhandling laws to harass citizens and discriminate against groups in the past, [and] since policing teeters near the edge of militarism in so many locations." Still, the only response to these concerns remains that somehow 'police discretion' will avoid such outcomes, notwithstanding the notable fact that "police are almost uniformly unable to articulate what they do, why they do it, and how they do it . . . virtually all of their order maintenance, peacekeeping, and conflict resolution activities are unofficial" (Kelling 1999).

Beyond the critiques suggested (and weak responses offered) by the theory's primary architects and apologists, many scholars and commentators have denounced *broken windows* as discriminatory in both intent and application, fundamentally unfair, logically flawed, and unsupported by studies of criminality and behavior (e.g., Mitchell 2003; Harcourt 2001). Jeremy Waldron (2000), for example, asks two related and pointed questions: (1) "Relative to what norms of order are bench squatters or panhandlers or smelly street people described as 'signs of disorder'?" and (2) "What is to count as *fixing* the window, when the 'broken window' is a human being?" In addressing the first, Waldron's answer is in the form of a question reminiscent of objections raised to the *civility* proponents: "Are these the norms of order for a complacent and self-righteous society, whose more prosperous members are trying desperately to sustain various delusions about the situation of the poor?" In terms of the second, Waldron notes that 'giving him money' is not an acceptable response under the theory, nor is the provision of "public lavatories and public shower facilities. Instead, fixing the window is taken to mean rousting the smelly individual and making him move out of the public park or city square . . . as though the smartest way to fix an actual broken window were to knock down the whole building, or move it to just outside the edge of town." Let me also suggest that unless attention is paid to the factors that contributed to *what caused the window to break in the first place*, fixing the window is only a band-aid since additional broken windows are likely to develop out of the same social and economic conditions.

Pursuing these questions further, the 1999 NLCHP report on homeless criminalization asserts that the theory

> "raises serious concerns about basic fairness. First, punishing one group of people to prevent future criminal activity by others runs afoul of the basic notions of equality underlying our criminal justice system. More importantly, in relying on police to distinguish between desirable and undesirable elements in the community, there is no way to ensure that the criteria they use to make these distinctions will not be invidious or impermissible ones. . . . The likely success of the only safeguard suggested by [Wilson & Kelling] – appropriate selection, training, and supervision of police officers – is belied by examples of discriminatory enforcement of criminal laws and ordinances by police officers across the country."

Indeed, the theory is entirely premised *not* on the notion that 'a single broken window' will lead to additional or more serious crimes by the person who broke the window, but rather that *others* (including even passersby and 'ordinary' citizens) will somehow be tempted by the appearance of disorder into the commission of crimes of both property and person. Asking police officers to discern and even remove individuals based on the likelihood that their mere presence will cause *other* people to commit crimes is unfair, absurd, and almost certain to lead to the sorts of abuses to which the NLCHP report refers. A recent study of 'order and disorder' (Farrell 2005:1036) restates the theory:

> "Much of the criminological literature has identified *disorder* as a source of neighborhood problems. . . . Wilson and Kelling's (1982) 'broken windows' perspective argued that the physical elements of disorder . . . are indicators of weak social control and in turn invite crime and other social pathologies into an area. However, it is the presence of 'disorderly people' [including panhandlers] that truly undermines the social order of a neighborhood. Although not necessarily criminals themselves, these disorderly individuals are unpredictable and sometimes confrontational, feeding into the concerns of neighborhood residents. The presence of physical and social disorder provides visual evidence to residents that their neighbors are unwilling or unable to address problems of

> disadvantaged neighborhoods. This results in a self-fulfilling spiral of fear, powerlessness, and mistrust in these areas."

The author (Farrell 2005:1048-9) concludes that the theory's major premises are not empirically or sociologically valid, drawing upon prior research (noted above) regarding the 'contact hypothesis' in relation to the homeless: "If these descriptions hold true, residential exposure to homelessness should heighten fear among residents and frame their views of the local homeless problem and its impact on neighborhoods. . . . I do not find much support for disorder perspectives when considering the impact of residential exposure on fear of the homeless."

A related set of objections has been raised by Maria Foscarinis (1996:57), who observes that "the evidence is that homeless people are not more likely to be perpetrators of serious crime than anyone else; in fact, they are more likely to be victims. Further, there is evidence that the majority of the public does not perceive homeless people as perpetrators of crime." Another study (Smith 1994) concurs that "the fear of homeless crime that prompts police sweeps is grossly disproportionate to the levels of homeless crime suggested by available empirical evidence," noting that "with an arrest rate for violent offenses significantly lower than that for domiciled males, it would appear that the homeless certainly are no more, and probably less, likely to commit crimes of violence than the general population," and that, for example, "police in Austin, Texas are 'keenly aware that neighborhood claims and fears [regarding homeless criminality] had little empirical substance.'" As Kress (1995:97) opines, "the correlation between homelessness and crime is, at best, tenuous. . . . Several studies have been conducted that lay to rest the belief that homelessness causes crime. According to [one study], among the homeless, arrestees were more likely to have committed trivial, victimless crimes, and to have engaged in acts related to surviving in the absence of housing." The net effect is that the homeless are being persecuted not only for crimes they didn't actually commit, but also for crimes others have not yet committed, which flies in the face of equity and fairness.

A final objection to *broken windows* as social policy is suggested by Waldron (2000) in the implicit derogation that comes when human beings are compared "even figuratively to *things*," wondering what would have ensued if Wilson & Kelling's article had been titled 'Broken People.' The central premise of the theory thus rests on a blatant form of *dehumanization*, figuratively in its principles but literally in their widespread deployment as the cutting edge of urban social policy. This is all another way of expressing that tired and dangerous characterization of the homeless as either pathological deviants or structural victims, and represents an additional method of undermining their agency and dignity. The impressive adaptability, noted inclusivity, and inherent resistance demonstrated by street people and their communities, however, can effectively rebut such dominant conceptions, as Mitchell Duneier (1999:315) contends in *Sidewalk*:

> "Because Americans ruthlessly use race and class categories as they navigate through life, many citizens generalize from the actual broken windows to all the windows that look like them – and assume that a person who looks broken must be shattered, when in fact he is trying to fix himself as best he can. Only by understanding the rich social organization of the sidewalk, in all its complexity, might citizens and politicians appreciate how much is lost when we accept the idea that the presence of a few broken windows justifies tearing down the whole informal structure."

Duneier goes on to suggest that allowing survival activities such as panhandling can actually *prevent* more serious crimes, implying a sort of 'reverse broken windows theory,' one that Tempe's Kevin (2000) intuitively grasps: "Would you rather have me spare-changing – or selling drugs to your kids or breaking into your house?"

Policing *Pleasantville*: The Private Security Matrix

Many of these themes are illustrated and extended in an article on 'Policing Entertainment Districts' (Berkley & Thayer 2000), which analyzed the practices and policies utilized in "every entertainment district known to the authors" (nearly 40 in all, then), in cities such as Houston, Cleveland, New Orleans, Denver, Seattle, Austin, Philadelphia, and including Tempe's Mill Avenue. The study begins by noting that "urban redevelopment [is] now driven by entertainment" (cf. Zukin 1997), that "responsibility for managing entertainment districts inevitably falls on the police department," and that such districts "are naturally appealing to transients and panhandlers [who] contribute to a perception of lawlessness and are primarily a problem during the day when they sit in front of businesses and scare away patrons." The authors go on to observe that "business owners want officers to maintain a friendly profile while simultaneously running off gang members and those with no money to spend," which leads to a process where 'undesirables' are "contacted and discouraged long before they reach core entertainment areas," and, in the case of those who make it into the district, can be "marked for surveillance or shadowed." In terms of how undesirables are identified, the study (based on responses from police managers in 30 districts) concluded that "troublemakers expect trouble and dress accordingly, while those in fine clothes" tend not to be a problem. In terms of issues identified by the police managers, "transients and panhandlers" were reported as the most problematic, while "police department interaction with merchant associations" was deemed the most effective method for preventing problems in the districts.

This last point leads naturally to a discussion of the role of BIDs (business improvement districts) in policing entertainment areas in particular and urban space in general, since "the typical BID involves a quasi-law enforcement force whose job includes, in large part, removing people who appear to be homeless from the BID areas" (NCH/NLCHP 2002). In addition to "arresting beggars" (Parenti 2000:96), BIDs "typically focus on 'broken windows' in the literal sense, cleaning streets and providing a visible, uniformed presence, all toward the goal of making public spaces more inviting" (Conner 1999; see also Mealer 1999 and Jackson 1998, directors of BIDs in Austin and Houston, respectively, both 'firm believers' in the broken windows theory; the DTC in Tempe likewise seeks "ordinances that advance our 'Fixing Broken Windows' strategy of order and civility in the public space"). In terms of the 'uniformed presence' that many BIDs maintain, Kelling & Coles (1996:199) note that they often serve as the "eyes and ears" of the police, are in "radio contact with the police, and are trained to report suspicious behavior." Christian Parenti (2000:96), however, asserts that such "private security forces [have] surpassed the cops as the main violators of street peoples' rights," yielding a "private security matrix . . . where rent-a-cops are imbricated into the larger policing project through a delicate division of labor: private forces control interior spaces, aid the police in holding pacified streetscapes, and even launch offensives against non-violent undesirables." As such, Jones & Newburn (1999:106) discern the possibility that "a 'new feudalism' is emerging, in which private corporations have the legal space and economic incentives to do their own policing. In this view, mass private property has given large corporations a sphere of independence and authority which can rival that of the state." The net result, as identified by Hil & Bessant (1999:42), is that "police and [private] security personnel seek to exclude [undesirables] from such places so that they can be 'purified' and 'reclaimed' for more 'legitimate' consumptive purposes." As the 2004 NCH report concludes, "A growing problem in the United States is the rise in private security forces that wear uniforms and harass homeless people." Parenti (2000:97) appropriately terms all of this "free-market social hygiene."

In Tempe, the DTC/TEAM embody these practices, as noted in the article on 'Policing Entertainment Districts' (Berkley & Thayer 2000):

> "Private security can be effective, even on public streets, as a presence and deterrent, as a means of urging voluntary compliance, and as a first stage in an escalation. If they cannot gain voluntary compliance, they simply call the police. For example, the Downtown Tempe Community, Inc., uses private security (TEAM) to serve as eyes and ears for the police department and to provide a low-contact variety of security. TEAM guards are young, mostly untrained, and unarmed, but effective nonetheless. On Friday and Saturday nights, TEAM makes 60 percent of all calls to the police department from the downtown area. When bicycle officers arrive to trouble spots, TEAM watches the bicycles. [Thus,] the effectiveness of private security is furthered by police efforts to build communications and relations and incorporate private security into community policing."

The DTC's literature trumpets that it has "increased relations with the Tempe Police Department to ensure criminal activity within the homeless population was curbed," and that it was able to "directly affect the arrest of 8 individuals engaged in illegal activity and provide information on criminal activity to the police officers assigned to the downtown." The DTC website (circa 2001) also noted that, "through our Downtown Ambassador Program and private security contractor, we serve as crowd watchers and crime reporters for the police."

As to the origins of private security in downtown Tempe, an article in the DTC 'newspaper' *The Downtowner* (2000a, 'TEAM Helps Tempe Grow') explains:

> "Mill Avenue and downtown Tempe have seen many changes in the last century with the most dramatic coming in the last ten years. As Tempe has evolved, so has Total Events and Management (TEAM) to meet the needs of this growing community. . . . During the weekly gatherings of eclectic and diverse groups, conflicts arose. Several business owners asked Mick Hirko to help and TEAM was started to provide security for downtown Tempe. . . . Today, 250 TEAM members do everything from keeping parking safe to answering visitors' questions and providing security services to businesses. 'TEAM exists because of downtown Tempe,' said Hirko. 'And we're dedicated to its future.' Hirko sees Tempe's future in the positive – with Tempe Town Lake and more business development, TEAM will continue to evolve as downtown Tempe does to ensure the safety and livability for everyone."

A subsequent article (DTC 2000b) goes on to add:

> "TEAM watches the Tempe community as if it were their home – because that's exactly what it is. . . . TEAM's patrol service roams the downtown Tempe area, checking properties on a regular schedule seven days a week. Late in the night, after restaurants and bars have closed and most people have gone home, TEAM can be found looking for break-ins, checking doors, observing suspicious behavior and coordinating with the Tempe Police Department to keep the downtown area safe. . . . After the Andre Building fire last August, they watched over the property 24 hours a day during reconstruction. Another construction project that was under their constant watchful eye was the Tempe Town Lake."

Nonetheless, despite their efforts on behalf of redevelopment, the DTC severed official ties with TEAM in early 2001. TEAM was then hired by DMB Associates, the commercial development company with one of the largest private property stakes in downtown Tempe, including Centerpoint. As Rod Keeling (DTC 2001a) explains:

> "The DTC has a long standing relationship with our Police Department. Over the years, the relationship has evolved and refined to the point where other cities around the country are

> looking at how we work together. . . . Earlier this year, the DTC made a fundamental change to our downtown safety program. We discontinued contracting with a security guard company and turned our focus on our Ambassador program. Our DTC Ambassadors are crowd watchers and crime reporters for the police but they are not security guards. We want to assist the police, not take the place of them. We believed then and are convinced now that our move from street security to street concierge presents a better image for downtown Tempe without compromising safety. In fact, downtown is safer than ever before. Now it's friendlier too. Just look for the teal shirts."

With all those 'crowd watchers' (i.e., *voyeurs*) and 'crime reporters' (i.e., *snitches*) in place, the feeling of *security* is indeed palpable.

Cleaning Up, Cracking Down, and Ordering Out

The Orwellian face presented by such scenarios isn't quite so 'friendly' for Tempe's homeless residents, who have experienced regular 'sweeps' and "ID and warrant checks" (Kevin 2000), as well as episodes where "the cops'll go out and find our squats and burn all our clothing, our IDs . . . they harass us all the time" (Katy 2000). As the Salvation Army's Julie Cart noted (2001), "everyone out there living on Tempe streets has been arrested . . . it's part of their lives." While the mood in Tempe has softened somewhat in recent years, the reality of being policed and harassed still exists for the street people there. The 2002 joint report by the NCH & NLCHP on homeless criminalization confirms the prevalence and indicates the full implications of such practices: "People who are homeless routinely report losing their possessions, identification, medication and employment as a result of being arrested. When homeless people are arrested, they lose whatever tenuous hold they have on getting their lives 'back together.' Incarceration and police harassment perpetuates homelessness by leading to missing appointments with health care providers, caseworkers, job interviews, children, partners, and family members, disrupting their lives in countless ways and reinforcing a sense of alienation and hopelessness" (see also Lelchuk 2001, noting that San Francisco often "throws out personal belongings and medication").

In this regard, Gregg Barak (1991:85) reports the results of a study of police harassment of the homeless in San Francisco. Based on a survey of almost 300 street people, 96% reported having been told to 'move along' when doing nothing wrong; 93% had been ordered to produce identification without cause; 80% said that their body, clothes, or possessions had been searched for no reason; and 50% had been "physically beaten or brutalized by a police officer." Recent articles and blogs (Street Sheet 2007b; 2007c) indicate that the situation in San Francisco has not improved very much since Barak's study in the early 1990s. As one possible explanation for why the homeless suffer such affronts and attacks at the hands of the police, Don Mitchell (1997b:393) observes that "the homeless so effectively challenge the *authority* of the police. They challenge the police's *competence* to control space." In Tempe, Kevin (1999; 2000) in particular was a frequent target of this spatial battle, having been arrested 43 times in a three-year period (1997-2000) for offenses such as public consumption of alcohol, trespassing on private property, and public urination.

Homeless crackdown

Here are some rules for cops from the NYPD's "Operational Guidelines for Homeless Outreach Unit" manual:

- Interview homeless only to assess need for services.
- If individual is deranged or dangerous, take into custody and to hospital.
- In freezing weather, offer ride to shelter or take into custody.
- If person blocks doorway, force to move.
- If person is ill, request ambulance and supervisor.
- Take to detox only on person's request.
- Refer uncooperative cases to Homeless Services.
- Homeless person who is physical and mentally normal and refuses services is free to stay put or move on.

N.Y. Post: Luiz C. Ribeiro

Fig. 3: New York newspaper headline re: 'Homeless Crackdown'

An episode that I witnessed in May 2001 (on the same night that I was confronted by TEAM for sitting on a sidewalk that was actually 'their' property) is emblematic. A man with a bushy beard was playing the guitar by the fountain behind the Coffee Plantation, smack in the heart of Centerpoint's private property domain. A TEAM guard – who later said of the guitar-playing man, "He scared me!" – asked the man to leave the area, since he was a known trespasser on Centerpoint property. The man offered no response, but continued to strum impassively on his guitar. The guard called the police on his two-way radio, and in a matter of minutes, the man was escorted by a police officer to a small open area directly adjacent to the busiest downtown corner, Mill Avenue and Sixth Street. As a crowd began to gather around and watch, the officer made the man kneel down, had him place every article of property he had on his person on the sidewalk, ordered him to open his backpack and guitar case to be searched, and proceeded to handcuff the man behind his back. By this time the crowd had grown to 25 or so. Someone in the crowd yelled out, "Hey man, give the guy a break, he didn't hurt anybody" – to which the officer replied, without glancing back toward the crowd, "I'm just doing my job here." A few moments later, the police paddy wagon arrived, and the man was taken away, head down and handcuffed.

Scenes such as this were not uncommon in Tempe, so much so that the lead researcher on a city-sponsored 'homeless needs assessment' study in October 2000 (discussed in Chapter One) felt compelled to state to the city council on the night the report was submitted:

> "Doing the report has been a real eye-opener. It is very disturbing as a Tempe resident to see the harassment of people who are homeless in Tempe. Being homeless has itself been criminalized. I have seen people harassed by the police and TEAM in Tempe. Where is our public space? The dehumanization of it all really disappoints me, and I hope that tonight is the first step in stopping this criminalization. These are our residents and they shouldn't be treated as they are."

Despite such sentiments, the enforcement situation in Tempe got worse following the 'needs assessment,' with private security increasing its profile and criminal justice travesties continuing unabated. More recently, the city has begun to seek alternatives including outreach and intervention (James 2008). Still, the homeless are in a vulnerable place.

One particularly sinister trend has been the imposition of fines on homeless defendants convicted of petty offenses. Katy (2000), for example, incredulously describes how she received a fine for drinking in public: "A $285 ticket! Where the heck is a homeless person gonna get $285 to pay them off? That's pretty stupid, I mean get real." Bill (2000) likewise refers to such fines as "extortion money," and notes that the result is usually that "an unpaid fine then becomes an arrest warrant, so the next time they run your ID, you're goin' to jail" (cf. Howland 1994). As Gary Blasi (2007:34) notes in his recent study of policing the homeless in Los Angeles, "for thousands of persons cited who are unable to pay the [fine], the result is an arrest warrant for failure to appear." More to the point, the 2004 NCH report discerns that citations and fines in fact perpetuate the cycle of homelessness:

> "Once homeless people have been arrested for 'quality of life' violations, their criminal records grow, and as a result they may be excluded from jobs and housing. Anyone incarcerated at least 30 days loses Social Security benefits during incarceration. Also, if an individual receiving benefits is found to have an outstanding warrant, she or he can be denied benefits. . . . In addition, when homeless persons do not follow through with the process of criminal justice, such as failing to pay traffic tickets or not appearing in court, warrants are issued for their arrest and they may be subjected to further charges and/or jail time. Money used to pay fines might otherwise be used for housing or other needs. . . . Many homeless people lose all their possessions, even difficult-to-obtain IDs, when they are arrested. . . . Policies of criminalization defeat their own goals of removing homeless people from public visibility because they simply create further barriers for survival and undermine individual efforts to escape homelessness. Such policies keep more people on the streets and increase problems related to homelessness. When individuals are released from jail, they are still homeless, and they have even more barriers and obstacles to overcome than before."

In this light, offhand comments such as Kelling & Cole's (1996:15) that public disorder laws are usually "punishable *only* by fines or community service" come across as particularly cruel when the full implications of a fine are considered. As for the 'community service' option, the DTC (circa 2000) noted that it had "increased relations with the Tempe City Court to allow the homeless to complete their community service by working to clean up the downtown under the direction of the DTC." Apparently, the unelected micro-republic of the DTC now possesses the power of punishment and criminal corrections. In fact, the 2002 NCH/NLCHP report properly criticized such 'alternative sentencing' schemes as "the newest marketing tool for public safety advocates who cloak their 'urban cleansing' policies in social service language." Similarly, the appearance of 'homeless diversion courts' such as the Downtown Community Court in St. Louis are mixed blessings at best and cynical marketing ploys at worst:

> "Homeless people are being hauled into the fledgling court that hopes to rid downtown of annoying behaviors such as public drinking, public urination and defecation, panhandling, trespassing, and petty larceny, crimes that degrade the quality of life. Trouble is, the process unfairly targets the poor and homeless, according to New Life Evangelistic Center, a homeless shelter and advocacy group. . . . St. Louis joins an estimated dozen other U.S. cities with similar court programs, and is fielding calls from cities such as Phoenix, for advice on launching their own. . . . 'The infractions may seem minor, but in the aggregate, studies across the country have shown they're a precursor to more serious crimes and detract from the quality of life in the area as a place to live, work, or be,' said Jim Cloar, president of the downtown partnership. . . . Sentencing options include fines, community service, time in the city workhouse, or treatment programs. . . . [Judge] Burke said the primary goal of Community Court is making the downtown more user-friendly, but if, along the way, a violator's life gets changed, all the better" (Wittenauer 2003).

Phoenix did in fact set up its own version, in partnership with the city of Tempe, in 2006. The 'Regional Homeless Court,' according to the phoenix.gov website, "was established to resolve outstanding misdemeanor warrants for homeless individuals demonstrating a significant commitment to ending their homeless lifestyle." Aside from the interesting choice of the word 'lifestyle,' the program involves many restrictions for eligibility, including that "defendants can only be referred to the Homeless Court by one of six programs after they have completed a rigorous transitional program. Defendants must also have a qualifying misdemeanor offense and no history of violence." The challenge of meeting these terms became evident when the *Arizona Republic* ran a story about the court's one-year anniversary (Heath 2007), noting that "it is difficult to find candidates who have who have completed their assigned programs and are qualified for the court," and finding that in its first year of operation the court heard just *four* cases. As Blasi (2007:35) likewise found in Los Angeles, "[o]f the thousands issued citations, only a small fraction will qualify, [and] it is clear that 'Homeless Court' offers scant amelioration . . . ."

Thus, despite more frequent rhetorical shifts to a language of 'alternative sentencing' and 'downtown ambassadors,' and away from phrases like 'zero tolerance' and 'private security,' the upshot is similar in terms of the treatment of and impact on homeless people. Criminalization, in short, has not been abandoned, but has become more conscious of appearances and better at couching itself in a cloak of friendliness and fairness, making it all the more perverse as a social policy. Enforcement reports from Tempe (1997-2001) are revealing of this sense of perversity and the utter futility of criminalization policies, whereby street people are repeatedly arrested for basic life-sustaining activities including sleeping, eliminating, and simply just being 'out of place.' From the 'police blotter reports' of the *ASU State Press*, then, come these selected and illustrative arrest narratives in Tempe, which speak volumes as to the plight of homeless people everywhere and the patterns of enforcement that figure so prominently in their lives:

- A 40-year-old male transient was arrested on three charges of theft from Tempe Mission Palms on 60 E. Fifth St. He stole $2 from a food cart, two towels and a coffee mug (2/14/01).
- A 26-year-old male transient was cited for jaywalking and a dog license violation on South Mill Avenue (10/16/00).
- A 30-year-old male transient was arrested on charges of disturbing the peace at Sixth Street and Mill Avenue. The man was yelling obscenities and physically challenging passing pedestrian traffic to fight him. He was issued a citation and booked at Tempe City Jail (10/16/00).
- A female transient was found sleeping on top of the Human Resources building at 20 E. Sixth St. She was arrested for trespassing. She claimed she entered the roof by an unlocked

door, but the door is always locked, according to police reports. The subject was booked into Tempe Jail (9/27/00).

- A 19-year-old male transient was arrested at the corner of Mill Avenue and Sixth Street for possession of marijuana and drug paraphernalia. The subject was stopped for riding his skateboard on the sidewalk. Further investigation revealed he was in possession of marijuana and a pipe (9/22/00).
- Police arrested a 40-year-old homeless man drinking a beer with a friend outside an office at the 1800 block of East Apache Boulevard. He was transported and booked into Tempe City Jail (2/3/00).
- A 28-year-old homeless man was arrested on charges of urban camping after an officer found him asleep in a sleeping bag near a railroad track. The man was transported and booked into Tempe City Jail (2/1/00).
- A 39-year-old man was arrested for giving false information to a police officer after he was found sleeping in an alley. The transient had prior warrants and numerous warnings for urban camping. He was booked into Tempe City Jail (12/2/99).
- Police arrested a 29-year-old man for urban camping on the north side of 'A' Mountain. His only possessions were a backpack and sleeping bag. Police said he had been warned five previous times not to camp out in the park. The man was booked into Tempe City Jail and held to see a judge. Police confiscated his belongings (12/1/99).
- A 19-year-old male transient was arrested on the charge of giving false information at 100 E. Third St. He was arrested for providing a false name and date of birth to a police officer on the north side of Tempe Butte Mountain. He was initially contacted for an urban camping violation (11/12/99).
- Police arrested two Tempe women Wednesday at 401 W. Baseline Road on charges of urban camping. An investigation showed they were sleeping on a rug. Both had been warned by officers before (4/19/99).
- A 62-year-old Texas man was arrested Tuesday at East Baseline Road and I-10 on charges of criminal trespassing. Officers said he was standing on an island marked "No Trespassing," panhandling motorists exiting the freeway. He was booked into the Tempe City Jail (3/26/99).

- Police arrested a 21-year-old Missouri man Monday at Papago Park, on charges of urban camping. Officers reportedly saw the man's clothing, underwear and food strewn out on several picnic tables and a pavilion floor and observed him sleeping on the ground near the lake. He had been previously warned about camping at that spot and told officers he was "purposefully protesting the urban camping ordinance." He was booked into the Tempe City Jail (3/25/99).
- A 22-year-old male transient was arrested Thursday at Centerpoint, on charges of criminal trespassing and possession of dangerous drugs. Police said the man was previously warned not to return to the property. A search following arrest revealed what police believe to be psilocybin mushrooms on his person. He was booked into the Tempe City Jail (2/8/99).
- A 37-year-old male transient was arrested on charges of providing false information to police at 3232 S. Mill Ave. Police contacted the man for trespassing and urban camping. He was booked into the Tempe City Jail (1/20/99).
- Officers arrested a 41-year-old transient woman for possession of marijuana Tuesday. They contacted her at a pavilion picnic table in Canal Park, and found a small plastic bag of what they believe to be marijuana. The woman claimed a set of tools next to the bag were hers, but denied knowledge of the presence of marijuana. Her belongings were spread out on the table and the ground around the pavilion. She has had four previous urban camping warnings and was transported to Tempe City Jail, where she was booked and released. The tools were impounded (10/30/98).
- A 22-year-old New York woman and a 24-year-old Indiana woman were arrested on charges of urban camping, Tuesday, after officers reportedly found them camping near South Farmer Avenue and East Rio Salado Parkway. According to reports, both women had been warned previously. They were booked into Tempe City Jail (10/29/98).
- A transient was arrested near McClintock Drive on charges of public consumption of alcohol. He was observed sitting at a bus stop on the southwest corner, drinking beer from a Milwaukee Ice can. An officer approached him and saw an empty case of beer and five to six empty cans on the ground.

When the man couldn't provide an address, he was arrested and booked into Tempe City Jail (10/21/98).
- Officers arrested a 20-year-old Kansas man Wednesday on charges of urban camping after he was found to have set up camp under the Priest Drive bridge. Officers found the man with a sleeping bag laid out and a backpack with clothes next to him, according to reports. The man was reportedly arrested on the same charges in May of this year and warned Monday for camping in front of a storefront on Mill Avenue (9/4/98).
- A clerk saw a man sleeping on the sidewalk close to a convenience store. He attempted to wake the man up for about five minutes, but the man continued to ignore the requests by turning his head and falling back asleep. An officer came to the scene and asked the man to move for three minutes. The subject was arrested and transported to jail (3/24/98).
- A 22-year-old female was arrested on Mill Ave. on charges of urinating in public. A police officer reportedly saw the woman go behind a trash Dumpster and pull her pants down. When he contacted her, she was in a squatting position and urinating. The location was 30 yards from Java Road and 20 yards from Jack-in-the-Box, heavily populated areas. She had no address or identification and was booked in Tempe City Jail (2/12/97).

These selected arrest reports were merely the 'highlights' from a five-year period in Tempe. The patterns of enforcement in this time span finally culminated in a joint pronouncement by the DTC and the Tempe Police Department that a "new crackdown on panhandlers and sidewalk sitters" would commence in early 2002 (Davis 2002). A new wrinkle in this plan specifically included the police "encouraging businesses to act as witnesses to help make arrests" (Davis 2002). "Right now we are on a mission to re-educate businesses that they can be witnesses," Tempe police Sgt. Noah Johnson told the *State Press*. "Businesses can aid in arrests like individuals can," he said. For their part, the DTC (through operations manager Chris Wilson) stressed that "now, businesses can call police if one of their customers is panhandled, as long as someone saw it happen" (in Davis 2002). In their own 'DTC Insider' publication, the DTC (2002b) noted that, "thanks to clarification of a city code, Tempe police officers no longer need a victim's account of aggressive panhandling to make an arrest –

businesses, or individuals may act as witnesses. Downtown businesses may now notify police of aggressive panhandling themselves, rather than waiting for someone else to report these activities. The reports may be made anonymously, as well." The article continued: "The police are finally coming around," Wilson said. "They realize that if they can get rid of low-level crimes and criminals, then the big crimes will disappear with them." Despite repeated invocations, in light of the inherent illogic of 'broken windows' policies the self-fulfilling nature of such constructions of 'crimes and criminals' is only too apparent.

The DTC's own account of this new 'Police Crackdown on Aggressive Panhandling' (DTC 2002a) is similarly revealing:

> "Thanks to the Tempe Police Department, downtown Tempe may become a safer and more friendly place. On Thursday, Dec. 27, Officer Whit Roesch made an important arrest. He took into custody a young man who was aggressively panhandling on the corner of Fifth and Mill Avenue in front of Starbucks. This arrest marked the first of a new campaign to crack down on aggressive panhandlers. The new crusade has sprung from clarification of a certain city code that states that officers need only have witnesses to the panhandling, not necessarily the victim. This will allow many more arrests of aggressive panhandlers, making Tempe a safer place."

This 'new crusade' also included an additional punitive and exclusionary twist called an 'Order Out,' which is "a stipulation to the parole of people arrested under the panhandling city code [mandating] that the person arrested could not return to that district, in this case downtown Tempe" (DTC 2002a). A *State Press* editorial (2004) further noted that the 'order out' concept has been extended to other anti-homeless laws as well, and that "city attorneys are striking plea deals with some of [the homeless], telling them that if they pack up and move out of town, the city won't press charges." Similar tactics have been used recently in cities including Seattle, Cincinnati, and Portland, Oregon, and are sometimes referred to as "off-limits orders" (Beckett & Herbert 2007:15). Even more telling is a recent analysis of "hate crimes against the homeless" that includes an historical perspective on such practices, previously known as "warning-out" (Wachholz 2005):

> "Homeless wanderers in the 17th and 18th centuries were ordered to leave communities in which they did not have legal residence. . . . Although there is now a broad array of informal and formal social control mechanisms that impose spatial constraints on the homeless, these practices are neither simple nor new. At their core, they reflect the character and objectives of the English warning-out laws that were imported in the 17th century. Essentially, these laws provided colonial towns with means to legally exclude people from communities . . . . However, similar warning-out mechanisms persist. The most obvious are statutes that criminalize behavior which is part of the survival strategies of the homeless – i.e., sitting or sleeping on sidewalks and asking for donations."

Undoubtedly, this isn't the sort of 'ordering out' one might ordinarily think of in a city full of restaurants and eateries – an irony evident in the fact that many homeless panhandlers are actually begging for food or money to buy it. Then again, perhaps starvation is an (un)intended 'benefit' of such blatantly discriminatory and exclusionary schemes.

From Criminalization to Extermination

A particularly pointed example that is indicative of all of these enforcement patterns observed in Tempe (and elsewhere) arose out of a 'battle' between merchants and street people in Asheville, North Carolina. A local paper detailed the conflict (Barber 1998):

> "'I started hearing how kids were being chased away by police for sitting downtown during the day,' [a local resident] relates. 'There were a lot of stories floating around, too, about kids being "shook down" by cops – which means they run your ID or flip through your bags for no apparent reason, other than you're sitting there and you look different.' According to Police Chief Will Annarino, these young people's behavior (for example, playing music without a license) often violates specific city ordinances. He denies that the police are harassing the kids, saying officers are merely doing their job by responding to merchants' complaints. . . . Annarino admits that certain selective law-enforcement practices come into

> play, but he insists that those practices are based not on cultural biases but on economics. 'We have to make tough decisions every day on how to best utilize our personnel in direct reaction to complaints from citizens,' adding that the majority of complaints come not from kids who feel harassed but from merchants and tourists. 'The merchants demand that their rights not be violated,' Annarino explains. . . . Some kids charge that the police are using far more force than necessary to respond to non-violent crimes, crossing the line into undue aggression and outright harassment. Annarino admits that some ordinances are now being enforced more aggressively than before, but he says this is simply due to the increased police presence. Annarino denies knowledge of any such incidents, adding that he has never taken a discriminatory approach toward law enforcement. 'All I can say is that officers sometimes use their discretion in matters like these'. . . . Some merchants say they have no interest in compromise: They just want the street people cleared out, period."

And so we return to the 'extermination' scenario that keeps rearing its head – unsurprising, after all, since eradication is the logical aim of these myriad policies and practices of *criminalization.* As Madeleine Stoner opines, "the images of homeless sweeps are reminiscent of holocaust roundups in Nazi Germany. To dramatize the message that homeless people are not welcome, police officers frequently conduct large-scale campaigns in which they arrest homeless people, handcuff them, mark their arms with identification numbers, drive them to the police station where they await formal charges for hours without food and water, and finally drive them to the edge of town after detention, drop them off, and tell them not to return" (1995:161). Samira Kawash likewise describes an "increasingly vengeful war on the homeless" in which "both threats and acts of violence are necessary to maintain this exclusionary force," and suggests that homeless advocates "discover ways to make the violence written on the homeless body legible" (1998:336-7). Throughout the many incarnations my investigations of and participations in homeless issues have taken, I remain guided by principles such as this that are grounded in the material conditions and lived experiences of street people themselves, hoping through discourse and activism to 'make the violence legible.' If this work is useful in accomplishing even that much, it has been well worth the effort.

CHAPTER FOUR

Mapping the Territory

Meanings, Methodologies, Means and Ends

How and why exactly does one come to investigate a particular 'social problem' such as homelessness? Can a scholar also have a bias, or more to the point, can a scholar ***not*** *have a bias? This chapter details the motivations and methodologies inherent in this interdisciplinary study that draws upon official records, media reports, interviews, and participant observations connected with the homeless community in Tempe, Arizona as its empirical foundation. Moreover, in-depth explorations of the extant literature, including case studies from other locales, serve to locate the issues within the context of everyday life on the streets and the unique perspectives of homeless people, their advocates, and those who choose to study them. What I strenuously argue for here is a methodology that accords with both the issues and people being studied, in the belief that this is a necessary ethical component of any inquiry into social phenomena.*

Meanings

"We travel on the surface of meaning, which slides a little further away with each step we take to approach it."

-- Pierre Clastres (1994:36)

The production of a 'text' is a hopelessly inadequate yet essential component of any research venture. At some point in time, it nonetheless becomes necessary to communicate one's findings, theories, and analyses, for instrumental purposes in the present as well as for posterity's sake. In undertaking such a project, it is important to specify one's intentions, understandings, and biases as they relate to the subject of study – in other words, the *meanings* one attaches to the subject. By this I do not refer simply to 'definitions' or 'terminology,' but rather to the more subjective aspects of epistemology and ontology that simultaneously enable and constrain the researcher's efforts. In this regard, it is worth noting that "the meanings of things are not always contained in what is communicated in a text, but rather, the context, awareness, and experience as tacit knowledge sets the tone" (Altheide & Johnson 1994:497). Accordingly, the central aim in this work has been to convey a sense of those experiences and moments of awareness that define the project, and not necessarily to reproduce a literal translation of the researcher's findings and theories.

With this in mind, it is possible to provide an overview of this project unburdened by the false aim of comprehensive clarity. Instead, I will indicate here the 'spheres of inquiry' that have been explored in this endeavor, and let the text largely speak for itself. Initially, in further debunking definitional terminology, the oxymoronic nature of some of the key concepts analyzed here becomes immediately apparent. For example, this is a study of *street people* – variously referred to in the literature and media as 'transients,' 'vagrants,' 'slackers,' or 'the homeless' – which immediately raises questions of how and why people would be associated with the street, let alone live there. Equally problematic is the construction of a category such as *homeless people*, since homelessness is really a condition more than a personal attribute. This work also explores phenomena such as *sidewalk sitting* – both as a criminalized activity and a strategy of resistance to authority – which again raises questions of why and how a person would resort to sitting in a space seemingly designated for walking. In exploring these themes, methodological attributes including *participant observation* have been employed, giving pause as to how one can simultaneously participate in and observe a social issue, further illuminating the terminological conundrum and oxymoronic qualities implicit in any research endeavor.

Rather than agonize over this, providing a sense of the spheres of inquiry guiding this effort will be sufficiently instructive at this juncture. The impetus for this study grew out of an experiential and academic interest in subjects including *anarchy*, *community*, *ecology*, *utopia*, and *resistance*. The aim in my early academic work was to ascertain and describe a coherent vision of anarchy-in-action that could serve as a tool for deconstructing and challenging the hegemonic nature of 'reality' while at the same time providing a basis for envisioning and constructing new 'realities' that might exist above, beyond, and within the cracks of the dominant framework of the State. This quest necessitated an investigation of the spatial nature of hegemony, since any attempted utopian experiment would have to be located *somewhere*. It soon became apparent that the essence of *open space* for imagining and constructing such endeavors was sharply limited by the "colonization of the lifeworld" (May 1994:31) that defines late capitalist society in all of its totalizing fullness. Thus, I began to search for spaces that presented opportunities for contestation and community building, even as I understood that such spaces were diminishing both ideologically and materially.

By itself, this turn to spatial thinking might have proved an interesting diversion or addendum to my anarcho-utopian project. But a series of events in the summer of 1998 moved the work to a new level, when the City of Tempe announced plans to adopt an ordinance that would make it a crime to sit on the sidewalks in the 'downtown commercial district.' No attempt was made at that point to mask the fact that this ordinance was specifically intended to remove a small enclave of loosely-associated homeless 'slackers' from the rapidly gentrifying downtown area, or to conceal the intention of commercial enterprises to 'take back' the public spaces of the city from the street people who were constrained to pass the days there. By this time I had already made the connection between the people on the streets and those involved in the anarchist community experiments I had been considering, such as the *Rainbow Family of Living Light*, intentional communities, and squats. I soon began to make a spatial connection as well, namely that the street people, like the anarchist avatars, often occupied areas designated legally and metaphorically as *public space*, and did so in a manner that challenged conceptions of *private property* and *law and order*. The appearance of these exemplars reinforced my anarchist explorations through their overt contestation of consumerism and commercialization, as well as through the incongruous nature of their very existence on the streets and sidewalks of the city. Indeed, this formed the basis of my perception of street people and sidewalk sitters as *spatial anomalies* – entities who are '*out of place*' in a seemingly well-ordered world, and ultimately becoming '*lost in space*.'

In this manner, what began as a consideration of anarchy, community, and resistance had morphed seamlessly into an exploration of *public space*, *homelessness*, *criminalization*, *gentrification*, and *contestation*. Along the way, elements of social praxis and community politics began to cohere, and the project took on new life as a subject of academic study as well as a topic of substantial media attention, legal analysis, and personal commitment. In terms of documentary material, I have collected and coded reams of *media reports* bearing on the salient issues locally, nationally, and worldwide, as well as compiling files of *government documents* including legislative histories, city council minutes, and police memoranda. I have also undertaken an exhaustive review of the *scholarly literature* on homelessness and public space, including books, social science journals, and law reviews. All of this material largely comprises the foundation for the extensive 'literature review' that is essentially presented in the first three chapters of this work. As such, this is a key aspect of the substance of this study, but it is equally necessary to consider the methodologies and procedures utilized *en route*, both in a theoretical sense and as applied to the many facets of this open-ended, ongoing project.

Methodologies

Social science inquiry is never undertaken in a vacuum, but is instead contextual, subjective, and, despite certain claims to neutrality, *always* biased. Indeed, it might be said that a researcher without a bias is either dishonest, disinterested, or dead. Of course, we *all* bring our predispositions, hang-ups, and agendas with us when we go out into the field, and the only things worse than having these objectivity impediments in the first instance are the frequent attempts by social scientists to either deny this inherent condition altogether, *or* to fail to make such biases apparent in the written reports of their observations. Good field work should be a product of the researcher's interests and subjectivities, or else one runs the risk of embodying the kind of instrumental rationality and dispassionate logic that qualitative research methods implicitly reject in their explicit rejection of positivism. In short, bias is essential to research, and the best way to constructively incorporate such bias is to make it apparent in our work – both in what we choose to study and in how we present what we have found (cf. Becker 1970:5,13,77). Some writers, such as Altheide & Johnson (1994:490), have even gone so far as to formulate this quality of "bias disclosure" as an "ethnographic ethic." Still other characterizations of this inherent-bias phenomenon include developing an "epistemological lens" or "interpretive framework" (Denzin & Lincoln 1994:13), and the concept of "*foreknowledge* of the historical situation or context of the text" that arises in hermeneutics (Diesing 1991:121).

In this regard, as intimated above, my focus initially was on questions of identity and culture, forms of living, utopian social movements, and various resistance strategies to the dominant Western paradigm that is characterized by market economies, private property, and state authority. Of particular interest in this regard are vagrants, vagabonds, and other transients and 'drop-outs,' who (from a utopian perspective) often appear as picturesque outsiders and gadflies in the ointment of consumer capitalist society, helping to preserve a discursive space that exists beyond the reach of hegemonic forces of social control. In addition, the quest to maintain a transient identity and a subversive ideology raises issues of agency and volition that are especially relevant in the face of diminishing privacy rights and the decline of public space. Such issues bear further on the question of whether utopian imaginaries can still be relevant in promoting social transformation, or represent mere romantic longings that are rapidly being mooted by globalization, surveillance technologies, and the death of open spaces (cf. Mander 1991; Hetherington 1997). The vagabond and the transient serve as potent exemplars of what a 'nomadic utopia' (Niman 1997) portends, and provide a pertinent bridge between notions of resistance and the preservation of spaces for the construction of alternative futures. This celebration (indeed, romanticization) of transient and other anti-systemic life-ways is plainly a bias, which I offer unabashedly as a counter-position to the pro-systemic bias that is apparent but often undisclosed in a great deal of 'social science.'

It is through this theoretical and epistemological lens that I set out to locate the transient pulse in and around the vagabond haunts of a particular southwestern college town that, because of its mild climate, crossroads location, and health food co-op (with its subsidiary 'Free Store') seemingly attracted more than its share of 'unsavory' types. One could often find these rogues along the town's main drag, huddled under a kiosk, drumming, and occasionally 'spare-changing.' They were also plentiful at the co-op, pulling in and piling out of their funky buses and cars, dreadlocked and pungent and happy to hug you for a smile {note: the co-op has since been replaced by a planned high-rise}. Sometimes you see them outside supermarkets and convenience stores, with buzzed blue hair, multiple body piercings, and unspecified gender, holding a scruffy puppy on a tattered hemp leash and asking for a cigarette or directions to the nearest blood plasma donation center. Every now and then you'll spot a pair sleeping on cardboard boxes in the shadowy regions of a neighborhood park. Sporadically, they can be found camping in a remote spot by the river that no longer runs, or 'car-camping' in a semi-industrial section of town that might be known as 'the docks' if the riverbed actually held flowing water. These are the sorts of individuals and locales whose voices and vistas emerge in this work, suggesting the utility of an *ecological* perspective that explores the reflexive nature of the relationship between people and place.

In conducting this research, my overriding aim has been to maintain a correspondence between the methodologies employed and the particular subject under investigation; as Becker (1970:62) observes, "we should use methods appropriate to the form of our problem and to the character of the world we are studying." Methods employed in anarchic settings such as street life should be fluid, spontaneous, and open-ended in order to cohere with the life-ways of the individuals and groups being studied. Despite the recent increased interest in anarchism as a political and cultural phenomenon, I have yet to encounter a discussion of anarchist research methodologies *per se* in either the social sciences or the body of anarchist literature, although Jeff Ferrell's excellent work on 'anarchist criminology' (1993, 1999) does begin to get at some of these issues. Philosopher of science Paul Feyerabend is sometimes taken as a methodological 'anarchist' because of his 'anything goes' stance, although it probably would be more accurate to refer to him as a 'pluralist' in the sense of embracing a multiplicity of methodological possibilities (see Diesing 1991:47-52; Ferrell 1994:175; Ferrell & Sanders 1995:305). In a review of various qualitative 'interpretive paradigms,' Denzin and Lincoln (1994:13) include feminist, ethnic, Marxist, and cultural studies frameworks – all of which have some features in common with what might be termed an *anarchist methodology* – but the authors do not specifically make reference to anarchist theories or methods. Still, some of the useful connective strands among these interpretive paradigms include a praxis-oriented approach that emphasizes lived experiences, a critical posture, and the promotion of emancipatory aims (cf. O'Leary 2004).

In the anarchist literature, an article by Brian Morris (1998:35) promisingly takes up the subject of 'Anthropology and Anarchism,' but turns out to be a substantive overview of anthropological works with anarchist strands and not an analysis of the methodologies themselves. Subsequently, David Graeber addressed the subject, producing an influential essay on 'Fragments of an Anarchist Anthropology' (2004), yielding important insights into praxis, ethnographic investigation, and the production of knowledge. Focusing on anarchism as a method for challenging present structures and imagining new possibilities, Graeber's important work is nonetheless not intended as an exploration of social science research methodologies. Accordingly, in tracing the contours of an 'anarchist methodology' that is appropriate for a study of vagrants, transients, and street people, I will rely on (re)sources from other interpretive paradigms, including various qualitative methods, alternative 'ways of knowing,' and even quantum physics. The overarching aim, again, is to develop a methodological perspective that coheres with both the issues being explored and the researcher's biases.

The Role of the Researcher

Research is a social activity as well as a meaning-making enterprise, and "as researchers and observers become increasingly aware that the categories and ideas used to describe the empirical (socially constructed) world are also symbols from specific contexts, this too becomes part of the phenomena studied empirically, and incorporated into the research reports" (Altheide & Johnson 1994:489). In other words, the ways in which researchers describe the world become part of that same world that is being studied. Moreover, as noted above, a certain methodological and epistemological bias is built into all research, embedded in the theories and symbols relied upon in framing the issues and the study design. Far from being avoided as threats to scientific objectivity, such bias is crucial to understanding the perspective of the researcher and the researched, and thus ought to be included in reports and write-ups as a necessary counterpart of the 'data.' Beyond this, our subjective intentions and understandings as researchers help create the things we are investigating. As long as we maintain a veneer of methodological consistency in our observations and disclose our positions relative to the phenomena being studied, then we have achieved a certain *reliability* in the form of forthrightness (cf. O'Leary 2004), by being up front about our activities and agendas.

Bricolage

A *bricoleur* works with the materials at hand, creating analogies and arguments (see Quinn 1996), becoming a "Jack of all trades or a kind of professional do-it-yourself person" (in Denzin & Lincoln 1994:2):

> "The bricoleur produces a bricolage, that is, a pieced-together, close-knit set of practices that provide solutions to a problem in a concrete situation, deploying whatever strategies, methods, or empirical materials are at hand. The bricoleur reads widely and is knowledgable about the many interpretive paradigms (feminism, Marxism, cultural studies, constructivism) that can be brought to any particular problem. The researcher-as-bricoleur-theorist works between and within competing and overlapping perspectives and paradigms. The product of the bricoleur's labor is a bricolage, a complex, dense, reflexive, collagelike creation that represents the researcher's images, understandings, and interpretations of the world or phenomenon under analysis. This bricolage will connect the parts to the whole, stressing the meaningful relationships that operate in the situations and social worlds studied" (Denzin & Lincoln 1994:2-3; see also Clifford 1988:13, on the radical centrality of 'collage' in ethnography).

As Becker (1970:6) similarly observes, such methods involve "the knitting together of diverse kinds of research and publicly available materials," which have the advantage of "allow[ing] human judgment to operate, unhampered by algorithmic procedures." Significantly, homeless people often appear as 'bricoleurs,' as observed in Chapter One, and I have drawn extensively on a diverse range of publicly-available works in order to produce this collage-like text.

Everyday Life and Studying the Public Realm

An essential theoretical notion often advanced in qualitative methodologies is that *all* activity is social, and as part of that network of relation and communication that we call 'everyday life,' research is likewise implicated as a social activity. In this regard, David Altheide (1996:8) identifies three primary tenets of social research: (i) the social world is grounded in a *symbolic order*; (ii) research is "part of the social world we study" (a phenomenon often termed *reflexivity*); and (iii) "*process* is key because everything is, so to speak, under construction." In particular, when methodological techniques such as *participant observation* and *active interviewing* are utilized, it becomes clear how research is both descriptive *and* constitutive of the social world and of the nature of 'reality' itself. What is asserted in this scheme is akin to a 'constructivist' view, and includes the concomitant role that research techniques play in reflexively constituting meaning (see Denzin & Lincoln 1994:4) – in short, the related notions that research is a social activity and that everyday life is a legitimate focus of social research (cf. Ward 1973:11; Thomas 1993:36).

As a consequence of championing *everyday life* investigations, it is important to consider the *public realm* as a central site of observation and analysis, since much of modern life takes place in myriad 'public' settings (although these are not necessarily the same as legally-defined 'public spaces'). Perhaps the best known proponent of such studies is Erving Goffman, who focused much of his gaze on behavior in public space as a means of analyzing concepts such as the nature of moral ordering, norms of conduct, presentations of self, and spatial arrangements in society (Goffman 1963, 1971; see also Adler 1994:384; Lofland 1998:2-3). Following Goffman, Lyn Lofland "employed a mixture of intentional and serendipitous research strategies" (Adler 1994:384) to explore the spatial and social features of the public realm (Lofland 1973), utilizing methods such as direct observations, interviews, newspaper stories and columns, and literature from geography, history, anthropology, architecture, and sociology (Lofland 1998:xii). The lessons here are that "the public realm is a social territory" (Lofland 1998:3), defined as much by its spatial qualities as its everyday life actions, and is always under construction.

Intuition, 'Verstehen,' and The Trouble with Maps

In developing an appropriate methodology for a study of transients and wanderers, it is worth recalling the axiom that "the *map* is not the *territory*" (Wilber 1977:42). In epistemological terms, this leads us to perceive that *all* knowledge acquired and disseminated through the *rational* processes of intellect, sensation, and linguistics, is only an "approximate representation of reality [and] is therefore necessarily limited" (Capra 1991:28). In contrast, knowledge received through *intuitive* or *mystical* processes – including *non-ordinary states of consciousness* such as meditation, yoga, shamanic trances, psychedelic altered states, or pranayama (e.g., Weil 1972; Huxley 1954; and Wilber 1977:24 on William James) – is often described as an *absolute knowledge* that, in Buddhist terms, is the "direct experience of undifferentiated, undivided, indeterminate 'suchness'" (Capra 1991:29; see also Hesse 1951). These two great epistemic principles, what Ken Wilber calls the "two basic modes of knowing" (1977:43), the rational and the intuitive, comprise a dichotomy that is "sewn into the very fabric of the universe" (1977:35), and manifests in myriad socio-philosophical antinomies such as *appearance-essence, fact-value, empirical-mystical,* and *patriarchal-matriarchal.* The common conclusion of the theorists cited in this discussion is that the great travails and grave perils of civilization are largely due to the misguided overemphasis of the *rational* principle almost to the exclusion of the *intuitive*, leading inevitably to "the confusion of our perceptions of reality with reality itself" (Weil 1972:147) – that is, to mistaking the map for the terrain. Thus, despite all of our attempts at *validating, confirming, rationalizing, regularizing, legislating, computerizing, predicting*, and *controlling*, 'absolute knowledge' or 'wisdom' often eludes us (cf. Nietzsche 1996; Spinoza 1991; Emerson 1969).

In this light, it seems that if we are to 'know' something, we must of course study it, think about it, and analyze it, but we may also endeavor to *experience* it. And if we are thereafter inclined to communicate our experiences, we need to comprehend that words are abstract, inaccurate, and incomplete (Garfinkel 1987), but that the use of symbolic forms such as *myth, metaphor, poetic imagery, allegories, paradoxes,* and *koans* can begin to 'point' the receiver in the direction of their own *direct experience* with the phenomena under investigation (Capra 1991:43). This, I think, begins to get at the qualitative turn to (re)sources such as "ethnographic prose, historical narratives, first-person accounts, still photographs, life histories, fictionalized facts, and biographical and autobiographical materials" (Denzin & Lincoln 1994:6), "visual sociology via photography" (id. at 390), "storytelling" (Altheide & Johnson 1994:486), and "poetic readings, one-act plays, and dramatic presentations" (id. at 498). It also begins to explain sociological turns such as Marx's "early insistence on the transcendent power of the imagination" (Solomon 1974:467), as well as why "for most Critical Theorists, the one space left open for resistance was that of art" (May 1994:26). Such symbolic forms, while still only *maps*, begin to connect the rational, intuitive, and direct ways of knowing.

Another way of making these connections is through an emphasis on processes of "experiential immersion" (Ferrell 1997:3; Ferrell & Hamm 1998:13), "empathetic understanding" (Ferrell 1997:10), and "epistemic enlightenment" (Ferrell & Hamm 1998:14) – sometimes attributed to and analyzed under the rubric of 'verstehen,' which traces its roots in social science back to Dilthey (Clifford 1988:35) and Weber (Ferrell 1997:10; Ferrell & Hamm 1998:14). By invoking concepts of empathy, intuition, involvement, commitment, emotion, subjectivity, meaning, understanding, and experience, *verstehen* is deployed not as a crude device that "often smacks of mystification" (Clifford 1988:35), but rather as a mode of knowing that challenges dominant forms of rationality and positivism (cf. Garfinkel 1987:3-4; Fernandez 2008:38). The aim is not so much to replace the authority of rationality with that of intuition, but instead to achieve a methodological synthesis that accords with principles of justice and compassion.

Spontaneity

This phenomenon raises the more general point, as noted above, about the utility of maintaining a correspondence between the *methodologies* employed and the particular *subject* under investigation. Methods employed in anarchistic settings such as the 'street scene,' for instance, ought to be fluid, spontaneous, and open-ended, whereas more structured, routinized, and systematic methods might be appropriate in settings where analogous values predominate. As Diesing (1991:52) notes in discussing Feyerabend's famous remark that 'anything goes,' the true meaning of the phrase is that "the method to be used should be appropriate to the research situation, including subject matter, theory, audience, and personality of the scientist." Anarchistic social settings, if they possess any common strands at all, are often united in a belief in "the theory of spontaneous order" (Ward 1973:28), sometimes analogized to the tendency of biological organisms and communities to be self-organizing and self-regulating, and generally expressed in the view that left to their own devices and placed on equal footing individuals will voluntarily and spontaneously undertake mutually beneficial cooperative endeavors (see May 1989:171, discussing the same as the '*a priori*' of anarchism). An *anarchist methodology* ought to abide by this fundament of anarchist social theory and practice.

Truth, Ambiguity, and Uncertainty

The methods employed in anarchist research are partially informed by principles often identified with *symbolic interaction*, which establishes a framework for interpreting and understanding the social realm. Whereas positivistic methods of analysis focus on objective 'Truth' as evidenced by epistemologically pure 'sense data,' symbolic interaction views 'truth' as subjective and therefore susceptible of no absolutely correct or privileged interpretation. The epistemological implications are that truth is relative dependent upon one's frame of reference and, accordingly, that there exists no privileged perspective for the observation and analysis of 'reality' (cf. Ferrell 1999:95; Jorgensen 1989:14-5). Thus, in a world where "all knowledge is perspectival" (Altheide & Johnson 1994:490), all truth-claims are therefore inherently 'valid' (cf. Jorgensen 1989:26-7), and "since there are many perspectives there can be many true interpretations" (Diesing 1991:54). And as Nietzsche (1996:15) succinctly exhorts, "there are no eternal facts, nor are there any absolute truths."

It must be noted here that I am not unaware of or unmoved by the potential implications of this position, namely that it appears as a form of *moral relativism* that might be used to justify even acts of barbarism and brutality under the guise of 'truth.' The difficulty comes in attempting to articulate a reasoned basis for accepting some truth-claims and not others – a process that has often worked to the disadvantage of marginalized people throughout history. For example, while fascism or racism are certainly not positive social processes, the question is whether such practices can be dismissed as 'untrue' or 'invalid' simply because they appear to serve the ends of oppression and injustice. It may well be the case that to their practitioners, such philosophies are not only 'true' but are even seen as beneficial and just. The saving grace of the position articulated here that 'truth is dependent upon perspective' is that the one basis it leaves open for rejecting a particular perspective occurs when a claim to truth is advanced in such a way that it denies other claims – in other words, when a claim is made to an immutable or totalized 'truth' such that other claims are declared invalid (which historically has at times led to marginalization, colonization, and genocide). Thus, the point of saying that all truth claims are valid is substantially equivalent to saying that none are, since this position maintains that any such claims are limited in their utility to an observer located at a particular point in space and time.

This relativistic condition requires that we come to accept, even revel in, a large dose of *ambiguity* in navigating the social and material terrain(s) (see generally Ferrell 1993:161 and 1999:91, observing that "ambiguity is the stance, the subtext, of anarchism; [it] is the essence of life"). As Andrew Weil notes in his early work on consciousness (1972:153), we must achieve an "acceptance of the ambivalent nature of things." Quantum physics has told us, moreover, that electrons exist as either/both "waves or particles, energy or matter" (id.), and thus that there is a fundamental *uncertainty* built into the fabric of the universe; in Einsteinian terms, all observations are relative to the observer's 'coordinate frame of reference' (cf. Massey 1994:261), and, at the subatomic level, all interactions can only be expressed in terms of 'probabilities' (see Capra 1991). Similar themes have been propounded through invocations of 'chaos theory,' which holds that "there are no essential structures and no permanent stabilities governing space or time" (Arrigo 1998:76). In the context of social science methodologies, this means that there is little if any point in ever trying to 'prove,' 'confirm,' or 'validate' anything; rather, the aim should be to discern *patterns* in the chaos, to elicit a *dialogue*, and to stimulate *thought* and *action* in ways that 'point' to our particular conceptions of 'reality' without trying to provide precise, repeatable instructions as to some generalizable 'truth.' Ultimately, messages received in this way tend to inhere deeply if at all, mostly because the truths gained through dialogue, pointing, and ambiguity are due primarily to the receiver's own internal processes and not the sender's marshalling of data, status, influence, or purported methodological rigor. More to the point, all of this places research in the useful posture of offering descriptions of social processes that can help others formulate their own truths.

Symbiosis, not Dualisms

A further aim of symbolic interaction is the uncovering of people's subjective meanings, and accordingly the theory generally is framed by the suppositions that (i) people act on the basis of meaning, (ii) meaning is produced by social interaction, and (iii) meanings are modified, molded, and refined through an interpretive internal process (Blumer 1969:2). The social realm is seen as a 'life-world' in which meaning is created and shared by a *reciprocity of perspectives* in which commonalities in orientation (e.g., speech patterns, signs and symbols, and 'normal forms') enable the mutual constitution of reality through processes of social communication. In this lexicon, we come to understand the 'process of the life-world' as both a *topic* (i.e., a subject meriting investigation) and a *resource* (i.e., a tool for understanding and interpreting meanings, symbols, and actions). In essence, symbolic interaction offers both an ontological account of the social world, and an epistemological method for understanding that world.

Still, I would be remiss here if I did not address some of the limitations of symbolic interaction, even as I draw upon parts of the theory in describing an *anarchist methodology* premised on sociality, spontaneity, and ambiguity. In a critique of "symbolic culture, with its inherent will to manipulate and control," John Zerzan (1994:27) observes that the development of symbolic forms in human societies was intimately connected to the "domination of nature" (1994:35), in the sense that the advent of symbolism and its equation with 'culture' allows a reduction of the world to human abstractions while simultaneously placing human perceptions and descriptions (i.e., culture) over and above the processes and practices of non-human life (i.e., nature). In other words, Zerzan perceives that "domination within a society is not unrelated to domination of nature" (1994:35), and that it is our modern fixation on seeing the world solely through human eyes and in human terms that leads inexorably to a rejection of natural processes and to the promotion of hierarchies within society. The extent to which symbolic interaction reifies any of this remains a matter of debate, and in fact the theory can be deployed to challenge the entrenched hierarchies of which Zerzan is so acutely and eloquently aware. As with anything, the ambivalent nature of things means that theories can be liberatory or repressive, emancipatory or complicit, with the critical factor being how an idea is used and in what spirit it is deployed. Zerzan's argument, for instance, can be taken as further exacerbating the rift between nature and culture by viewing humans as antagonists of nature rather than as part of it; but since he likely doesn't intend this outcome, I read his point as a corrective to the predominance of human culture and the rapid extinction of nature.

All of this indicates the applicability of an *ecological* perspective on reality that prizes reflexive, reciprocal, and even radical ways of understanding the world that we both inhabit and construct. In generating a sense of *reciprocity* and pursuing socially useful aims, active interviews (Holstein & Gubrium 1995), participant observations (Jorgensen 1989), and hermeneutics (Diesing 1991) are properly viewed as methodological cousins in which the rigid positivistic lines between observer and observed are obliterated in favor of a more holistic, inclusive, and egalitarian approach that privileges no perspective over another and removes the white cloak of objectivity that seems to me misplaced in any 'science' that calls itself 'social' – opening a space for "the dismantling of dualistic epistemic hierarchies which position the researcher over and apart from research subjects" (Ferrell & Hamm 1998:14). This is what Dewey perceived in his insight that "there is no *external* world *separate* from us" (in Diesing 1991:77); as Diesing goes on to note, "the spectator theory assumes a separation between us and the object to be known, nature or society, so that our efforts to know it do not affect the object. . . . Against this Dewey asserted that since we participate in our 'object,' society or nature, knowing involves interaction with the known" (1991:78). Of course, this is just what the Eastern philosophers, indigenous cosmologies, and physicists have been telling us, that the universe is "a system of inseparable, interacting, and ever-moving components with the observer being an integral part of this system" (Capra 1991:25). As Ken Wilber (1977) notes, there is an inescapable sense of *symbiosis* that is woven into the very fabric of *nature:* "Objective measurement and verification could no longer be the mark of absolute reality, because the measured object could never be completely separated from the measuring subject – the measured and the measurer, the verified and the verifier, at this (quantum) level, are one and the same. The texture of reality is one in which the observer and the event, the subject and the object, the knower and the known, are not separable." This to me is the essence of *ecology*, and it guides all of my research efforts.

Moral Implications

A further matter that merits attention here is the venerable *fact-value* (or 'is-ought') conundrum that has plagued philosophy, science, and all the social disciplines since their inception (see Harvey 1973:14): Is 'human nature' discoverable by means of 'scientific' inquiry such that it makes sense to think in terms of establishing laws, norms, or principles of conduct? Einstein (1954:42-5) emphatically avers that:

> "Knowledge of what *is* does not open the door directly to what *should be*. One can have the clearest and most complete knowledge of what *is*, and yet not be able to deduce from that what should be the *goal* of our human aspirations. Objective

> knowledge provides us with powerful instruments for the achievement of certain ends, but the ultimate goal itself and the longing to reach it must come from another source. And it is hardly necessary to argue for the view that our existence and our activity acquire meaning only by the setting up of such a goal and of corresponding values. The knowledge of truth as such is wonderful, but it is so little capable of acting as a guide that it cannot prove even the justification and the value of the aspiration toward that very knowledge of truth. Here we face, therefore, the limits of the purely rational conception of our existence. . . . For science can only ascertain what *is*, but not what *should be*, and outside of its domain value judgments of all kinds remain necessary."

In this sense, it becomes apparent that moral statements of the *law-rule-injunction* type are necessarily arbitrary extrapolations from an untenable conflation of 'fact' and 'value,' sometimes referred to as a 'naturalistic fallacy' which occurs when a normative claim is defined in empirical terms – in other words when we say that something *ought* to be because it just *is*. The problem arises in such Western cornerstones as social contract theory and classical utilitarianism. Thomas Hobbes, for instance, based his conclusions about *human nature* – and hence his entire moral theory – on observations "confirmed by Experience" including that then-modern man "rides armed," "locks his doors," and "locks his chests": "Does he not there as much accuse mankind by his actions, as I do by my words?" (in Goldberg, ed., 1995:60). Evidence that men already living under a strong social state are possessive and suspicious is hardly likely to convince me that the remedy is a stronger social state. Likewise John Stuart Mill demonstrates the tautological nature of his moral claims in the assertion that "the sole evidence it is possible to produce that anything is desirable, is that people do actually desire it" (id. at 140). Since *utility* is taken as the most basic principle, it cannot be proven by reference to other principles, and so empirical evidence must be offered to support the proposition that each person ought to act so as to maximize pleasure and minimize pain. But what can empirical evidence tell us beyond the fact that people actually do or do not act in a particular manner? Even if every person so acted, it still doesn't tell us that people *ought* to be acting in this way (consumerism comes to mind in this regard). Utilitarianism suffers this fallacy precisely because it attempts to construct universal normative foundations on the basis of a version of *human nature* that is derived from observations of how people behave in a particular time and place.

This tendency is evidenced prominently in the Western paradigm as the colonization of the 'intuitive' (*ought*) by the 'rational' (*is*) (see Nietzsche 1996:45; Spinoza 1991:177; Emerson 1969:21; Thoreau 1965) – and notably manifested in the ubiquity and increasing intricacy of legislation and regulation today. Contrast this with Eastern cosmologies such as Taoism (Clark 1998; Legge 1962) and Zen (Capra 1991; Weil 1972), which emphasize the *intuitive* principle yet prescribe **no** moral injunctions. Similarly, compare anthropological and ethnographic studies of certain so-called 'primitive' cultures and their 'indigenous cosmologies' that similarly rest on *intuitive* modes of knowing and exist largely in societies where anything even resembling the 'rule of law' and coercive authority is virtually unknown (e.g., Barclay 1990; Clastres 1994; Mander 1991), as well as studies of certain 'alternative cultures' such as the *Rainbow Family* (Niman 1997), communes and intentional communities (e.g., Kanter 1972), and various cooperative and collective federations (e.g., Ward 1973) that manifest analogous tendencies. The clear import of this reasoning is that moral conduct cannot be prescribed, nor immoral behavior proscribed, and the more that one attempts to do so by imposing *laws,* the farther away *morality* recedes (cf. Bauman 1993). In other words: science, philosophy, and mysticism, from Einstein to Nietzsche to Lao Tzu, confirm the presence of an *inverse relationship between morality and law* (cf. Black 1976). The less that coercive and formal-rational 'Law' is extant in a given society, the more its members cultivate other instincts for acting in the world; the greater the presence of such 'Laws,' the lesser the moral impulse exists in the community.

The challenge here has been to explore the moral ramifications of a methodological orientation that is grounded in the theoretical and praxis-oriented tenets of *anarchism*, and to evaluate the prospects of deriving certain lessons from 'nature' that could shed new light on certain age-old queries of philosophy and social theory. Appropriately enough, it turns out that: (i) *knowledge*, and in particular *moral* knowledge, cannot be established with certainty due to an inherent subject-object reflexivity that is sewn into the very fabric of the universe; (ii) all pronouncements of the *law-rule-injunction* type are necessarily arbitrary and illusory; and (iii) both relativism and universalism are inadequate terms to describe the inherent ambivalence and moral ambiguity that pervades the human experience. Of course, all of this accords with the epistemological implications of *anarchism* (see Koch 1993), which eschews 'laws' and 'causation' and 'validity' in favor of a voluntary morality, a holistic world-view, and the kind of dialogue that makes communities embodying these ideals appear on the horizon of possibility. It is not a 'perfect science' by any means, but this view at least provides a framework for manifesting new visions.

Transformative Potential

Accordingly, as we enter a new millennium that portends a brave new world of hegemonic capitalist values and the Disneyfication of the globe (cf. Mander 1991; Sorkin 1992; Hannigan 1998), matters of resistance, freedom and volition, and open space take on a certain aura of urgency (cf. Ferrell 1993:192). The ideological and ontological issues raised in this study of transients, vagrants, and the processes of criminalization and sanitization that operate upon them, provide a framework for a further analysis of the continuing vitality of notions of *public space* and the viability of social movements in a new world order that is characterized by the globalization of capital and its associated technological and cultural logic(s) (see Harvey 1996; Mitchell 2003). This burgeoning global mono-culture, with its state/corporate control of space and the pervasive push of privatization, directly implicates issues of resistance strategies and forms of living, requiring of us (especially those who teach and/or publish) a position of 'advocacy' in order to bring about "the shift from an attitude of domination and control of nature, including human beings, to one of cooperation and nonviolence" (Capra 1991:334). Most emphatically, however, this is not to be taken as a call to replace one totalizing scheme with another, nor simply to deconstruct one set of practices without articulating a new vision. As Kropotkin notes (1993:144-45): "We are not afraid to forego judges and their sentences. We forego sanctions of all kinds, even obligations to morality. We are not afraid to say: 'Do what you will; act as you will;' because we are persuaded that the great majority of mankind, in proportion to their degree of enlightenment and the completeness with which they free themselves from existing fetters will behave and act always in a direction useful to society . . . . All we can do is give advice. And again while giving it we add: 'This advice will be valueless if your own experience and observation do not lead you to recognize that it is worth following.'"

Praxis, Activism, and Illegality

In pursuing such aims, it is essential that we develop a sense of *praxis* built around tenets such as 'human solidarity' and 'domination-free communication' (see Palmer 1993:582). In so doing, we are likely to brush up against the specter of *activism*, which I take simply to be the effective coupling of public advocacy with personal praxis. Of course, wearing these hats in addition to that of 'researcher' is bound to create difficulties, some of which are no doubt due to the false 'theory-praxis dichotomy' enforced by many academic 'disciplines.' Aside from traditional taboos about influencing the 'experiment' and corrupting the 'data' (which, hopefully, I have already dispensed with as nonsensical and, in any event, undesirable aims), the activist researcher studying marginalized populations is also likely to encounter official forces of law and order along the way. Indeed, as Jeff Ferrell (1997:18-20) notes, such outcomes are inevitable if we take our work seriously, and must be answered practically and personally with due regard to the nature of the problem at hand, as well as the researcher's values and intentions:

> "As new legal regulations of urban space and urban life increasingly criminalize the lives and actions of homeless people and dislocated urban populations, field researchers engaged in participant observation with those persons increasingly face situations in which their own activities also may be construed as violating numerous new or newly enforced ordinances relating to vagrancy, loitering, curfew, trespass, panhandling, public lodging, and public nuisance. If homeless and other inner-city populations continue to be marginalized and criminalized, where will we as criminologists draw the line between ethnography and activism, legality and illegality?"

Means and Ends

Now that I have expounded upon the theoretical implications of an *anarchist methodology*, it is equally imperative to address the particular 'means' employed in this study to achieve the 'ends' of empathy, exposition, and enchantment. At the outset, this project essentially entails a *case study* of street life and its associated socio-legal ramifications in Tempe, Arizona, with a particular focus on the downtown 'commercial' area near the local university. As such, this is not intended as a global pronouncement on forces of gentrification, redevelopment, and criminalization, nor is it meant to portray the experiences of homeless people as monolithic and unitary. Nonetheless, readers are free to explore the implications of generalizability to their own advantage but also at their own peril. In other words, I make no claim that the phenomena studied here are 'typical' such that it makes sense to think about grand edicts, yet it is equally clear that every investigation of the 'particular' has aspects that bear upon a consideration of the 'universal.' Essentially, the question is one of levels of analysis, whereby micro-inquiries are sometimes employed in the service of macro-extrapolations (cf. Burawoy 1991:272). What I mean to reinforce here is the notion that research can be micro, macro, both, neither, or (at different points along the way) all of the above. The rest is up to the reader in terms of deciding what the implications are for grander theorizing and wider application.

As a final word on methods, it should be noted that my personal encounters, experiences, and friendships with many of the street people in Tempe have been equally integral to the development of this project; on many occasions I have joined their drum circles, chanted their chants, and just hung out with them in the public places of the city. Moreover, my own experiences of nomadism, dispossession, and 'opting out' have served not only to cultivate research rapport and communal kindredness, but also comprise part of the 'data' analyzed here. As an activist connected with Project S.I.T. (Sidewalk Initiative Team), the Phoenix Anarchist Coalition (PAC), and the Free to Camp Coalition, I have been part of numerous direct action and outreach endeavors both with and on behalf of street people. In the end, it is contemplated and hoped that these varied experiences and methodologies will serve to enhance the impact and import of this ongoing project. All of these values and experiences are reflected most directly in the story of Tempe's adoption of an ordinance that made it illegal to sit on the sidewalks in the downtown area. My personal involvement in challenging this law co-existed with my work as a researcher; along the way, some of the research itself became part of the public dialogue over and legal challenge to the ordinance. In this moment of research-activism *symbiosis* there is a hopeful potential that suggests the importance of drawing our own maps of the world.

CHAPTER FIVE

Case in Point

A Brief History of the Tempe Sidewalk Ordinance

An analysis of the origins, intentions, passage, and enforcement of an ordinance that prohibits sitting on the sidewalks in downtown Tempe is indicative of nearly all the themes and policies that have been considered thus far. As such, the sidewalk ordinance provides a unique opportunity for an intensive case study of the forces of development, privatization, demonization, sanitization, criminalization, and exclusion. In many of the episodes recounted here, the texts speak for themselves – that is, they are either consciously or inadvertently self-revealing in a way that makes the critique obvious – such as the newspaper column, called 'Time to Sweep Slackers off Mill,' that came out at the same time that city officials and business leaders were insisting that the sidewalk law was simply about public safety and pedestrian congestion, and that it had nothing to do with homeless people. Think of this chapter, then, as a 'case study within a case study,' taking one particular point from one locale and amplifying to a degree that reveals something of social policies and urban ecologies being plied elsewhere. Indeed, examining the life-history of even one single brick of downtown sidewalk might very well tell the story of all of Tempe's sidewalks, and perhaps even sidewalks everywhere.

Sizing Up a Sidewalk Law

On August 8, 1998, a memorandum on 'Sidewalk Usage' was sent from Mike Ringo, then-Lieutenant in the Tempe Police Department, to the Tempe city council, stating in part:

> The Police Department has received continuous communication from downtown merchants and the Downtown Tempe Community Inc. (DTC) that various individuals continue to disrupt business by sitting on sidewalks in front of or near their place of business. A primary activity of these people who position themselves near business entrances is to ask for money. The merchants feel that this affects their business because potential customers look to avoid these individuals or groups and steer clear of their locations. The issue has not been resolved, and the Police Department has been asked to conduct research on the possibility of implementing a city ordinance precluding this type of activity.
>
> Re-Development of downtown Tempe and its Mill Ave has been tremendously successful with ever-increasing numbers of people making it a point of destination. The downtown has commercial and retail elements with a high proportion of entertainment oriented establishments.
>
> The success associated with downtown re-development increased the number of transients who frequent the downtown. The behavior of these individuals has caused concern from the perception of downtown merchants and customers. One of the concerns has been the manner transients position themselves on sidewalks. The following is a summary of the actions taken and research conducted on this issue.
>
> - Transients/homeless have had a presence in the downtown for many years.
> - Tempe draws a younger age group of individuals who carry various labels to include transient, homeless, runaway, and slacker. There is also a fringe group who look and act the same as 'slackers.' They are local to the valley, they work, and many live at home with their family unlike slackers.

- Their numbers have steadily grown over the years though many are seasonal bringing the greatest number to the downtown from fall to spring.
- These individuals come from various locations. They normally enter the downtown and spend the day and evening along Mill Ave where they sit on the public sidewalk, benches, and planters. One of their primary activities is to panhandle from people who walk by.
- Initial re-development concerning public sidewalk features included park benches along Mill Ave. Most of the benches have been removed as part of a CPTED response to the problem. The transients were displaced to some degree but the planters and sidewalk are still available for sitting.
- The Police Department has responded to numerous complaints of individuals sitting outside of businesses. Complaints of the business being blocked in front of a business are easily handled with an existing city ordinance.
- These individuals are familiar with the law and local ordinances. They know they can sit where they want on public right of way if they don't obstruct the pedestrian traffic. Though they don't block it, their actions do constrict people as they walk by.

Now, if I told you nothing else about the sidewalk ordinance, you could glean a pretty fair idea of its purpose and intent just from this memorandum. Clearly the aim is to give the police the power – urged by the local 'business improvement district' (the DTC) and merchants – to contact and remove 'slackers,' 'transients,' and the 'homeless.' The origins of the law as presented in this memorandum reveal the intimate connection between processes of redevelopment and the desire to displace the so-called slackers. Noting that existing laws prohibiting blocking or obstructing the sidewalks cannot accomplish this end of eradication (because the homeless don't in fact block or obstruct), the memorandum recounts how strategies of removing "most of the benches" on Mill Avenue have been similarly ineffective at eliminating the problem (cf. Carr, et al. 1992, noting that, "by not placing benches in their downtown spaces, [many] towns discourage [certain] groups from hanging out"). Identifying downtown Tempe explicitly as an "entertainment oriented" district, the memorandum notes that the DTC and business community initiated the process leading to adoption of the ordinance, and that it was the police who had "been asked to conduct research on the possibility of implementing a city ordinance precluding" sitting on the downtown sidewalks. Subsequent events will reveal nearly every one of these original points being contradicted by those espousing the 'official' position as to the intent of the law, including Rod Keeling (former Executive Director of the DTC), former Mayor Neil Giuliano, and former Tempe City Attorney Marlene Pontrelli Maerowitz – all of whom figure prominently in this narrative.

The text of the sidewalk ordinance originally proposed by Tempe's 'Criminal Justice working group' (made up of Ringo, Maerowitz, and Keeling) is similarly revealing in both intent and function. Based on and nearly identical to Seattle's controversial sidewalk law, Tempe Ordinance No. 98.57 (Section 29-70 of the Tempe City Code) begins with a generic but remarkably revealing preamble:

> **WHEREAS**, public sidewalks in business districts are created and maintained for the primary purpose of enabling pedestrians to safely and effectively move about from place to place, facilitating deliveries of goods and services, and providing potential customers with convenient access to goods and services; and
> **WHEREAS**, during normal business hours, the public sidewalks in the downtown commercial areas are prone to congestion, and should be kept available to serve these primary purposes; and
> **WHEREAS**, except in places provided therefor or where reasonably necessary, sitting or lying on the public sidewalks in the downtown commercial areas during the hours of greatest congestion interferes with the primary purposes of the public sidewalks, threatens public safety, and damages public welfare; and
> **WHEREAS**, pedestrians, particularly the elderly, disabled, or vision-impaired, are put at increased risk when they must see and navigate around individuals sitting or lying upon the public sidewalks; and

> **WHEREAS**, the public welfare is promoted by economically healthy downtown commercial areas which attract people to shop, work, and recreate. These areas provide easily accessible goods and services, employment opportunities, the tax revenues necessary to maintain and improve property within these areas; and
> **WHEREAS**, there are numerous other places within the downtown commercial areas where sitting or lying down can be accommodated without unduly interfering with the safe flow of pedestrian traffic, impairing commercial activity, threatening public safety or harming the public welfare. These other places include city parks and plazas and common areas open to the public, in addition to public sidewalks outside the designated hours.

The preamble expressly identifies the "primary purpose" of public sidewalks as largely economic, links "public welfare" directly to economic health, and promises "numerous other places" to sit within the downtown commercial area. In addition, it claims that certain people are put at "increased risk" from having to "see" someone sitting on the sidewalk! However, as indicated herein, those 'other places' for sitting – including parks, plazas, or the mysterious "common areas" – either do not exist, contain their own criminal behavior restrictions, or are fast shrinking through patterns of privatization.

The actual text of the ordinance itself, in addition to imposing a maximum penalty (for a class 3 misdemeanor) of 30 days in jail and a $500 fine, reads as follows:

> **Sec. 29-70. Prohibited conduct; exceptions.**
> (a) No person shall sit or lie down upon a public sidewalk or upon a blanket, chair, stool, or any other object not permanently affixed upon a public sidewalk or median in the downtown central commercial district during the hours between 7:00 a.m. and 10:00 p.m. on weekdays and between 7:00 a.m. and 1:00 a.m. on Fridays and Saturdays.
> (b) The prohibitions in subsection (a) shall not apply to any person:
>
> > (1) Sitting or lying down on a public sidewalk due to a medical emergency;

(2) Who, as the result of a disability, utilizes a wheelchair, walker, or similar device to move about the public sidewalk;
(3) Operating or patronizing a commercial establishment conducted on the public sidewalks pursuant to a permit; or a person participating in or attending a parade, festival, performance, rally, demonstration, meeting or similar event conducted on the public sidewalk pursuant to a permit;
(4) Sitting on a chair or bench located on the public sidewalk which is supplied by a public agency or by the abutting private property owner; or
(5) Sitting on a public sidewalk within a bus zone while waiting for public or private transportation.

(c) Nothing in the exceptions enumerated in subsection (b) shall be construed to permit any conduct which is otherwise prohibited by law.
(d) No person shall be cited under this section unless the person engages in conduct prohibited by this section after having been notified by a law enforcement officer that the conduct violates this section.

The text thus notes that it applies only during certain (business) hours in the "downtown central commercial district," with exceptions for medical conditions and emergencies, patronizing an establishment's sidewalk seating area, and engaging in a demonstration pursuant to a permit. All of these themes raised by the text of the ordinance, its preamble, and Lt. Ringo's initial memorandum, will figure prominently in the ensuing debate over the legitimacy and utility of the ordinance.

Rotten to the Roots: Those Cursed Precursors

Let me to dispense with this chronological narrative and digress for a moment. Obviously there is a pre-history to all of this that informs the analysis. In Tempe, the most immediate chapter involved the passage of ordinances in August 1997 prohibiting 'urban camping' (Sections 23-90 and 23-91 of the Tempe City Code provide, in part, that it shall be unlawful to use a public park, street, or other public place for living accommodation purposes, including erecting tents or any structure to provide shelter, laying down bedding, storing personal belongings, regularly cooking or preparing meals, or living in a vehicle; violations are punishable by up to 6 months in jail and a $2500 fine) and 'aggressive panhandling' (sections 24-115 and 24-116 of the Tempe City Code provide, in part, that it shall be unlawful in a public area to solicit within 15 feet of a bank or ATM machine, to continue soliciting after a person has given a negative response, to obstruct the safe or free passage of the person being solicited, or to make physical contact with such person; violations are punishable by up to 6 months in jail and a $2500 fine) – enacted just one year before the sidewalk ordinance proposal was initially floated publicly. For reasons that have to do primarily with lack of public knowledge of the import and intent of those two earlier 'anti-homeless laws,' there was little discussion in city hall or the media about their passage and implementation. I personally was unaware at that time that the laws had been adopted, despite the fact that I regularly read the area newspapers and casually followed local politics. Shortly after the laws took effect, then-City Attorney Marlene Maerowitz, who wrote a regular column in the community section of the *Arizona Republic*, published a piece entitled 'Homeless Aren't Tempe's Responsibility' (1997), in which she argued:

> "The camping ordinance is not written or designed to discriminate against the homeless. All people, whether they have homes or not, are free to use the parks. The prohibition is about permanently appropriating public space for private use. . . . Some [of the street people] are homeless by choice. These are the so-called slackers. They suffer from no mental illness and could find work, but they refuse to do so. They enjoy life on the street. For them, panhandling is a good way of life. Yet, it does not mean that the rest of the community must support them by allowing unfettered use of the public parks. . . . Social conscience does not mean turning our front yards or our public parks into a homeless haven."

Squeezing out the 'slackers,' then, was not a new idea in downtown Tempe in the autumn of 1998 when the sidewalk law was being debated, and in many ways the die had already been cast by then.

Nor were such processes and policies unknown in the rest of the country. In many towns and cities, especially in the western United States, there were attempts to limit the access of homeless people to downtown commercial areas through use of a sidewalk ordinance. Santa Monica, California, is sometimes considered to be the site of "the nation's first sweeping crackdown" on homelessness in 1991 (see Wong & LaGanga 1998). Santa Cruz, California, also was one of the progenitors, having by 1994 already gone through a cycle of narrow passage by a divided council, student/citizen protests, and modification of an ordinance to prohibit only obstructionist sitting (Gaura 1994). Seattle of course was the site of the famous 1994 'Sidran Sidewalk Law' that was challenged in federal court, resulting in the decision by the Ninth Circuit Court of Appeals in *Roulette vs. City of Seattle* (97 F.3d 300 (9th Cir. 1996)), a case that would have national implications and empower cities in the western U.S. (the jurisdiction of the Ninth Circuit) to enact similar laws (see Teir 1998:275; Kelling & Coles 1996:213) – despite frequent criticisms that "the law blatantly criminalizes homeless people who have nowhere to go and forces them to be constantly moving" (Stoner 1995:154; see also Arrington 1996, noting that in the first 2 years of its application, the Seattle sidewalk law resulted in 107 citations and many more 'contacts' by the police). Early locales to flirt with the invitation to adopt a sidewalk law post-*Roulette* included Boulder (ACLU 1997) and Aurora, Colorado (Amole 1998), as well as Berkeley, which passed the ordinance in 1994, had it enjoined by a federal judge for two years, put it back into effect after *Roulette* was decided (Goodman 1996), repealed it, and then passed laws against sleeping and lying down (Wong & LaGanga 1998).

Two of the legendary and most emblematic sidewalk ordinance battles took place in Palo Alto (CA) and Philadelphia, with the former preceding Tempe's ordinance by two years, and the latter coinciding almost precisely with Tempe's time frame and in fact having its law take effect on the same day as Tempe's. In Palo Alto, critics blasted a "sidewalk civility" ordinance as "a recipe for creating division within the community" (Arrington 1996), as "a disguised and dishonest way of trying to get people off the streets when we don't like how they look," and as an attempt "to remove (indigents') presence from the sidewalk – it is not to effect safe passage" (Zinko 1997). Local newspaper editorials asserted that the ordinance "is not about sidewalk obstruction; it's about controlling and containing a problem that can't be legally targeted: homeless and other people who use our sidewalks for panhandling" (Palo Alto Weekly 1997a); and argued that it "represents another evolution in society's efforts to thwart begging and vagrancy, [dating] back hundreds of years" (Palo Alto Weekly 1997b). A college editorial (Stanford Daily 1997) concurred, noting that the ordinance "remains a harmful piece of legislation. The real objection that merchants and city council members have to sitters . . . is their presence alone." Interestingly, following a rancorous debate in the years after the ordinance was enacted, when a new police chief was appointed the city's policy toward the homeless was reoriented toward "treating the homeless with more respect and helping them solve their problems" (Zinko 1999). One homeless resident, however, couldn't discern any difference: "I haven't seen anything to help us – nothing but running us off and making us feel like we're just yea tall. A nurse and a social worker? That's just to make themselves feel better. What we need is a place to shower, wash our clothes, look for work and get a callback."

In Philadelphia, proponents of the sidewalk law – including Councilman John Street (who would later become mayor), prompting colorful critical cries of 'Street Sweeper!' – stated that the law was "designed to make sidewalk behavior more civil, to promote commerce and tourism, to provide an additional tool to police officers" (in Sarlat 1998), and to "increase Philadelphia's ability to attract tourists" (in Shaffer 1998). Critics noted, however, that "it would ultimately force the homeless from the city's downtown sidewalks," and warned that "many homeless people will ignore the citations – and their mandatory court appearances and fines – and, therefore, develop serious legal trouble" (Naymik 1998). Homeless advocates called the law "an attempt at criminalizing homelessness;" pointed out that "sidewalks are for everyone, even those who have nowhere else to go;" argued that the law "makes it impossible for a homeless person to live their life;" and maintained that "the city is more concerned about tourism, making money, and creating more business and profit than about its citizens" (Stiles 1998). Despite these concerns, the law was adopted and put into effect on the same day as Tempe's version.

In recent years, the use of a sidewalk ordinance as a street sweeping tool has proliferated. The NLCHP report *Out of Sight -- Out of Mind?* (1999) identified cities including San Jose, Virginia Beach, Charlotte, and Atlanta as then-additions to the roster; in fact, between 2002 and 2003, the NCH/NLCHP reports on homeless criminalization indicated an increase in the rate of cities surveyed that had a sidewalk sitting ordinance, from 33% in 2002 to 45% in 2003. Among participants in the trend at that time were Arcata, California – one of the most 'liberal' cities in the country (see Boxall 2001), where some have urged the city to "take a clue from the already-fought battles of many other cities and avoid divisive conflict and the threat of costly legal wrangling" (Meserve 2001). Tucson, Arizona, which actually had a sidewalk law in place as early as 1997, recently debated its future in light of events in Tempe that will be detailed below (according to police information services, 50 people were cited in the first four months of the law's application there). The Tucson city council considered easing the law to include an exception for people "exercising First Amendment rights" of speech, religion, or assembly (Tobin 2000a; 2000b). "It's a public place, so why shouldn't I be able to sit?" asked one homeless youth there. "We spend money in these businesses too" (2000a). An editorial (Tucson Citizen 2000) observed that "it's time for Tucson to rethink its ordinance banning sitting and lying on public sidewalks. . . . Instead of discriminatory laws that target undesirables, the city should focus on those who engage in criminal activity, then deal with them appropriately. . . . Trying to remove the threat with vague and sweeping ordinances rarely works. If it did, the City Council just as easily could accomplish its goal by passing an ordinance banning people with body odor or unkempt hair."

Despite these and other similar concerns from various locales, by 2004 the NCH reported 61 cities with sidewalk sitting ordinances. In Los Angeles, to take one example, the numbers are staggering, as Gary Blasi (1997:30) reports: "After the 2002 holiday season, the majority of arrests were for sitting or lying on the sidewalk. . . . In January 2003, LAPD presented 135 cases to the City Attorney, whose office prosecuted 116. . . . Between January 1, 2003 and March 4, 2004, LAPD had made 1474 arrests for violations of this [ordinance]."

Before returning to the Tempe case, I'd like to close this brief digression with a reminder of the stakes involved here, running the gamut from liberty, to the right of dissent, to having a place to do so, to embracing diversity, and finally to the very core of our cultural practices and policies. An eloquent statement of this appeared in a law journal article analyzing legal challenges to Tempe's sidewalk law (Houck 2000), which deftly makes the implicit connections explicit:

> "Unlike the more traditional homeless who may be glad to go to a shelter and accept help getting back on their feet, gutter punks [i.e., slackers] decline those services. They are rebelling; they do not want the nine-to-five life, nor do they want to be cloistered off out of sight getting services. They do not trust adults or see them as role models. Visibility is

essential if they are to communicate their rejection of the mainstream American lifestyle. Upscale commercial areas of major cities are the perfect place to communicate this message. . . . In driving out the messenger, cities also drive out the message. The message is that post-industrial American society has a very definite down side, demonstrated by the number of youths who think street life is better than home life. With this group of people out of sight, cities are free to display their yuppified, gentrified, Disney-like, consumer-driven version of postmodern society, in hopes of attracting more of the 'right' kind of people, i.e. consumers. These disaffected youth are the externalities of the very system trying to dispose of them. . . . Hopefully, the struggle over [sidewalk] laws will force Americans to acknowledge and deal with the alienated and disenfranchised young adults in our society, or perhaps be more tolerant and not label street people as 'problems,' instead of trying to put them out of sight, out of mind."

How a (Dollar) Bill Becomes a (Discriminatory) Law

Back in Tempe, things quickly began to heat up. Following Lt. Ringo's memorandum, an article appeared in the *Arizona Republic* (Petrie 1998a, 'Tempe Police Hope Proposed Law Won't Sit Well With Transients') which observed that, "the DTC and the police would like a law in place by the time the weather cools off and transients start heading to Tempe en masse. 'This is our ongoing effort to argue for the ease of civility in the downtown,' Rod Keeling said. [Chief of Police Ron] Burns said the police find themselves in a difficult situation in crafting and enforcing such laws. 'We're put in the middle here,' he said. 'One side is saying, 'Get rid of them,' and the other side is saying 'We're not doing anything wrong.'" A subsequent piece in the *ASU State Press* (Prendergast 1998a) was more bluntly titled 'City Proposal Would Eliminate 'Mill Rats.'' The article observed:

"'This is an ordinance that we are advocating the city to take a look at,' said Rod Keeling, executive director of the DTC. 'It promotes civility in public space by requiring people to sit on benches and not the sidewalk.' But the so-called Mill Rats, who spend their days on the sidewalks of Mill, seem to be the

> obvious target of the ordinance. . . . Jessica Greiner, a well-pierced, mohawked 17-year-old who frequents Mill Avenue, said this would be just another way of ostracizing 'street people' like herself. 'The police often come up to me, open my backpack and dump out my stuff and then tell me to put everything back in it,' she said. Shawn McCoy, a shirtless 18-year-old with pierced nipples, agreed with Greiner. 'They're just trying to chase us out of here,' he said."

Apparently, Mr. Keeling had read the propaganda put forth by the proponents of 'civility,' as discussed above in Chapter Three. Equally apparent is that he hadn't carefully read Lt. Ringo's candid statement that "most of the benches have been removed," leaving people on Mill Avenue to sit on either the planters (now arced or spiked), the sidewalks (public but prohibited), or in restaurant sidewalk cafes (private and costly). Or more likely, Keeling was well aware of the wholesale removal of benches but was hoping that the public wasn't.

Reading these two early articles is how I found out about the sidewalk ordinance. I had previously been studying issues concerning public space, including the Rainbow Family and the right to 'gather' in the National Forests. Earlier in the summer of 1998, while traveling through Berkeley, I obtained a copy of the homeless paper *Street Spirit* that mentioned the sidewalk battles there between street people, merchants, police, and the city. I returned to Tempe just days before the *Republic* and *State Press* articles came out, and immediately realized that the issue was precisely what I had been investigating in terms of spatiality, dissent, and exclusion, and had been foreshadowed by my observations in Berkeley. I first entered the political fray on the sidewalk issue (and Tempe politics in general) on September 3rd in a *State Press* guest column (1998) that was self-titled 'Taking a Stand to Keep Sitting Legal,' where I argued as follows:

> The proposed anti-sitting ordinance is the most recent pretextual attempt to eliminate the 'Mill Rats' [and] the setting in controversy here is the most public of places, the classic First Amendment forum for the development of a 'marketplace of ideas' – the sidewalk along a public right-of-way. When a group of rag-tag drummers, homeless vets, new age travelers, and young neo-hippies congregate publicly, they acquire standing to assert legal rights of free expression and

association that we all value, and serve as active defenders of civil liberties that are fast contracting with the rapid expansion of state and corporate control of space.

A healthy society requires elements of both consensus and dissent. . . . Are we prepared to say that the needs of business and commerce outweigh the rights of citizens to gather peaceably in public settings? Is the flow of dollars and merchandise the only indicator of value in deciding how to balance competing interests over public space?

Consider the vast amount of space occupied by business interests in our society. Compare it to the meager spaces these kids have to act out and assert their divergent ideologies, and ask yourself whether a few people sitting on small patches of public sidewalk is really a sufficient evil to justify further curtailing expressive activity. In my view, the proposed sitting ban is an unconstitutional and inappropriate response to the challenges raised by the so-called 'Mill Rats' and their particular brand of dissent. The ordinance ought to be rejected if it comes up for a vote in the Tempe City Council.

It didn't take long for Rod Keeling to respond. The following day, the *State Press* ran a letter entitled 'Downtown Tempe Gives Their Side,' in which Keeling (1998a) opined that the ordinance "is not solely a homeless issue, although many street kids do sit on the sidewalks of Mill Avenue congregating in large groups," but instead "is aimed at preserving the safety and comfort of everyone who lives, works, shops, plays, and goes to school in downtown Tempe." In terms of the space itself, Keeling added that "the community is in charge of the public space and each member has a right to an expectation of safety. The city of Tempe holds our sidewalks in trust for all the citizens of Tempe." (However, as detailed above in Chapter Two, many of those sidewalks supposedly 'held in trust' have either been sold or otherwise converted from public to private space.) Finally, Keeling invoked the slippery slope logic of the 'broken windows' theory: "Sitting on the sidewalk is not a standard of behavior our community accepts. We need to ask ourselves, 'If we allow this, what other unacceptable behavior do we allow?'" Presumably, when Keeling referred to 'our community,' he meant the DTC and their ilk, and was excluding the street people themselves from being members entitled to help define standards of acceptable community behavior.

The DTC czar was at it again in an October *Phoenix New Times* piece called 'Crusty Crackdown' (Holthouse 1998b):

> "This problem with what I term 'disconnected youth' really began about three years ago, and basically caught us off guard," says Rod Keeling, director of Downtown Tempe Community Inc. "We didn't know what the hell to do but now we're learning, and beginning to implement and use the tools that have worked for other communities with similar public-disorder problems. Keeling brought the idea for a new law before the Tempe City Council in August. The council directed Tempe's city attorney to draft an ordinance closely modeled after a sidewalk law Seattle passed in 1994.
>
> "Downtown Tempe is a public place," says Keeling. "If you were to go to another public place, such as a movie theater or a mall or Gammage Auditorium, and you saw dozens of people sitting and laying around, your reaction would probably be, 'Who's in charge here? Who's tolerating this on behalf of the citizens?' Well, the crux of any discussion of this sidewalk ordinance is this: Is our community willing to tolerate that kind of behavior in our downtown area? And I think the answer has become a firm 'No.'"
>
> Like Tempe's aggressive panhandling and urban camping ordinances, Keeling says, the sidewalk-squatting ban will likely produce few arrests. "It's more of a tool for the police. It will empower a cop to come up and say, 'You can't sit on the sidewalk, and I can cite you if you don't move along.'"

While empowering cops to remove the homeless is hardly a laudable goal, equally bizarre is Keeling's flagrant failure to grasp the meaning of public space. The examples he cites for places where "sitting and laying around" would be inappropriate – movie theaters, malls, auditoriums – are all *privately-owned* spaces that are open to the public (for a price) but are not public spaces in a legal or political sense. Keeling plied the same logic before the Tempe City Council Public Health and Safety Committee, whose September 3, 1998, minutes reflect him stating that "you typically don't see individuals sprawled out in a disruptive fashion at churches, schools and malls. What the DTC is saying is that it would like to afford downtown patrons the same expectations as they would have of other destination points."

Others would repeat this public/private error in the coming weeks, as well as that pervasive untruth about being allowed to sit elsewhere, as Keeling told the *East Valley Tribune* later that year (Schakel 1998): "All we're asking them to do is get up off the sidewalks and sit on something that was designed to be sat on." Since most of the benches had been removed, and with the planters eventually being privatized and then spiked, the 'somewhere else' that Keeling alludes to presumably means a restaurant's sidewalk café area – whose growing presence and encroachment, as then-Councilmember Hugh Hallman observed in the Issue Review Session of October 29th, "undermines the claims that this ordinance concerns impeding the flow of traffic, and makes this ordinance discriminatory against individuals who are not considered desirable by commercial interests; it's about impeding the flow of commerce – not the flow of traffic." Hallman and others also noted that Tempe already had in place at least three other city ordinances prohibiting sidewalk obstructions: (i) Section 22-4 states that "No person shall obstruct or place any obstruction upon, across or along any street, alley or sidewalk in any manner;" (ii) Section 29-21 states that "No person shall . . . obstruct . . . any street, alley or public right-of-way so as to hinder free and proper use thereof;" and (iii) Sections 24-115 and 24-116 prohibit 'aggressive panhandling,' defined as "obstructing the safe or free passage of the person being solicited or requiring the person to take evasive action to avoid physical contact." The presence of these ordinances belies the argument that the sidewalk law was needed to combat congestion; indeed, as noted in Lt. Ringo's initial memorandum, "Complaints of the sidewalk being blocked in front of a business are easily handled with an existing city ordinance."

Additional critical voices in this period included *Republic* community columnist Art Thomason (1998), who observed that

> "city officials are contemplating the adoption of an ordinance to cleanse Tempe streets of all sidewalk-sitting slackers. It's their way of saying: No Armani, no admittance. . . . Ordinances that virtually encourage selective enforcement are not the answer. They have too much potential for abuse. . . . I have an inkling that Mill Avenue's problems have less of a relationship to do with panhandlers and loiterers than they do with a picture-postcard downtown on the verge of losing its originality, individualism and creative charm."

Obviously, Keeling had his counter-punch ready once again, which came in the form of the infamous 'Time to Sweep Slackers Off Mill' column (1998b), where he concluded that "the city of Tempe holds the ownership of downtown sidewalks in trust for the benefit and non-exclusive use of all of the citizens of our city. To allow a small number of misbehaving individuals to 'run off' the citizens of this community from our finest public spaces, space that was paid for by those very citizens, is wrong. . . . Let's clean up Mill Avenue. It's time for a change and we need your help and support."

Nevertheless, as noted above in Chapter Two, that supposed 'trust' in those spaces "paid for by the citizens" had already been violated by the city in selling the sidewalks to private property owners, which inured to Keeling and the DTC's direct benefit. In a scathing critical response, Kathy Finberg wrote in the *Republic* (1998a):

> "The Downtown Tempe Community is at it again. It's after the City Council to ensure that Mill Avenue's $20 million face lift remains wrinkle free. If you believe Mr. Keeling, the slackers are part of an invading army of economic anarchists who have come to Mill Avenue to drive customers away and make downtown businesses fail. . . . [D]owntown interests have been more concerned with form and appearance than function. Even the appearance of Mill Avenue is increasingly disappointing. It has become my worst fear: a downtown mall. More of the old-time independents, which brought me to Mill Avenue initially, have been replaced by franchise operations. . . . If crowded sidewalks are a problem, deal with that. But don't single out an economic or social class of youth that don't fit your image of Mill Avenue. . . . Let's keep Tempe tolerant. I urge the council to reject this social street sweeping. When a face lift gets too tight, the result looks absurd."

Finberg reiterated these sentiments two weeks later (1998b), quoting Councilmember Hallman and expressing concern about "this movement to sanitize the sidewalks of undesirable characters."

Meanwhile, despite the vehement objections being registered, the city council was busy working to move the ordinance toward adoption. Another memorandum from Lt. Ringo was delivered on October 22, 1998, noting that "the Police Department had received complaints and concerns from merchants in the downtown concerning persons sitting on the sidewalk and interfering with their businesses and customers. This concern was also supported by the DTC who requested that the Police Department look into the use of a sidewalk ordinance." Then, on November 12th, a Staff Summary Report was issued by Lt. Ringo, Police Commander Kevin Kotsur, and Assistant City Attorney Maerowitz, which largely recast the issue in terms of sidewalk congestion instead of slacker-bashing: "There has been an increase in the number of people who sit or lie down on the sidewalk in the central commercial district. The result is that the sidewalks are congested by clusters of people that narrow the sidewalk and create a negative perception from people when such clustering occurs outside the business entrances. At night the clustering causes confrontations between people as they squeeze by each other." It was not specified from whose perspective this 'negative perception' was created, but since only the DTC and downtown merchants had been cited as complainants, we can infer that it was their perceptions that had been affronted, as well as Keeling's, who thus far had been the only person to defend the ordinance in the media.

In addition to the criticisms raised by columnists, Mr. Hallman, and myself, a number of citizens came out to a city council meeting on November 19, 1998, and spoke against the ordinance. One resident stated: "There's no place to sit downtown – the benches are all taken. I've been harassed on Mill Avenue outside of the Coffee Plantation, and I was a paying customer." Another citizen said that "the intent of this law is to remove undesirables from the street. The business owners wanted more people downtown – they need to take the good with the bad." And finally, a young man noted: "I sit on the bricks on the sidewalk. I'm polite, although there is a lot of animosity coming from shop owners and white collar workers. I've also been harassed and told to move on. Imposing $500 fines is not going to work. All that's being done is throwing money and handcuffs at the problem, and it's frightening." The minutes of the council meeting from that evening conclude with Hallman commenting that "if individuals who sit on the sidewalks are the real problem, then why not install more benches?"

An *Arizona Republic* article titled 'Sides Squaring Off on Restricting Youths in Tempe Public Areas' (Petrie 1998b) sensed the building momentum toward a community conflict:

> "Whether it's perception or reality, does the community feel comfortable with using their downtown?" asks Rod Keeling.

> Vocal critics, however, accuse the city of using laws to keep the slackers off the carefully manicured streets of downtown. Yet Keeling and others insist, vehemently at times, that they're not interested in ridding the town of slackers, or legislating Tempe into an idyllic community like the one portrayed in the movie *Pleasantville*, where perfection is law. "We're not asking them to leave, and we're not asking them to vacate the city," Keeling says. "We're simply asking them to get off the ground and sit on a bench." Some slackers say that there are fewer benches to sit on these days and that their rights are being infringed even more by the sidewalk ban. "It's *1984*. That's what they're doing," says 15-year-old Sponge, referring to the George Orwell novel about the fictional Big Brother and the Thought Police. . . .
>
> [Councilmember] Hallman says the argument that business isn't booming like it should because of the slackers' presence is hollow. "We're trying to get rid of a group of people they want to use as scapegoats for business problems," he says. Statistics recently released by the DTC belie that business is bad. Taxable sales on Mill Avenue are up 25% overall from 1997. . . . [Vic] Linoff says that today's DTC leadership may be trying too hard to craft a downtown atmosphere, rather than let it evolve naturally. "There's a tendency to program everything, and you lose the spontaneity," he says. That's how some Mill shoppers feel about the slackers. "You've got a lot more diversity [here]," says Bruce Johs of Tempe. "I kind of like the way it is now," Bruce adds. "You'd hate to see it become a Gestapo thing."

Perhaps most would agree that an Orwellian, neo-fascistic *Pleasantville* is something to be strenuously avoided. City Attorney Maerowitz, however, took a different view in a subsequent column (1998: 'Walking Only on Sidewalks is the Point'), where she attempted to portray the issue as purely one of pedestrian safety and traffic flow. Identifying herself as "one of the drafters of the proposed ordinance" – a fact mentioned since she was part of the city's August 1998 'Criminal Justice Working Group' for which, as Reed & Venable 2001 note, "the focus of this group was not to provide humane services, rather it was to eliminate the homeless as a whole from the area, or at least to remove them from public view" – Maerowitz opined:

> The proposed ordinance is not about controlling a particular segment of the population. Rather, it is about controlling inappropriate behavior. The proposal is simple. The ordinance prohibits lying or sitting on public sidewalks in Tempe's downtown commercial district. This doesn't mean there is no sitting in downtown Tempe. People can still sit and watch the world pass by, but the sitting must be done on planters and benches that are affixed to the pavement. In addition, sitting at outdoor cafes or on chairs provided by private property owners outside of their establishments is permitted. If the ordinance is adopted, access to all public areas in Tempe would remain the same. The ordinance does not prohibit slackers. In fact, slackers can still hang out and hang around. No one can, nor would anyone try, to stop them.
>
> The Tempe Police Department first proposed the idea of a sidewalk ordinance more than a year ago because police were finding it increasingly difficult to prohibit people from lying and sitting on the sidewalks. This was blocking the way of pedestrians who were attempting to enter businesses or simply walk down the street. . . . It is unfortunate that there is a need to legislate common courtesies. No one would consider it appropriate to lie down in a restaurant or grocery store. Sidewalks should be no different. Tempe's proposed ordinance merely seeks to preserve at least a portion of its sidewalks for walking.

As with many of Keeling's remarks, Maerowitz is similarly misleading as to the nature of public spaces (sidewalks, parks) versus private spaces (restaurants, grocery stores, sidewalk cafes). Statements about sitting on benches or planters are likewise disingenuous. And Lt. Ringo's initial memorandum raising the issue publicly for the first time plainly indicates that the problem, as identified by the DTC and not the Police as Maerowitz contends, was not about sidewalk congestion but about eradicating the slackers. A *Republic* editorial (1998b, 'Ordinance is Not the Right Answer to Mill Slackers') pointed out some of these inconsistencies and difficulties: "Tempe had better remember that ill-conceived laws also are a blight on the land. Tempe's elected officials are considering a balm that's worse than the irritation. Sweeping a beleaguered group of young people off the sidewalks through a no-sit ordinance is going too far. Besides, it's not likely to work. Months ago, in an attempt to deter slackers, the city removed many of its benches. With fewer places to sit, the slackers merely moved to the ground. . . . To get off the ground, these kids may need a hand up rather than a citation. Creating an ordinance to toss them off the sidewalk is simply a shame." As the editorial identifies, the slackers had been forced to take to the ground following the wholesale removal of benches, and once there, became targets of the next phase in their elimination *via* the sidewalk ordinance (see Houck 2000:1462).

Finally, the appointed day had arrived for the council to either adopt or reject the proposed ordinance. As that day's (December 17, 1998) *Arizona Republic* (Petrie 1998c) set the scene:

> "Tempe takes another step toward becoming *Pleasantville* tonight, as the City Council is expected to pass a law banning people from sitting on sidewalks along Mill Avenue. It would be the third Tempe ordinance aimed at restricting the homeless and those who spend hours hanging out on the streets. . . . 'The lifestyle we're talking about is horrific,' Rod Keeling said. 'The human carnage is unbelievable. Our community shouldn't let this behavior go on.' James O'Leary of Phoenix says the increasing regulations are robbing the area of its urban vitality. 'Do we want to supersanitize Mill Avenue?' O'Leary asked. 'Do you air-condition it or roof it over or put video cameras in there? Where does it all end?'"

Nonetheless, despite such concerns – including evidence presented and confirmed by city staff that 75 benches had indeed been removed under the CPTED (Crime Prevention Through Environmental Design) program – the council passed the ordinance by a 4-to-3 vote, indicating at least that two additional "no" votes had been picked up since the early days when Hallman clearly was the lone dissenter. Apparently, the two "nays" (Councilmembers Cahill and Lewis) were influenced by the diverse array of citizens who spoke out against the law during the three-hour council meeting that evening, as described in the *Tribune* (Riordan 1998): "About 25 people spoke during the hearing. Most were opposed to the law, including Arizona State University professor [sic] Randall Amster, who called it 'anti-homeless legislation.' 'We're going through this dance because a certain set of folks wanted to enact their own ordinance as part of a plan to get rid of undesirables,' Councilman Hallman said." Setting the tone for what would become a vigorous post-passage debate over the ordinance, the *Republic* printed a letter to the editor (1/8/99) that captured the sentiments of many: "Call Tempe's sidewalk ban what it is: legislated discrimination."

Street Wars: The Empire Lashes Back

As fate would have it, Tempe's sidewalk law took effect on January 18, 1999, which was Martin Luther King, Jr., Day. In the next chapter I will describe how some citizens of Tempe chose to commemorate that day, and its profound effects on the ordinance and the city itself. Also omitted for the time being is an analysis of the legal battle over the ordinance that began just before the law took effect, deferring the same to the discussion of civil rights struggles that follows. Rather, the focus here will be to continue the genealogy of the public discourse surrounding the law, interpreting events through the critical lens developed in the course of this study, and situating the unfolding debate within the larger framework of homeless criminalization and spatial sanitization. All of which, in one of those synchronous moments alluded to above, leads naturally into the next piece in the chronology, an *Arizona Republic* column (Svelund 1999, 'Sidewalk Ordinance Wrong') that began to expand the debate into these realms:

> "This is our new socio-spatial battle. Our new form of spatial apartheid. Do you allow public land, and, by extension, public interest, into the discriminating hands of a few store owners? The Tempe City Council says 'yes.' Naturally so do the store owners. I say no because the slackers and the homeless who convene on sidewalks remain sole witness to the testimony of public spaces as democratic environs. Access to public land is not a right we should easily forfeit. . . . The undesirables we want removed from our stores and our streets and our cities and our lives have broken only the unwritten law of conformity. . . . Let us admit that this has more to do with class than curbs. It has to do with the privatization of public land. About keeping people in their appropriate places. But worse than revoking public land from the very public who owns it, the ordinance promises to blur the already murky relationship between the private and public domain. And this is the real danger here."

In light of subsequent events in Tempe, statements such as this have come to appear positively prescient.

The *State Press* ran an editorial on the same day, January 19, 1999 ('New Ordinance Attacks Homeless'), observing that "Tempe city officials have demonstrated that Tempe will continue to be a heartless, disinterested city in the plight of the homeless," and even making a 'reverse broken windows' argument like that noted in Chapter Three:

> "By adopting this law, we've decided to say to the homeless: 'Hey pal. Down on your luck? Well, guess what. If you want to sit here, it will cost you 500 bucks and as an added bonus you get to spend a nice holiday in the city slammer. We at the *State Press* want to officially go on the record as saying that the city council is determined to create more criminals in our good city by forcing the otherwise-harmless transients to enter a life of crime in order to pay their $500 fines. These people don't have a dime to spend on a sandwich, let alone pay some ridiculous fine for sitting on a sidewalk – so get ready for higher crime rates, Tempe."

A follow-up column three days later (Whisler 1999) closed the criminalization circle once again:

> "The city council has been pressured by business interests to sweep its homeless problem under the carpet. Rather than seeking to solve the problem by providing assistance to those who need and want it, they have decided to tailor laws so as to sanitize public space in the hopes of making more money. Rationally, the criminalization of homelessness does not make sense. And yet the true intent of the sidewalk ordinance is absurdly obvious."

The final three relevant episodes from this time frame are all connected thematically. Let me take them in reverse chronological order to make the point clearly. In his State of the City address, Mayor Giuliano's reference to the sidewalk ordinance battle drew headlines in the *State Press* (Subramanian 1999). In his speech, the mayor "admitted that the issue has drawn the city's attention to the plight of its homeless." He also noted, however, that "the city's only objective in enacting the controversial law was to improve safety and access on Mill

Avenue." Similarly, City Attorney Maerowitz told the *Tribune* (Riordan 1999b): "It's kind of right in line with being progressive and thinking of ways to make the downtown area available to everybody. It's really just governing behavior." Since both the mayor and city attorney were aware of the actual genesis of the ordinance as related in Lt. Ringo's opening memo, it is clear that this 'public safety and access' justification arose more out of revisionist damage-control tactics than any real threat to safety in the downtown area. A *Tribune* columnist (Dunn 1999a) must have read Ringo's 'smoking gun' (cf. Houck 2000) as well, echoing these themes: "Of course, the people responsible for the ban maintain the new law is strictly about public safety. That sidewalks littered with sitting bodies are dangerous to walk on. They'd have you believe that there's a mutant strain of navigationally challenged citizens stumbling down Mill Avenue and that our elected officials are merely legislating some obstacles away. Make no mistake: This law addresses public uneasiness, not security." A subsequent scholarly treatment (Brinegar 2000:504) likewise notes that "the official reason for implementing the sitting ban was to secure sidewalk safety for citizens downtown," but points out that the city "attempted to remove the homeless from downtown by passing an anti-sitting ordinance. The exclusionary and punitive actions are strongly supported by local merchants who view the homeless as social deviants and criminals. The DTC endorses official actions against the homeless, particularly those measures aimed at Mill Avenue 'slackers.' Tempe's popular downtown attracts a homeless youth population (called slackers or Mill Rats) who have become the focus of punitive actions."

As usual, ebb followed flow, and in this case the ebb came in the form of a backlash, both perceptual and tangible. For instance, a blatant propaganda piece in the *Republic* (Barajas 1999, 'Tempe's Got the Hookup') noted how much better things were on Mill Avenue since the sidewalk law had gone into effect over six months earlier (the law had actually been suspended for three of those months, but that's another story): "The drastic improvement in scenery has been noticed. Rod Keeling says a recent survey by his organization indicates that 89 percent of Tempe residents think downtown is safe, adding that 'everybody that I've talked to over the past six months has noticed a marked improvement.'" (At least he's consistent, having previously argued that when it comes to crime and safety, perception is equivalent to reality.) Also in the realm of perceptual propaganda, an opinion piece in the *Tribune* (Nelson 2001, 'Sidewalk Sprawlers Deserve the

Road') argued that "people ought to be able to get from one place to another without having to stumble over sleeping bags and space-cadet panhandlers. . . . Why anybody would want to sit or lie on a public sidewalk is beyond me anyway. Compared to a public sidewalk, the 30 days in jail you could get for violating the ordinance seems like a pretty good deal." (The 'why' of course is obvious: because for many of the street people there's no place else to go. As for jail being preferable to a public sidewalk, well, that's just downright uncivil.)

Speaking of things lacking civility, in terms of comprising a tangible backlash, we have already seen how the public quality of the sidewalks became private, how the planters were made 'homeless-proof,' how the downtown benches were removed, and how out-turned metal spikes had been strategically deployed against the street people (see, e.g., Reed & Venable 2001). The downtown's private security force, TEAM, got its share of retribution in as well, reflected in a guard's cheerful comment to me (TEAM 2001) that "the sidewalk ordinance is basically a no-loitering law – it gives me a way to move those kids off my owner's property," which he proceeded to follow up later that night by having a bearded guitar-playing man removed from the Centerpoint domain and humiliated by the police on its doorstep. It seems clear that the aim was to make Mill Avenue as unfriendly as possible to the street people, primarily through the creation of a downtown urban zone where the only place left to sit down is at a merchant's outdoor cafe seating area. The DTC in fact later lobbied the city to "ease restrictions that inhibit sidewalk cafes," and specifically "to decrease the 10-foot sidewalk rule to allow for more sidewalk cafes" (Urquides 2002). In effect, then, the DTC – which consistently had claimed that slackers were causing massive *sidewalk congestion* – were advocating narrowing the public sidewalk corridors and extending the reach of private sitting areas. With entry into such spaces conditioned upon the owner's approval, and with the slackers being *persona non grata* in any event, it's easy to see the systematic way in which 'undesirables' were being excluded and erased in a process that too closely resembles an official policy of *ethnocide-by-attrition*.

Let me conclude this genealogical foray by quoting one of the last major pieces written about Tempe's sidewalk ordinance. The column ('Tempe Development Plan: Hello, Yuppies; Goodbye, Homeless') appeared in the *State Press* on July 10, 2001, and serves as an appropriate summary of what transpired, as well as indicating where the next chapter will go in its analysis. The authors (Reed & Venable

2001) were both ASU students at the time and managed to interview Rod Keeling, who told them that the DTC exists to make Tempe a "clean, safe and pedestrian-dominated environment" and to foster an "independent, self-sustaining regional economy." Noting, however, that "the DTC has favored a program including excessive police enforcement and heavy-handed development schemes [that] have squeezed out the original small businesses and radically altered the character of the area," the authors maintained:

> The imposed corporate culture cannot compare to the organic, quirky community that once thrived and is now struggling to exist. What was once a unique and still somewhat historically intact part of the Valley is now being eroded and replaced by a homogenous replica of its former self. . . . This process has also not lent itself to democracy. The city has consistently sided with the DTC, even in light of the vibrant public dissent surrounding the sidewalk sitting issue. The residents of Tempe have been not only excluded from the workings of the city, their voices have been blatantly ignored. A backyard mall is no compensation for the loss of a voice in civic politics. . . .
>
> Exclusion of one class of people leaves the door open for the exclusion of others who do not fit the DTC's corporate ideal. Don't be fooled: the homeless aren't the only ones threatened. Everyone from the poor to the eccentric, who might 'drive away business,' even students who might choose to pay their tuition instead of buying junk, are not welcome. When we allow entities such as the DTC to prey upon one class of people, we open the door to the possibility of more encroachments on all of our rights. . . . The fact is that very soon people are going to be arrested for resting on the ground. They may face fines they could never pay; they may face incarceration. Residents have realized the inhumanity of these laws in the past, and fought to abandon them. The question is, will the people of Tempe accept this, or will they continue the struggle for the dignity of their community?

Picking up on these themes, as the following chapter describes, the 'struggle for dignity and community' in Tempe began in earnest, took shape in tumultuous times, and in some ways still continues today.

CHAPTER SIX

The Ecology of Resistance

Human Rights Struggles and the Contested Realms of Public Space

The discussion thus far has mostly proceeded along a macroscopically increasing arc of 'levels of analysis,' moving from the realm of individual choices to that of structural processes. Here, it will be instructive to swing the pendulum back a bit, just enough to recapture the sense of the microscopic that is always present but often muted by larger forces at every succeeding level in the analysis. The vision of resistance presented here is grounded in small acts of individual will and community solidarity, cobbled together in recurring themes and images, fighting intensely local battles with implications ranging from the level of homeless bodies, to municipal policies, to national trends, to global developments. These nascent 'contested realms' of space are, much like the homeless themselves, everywhere yet nowhere at all, both dramatically visible yet often unacknowledged. Power and resistance, locked in an eternal dialectical dance, ebbing and flowing throughout time and across space, protean possibilities perpetually portending – this is both the horror and hope of any attempt to create and deploy resistance. Luckily, there is a safety net inherent in such moments, namely the irreducible nexus of people and place that all forces of contestation must by necessity embody, suggesting not only the utility of an ecological perspective on resistance but a comforting sense of inescapability as well.

Resisting Homelessness through Homeless Resistance

Before considering particular examples of resistance, including legal and direct action strategies employed in Tempe and elsewhere, a word about the purposes of contestation is in order. By this point in the analysis, the question of precisely what activists, advocates, and the homeless themselves would be struggling *against* should be abundantly clear: the sanitization of space, the criminalization of status, and the societal forces that render people vulnerable in the first instance. The strands of these struggles converge in the lives and experiences of street people, and in the changing nature of spatial relations in society; indeed this is the parallel that has been followed throughout, the realization that the people and the spaces they occupy are under concomitant and mutually reinforcing attacks. One of the keys for activists and mobilizers – homeless and domiciled alike – has been to discover strategies that simultaneously address the spatial and social components of the struggle. Legal strategies sometimes make this connection, as do direct action tactics of civil disobedience and political protest. Efforts toward homeless community-building, homeless-activist alliances, student outreach programs, food and clothing giveaways, housing occupations, and even weekly 'drum circles' have been deployed with varying degrees of success (cf. Howland 1994:34; see generally Wright 1997:225-251). The central aim of these strategies is the empowerment of the homeless, as well as the curtailment of the forces of sanitization and criminalization that continually seek to crush street people out of existence in the misguided belief that 'eradicating the homeless' is a more effective social policy than 'eradicating homelessness.'

In terms of criminalization, it is apparent that while the homeless are often the targets of laws about urban camping and sidewalk sitting, there is an element to such laws that is aimed at spontaneity and rebellion in general, representing an attempt to preclude possibilities of political organizing or social protest in the remaining public spaces of the city. This is a direct consequence of the anti-democratic tendencies evident in BIDs such as the Downtown Tempe Community (DTC) and their obsessive 'law and order' policies. The intent is to force everyone to participate in the 'community of consumption,' or be faced with imprisonment, humiliation, and banishment. One of the ways of accomplishing this forced socialization is through the foreclosure of non-commercial survival options, including criminalizing basic acts of necessity and privatizing space to such an extent that there is literally no place to locate alternative experiments in living. The point of this bureaucratic blackmail, then, is to eliminate the choice *not* to participate, achieving through coercion a modicum of legitimation that could not be gained by consent. As the IWW (1994) noted in a broadsheet against Santa Cruz's homeless policies, "the criminalization of the 'choice' not to participate in 'the system,' demonstrates the fascist strategy of current anti-homeless campaigns; to attack, manage, regulate and ultimately destroy perceived or actual social dissent." In the end, the salvo called for "a renewal of activism aimed at the entirety of gentrification and social regulation underway" in the city.

Nonetheless, the National Coalition for the Homeless (NCH 1997) has warned that "criminalization [contestation] efforts tear the focus of both homeless people and their advocates away from long term, permanent solutions in order to fight for the right of people who are homeless to simply exist;" as Mitchell (2003:209) further observes, there is something almost "perverse" about the fact that "homeless people and their advocates are driven, in the current urban context, to argue for the *right* to sleep in public, to lie on sidewalks, to beg on the streets, or to shit in alleys." Still, as Baron (2004:286) discerns, "it is no mystery why advocacy has moved in this rather limited direction making homelessness more tolerable. Begging, sleeping out of doors, taking up space in libraries – these are the few freedoms that still conceivably can be sought once the larger question of entitlements to housing and wealth are foreclosed." Perhaps even more to the point, Hafetz (2003:1239) notes the pragmatic aspects of anti-criminalization advocacy: "When a homeless person is arrested for sleeping on a park bench, her lawyer's first response is not to address the underlying causes of homelessness, but to respond to a concrete injustice. Indeed, prohibitions on begging or sleeping in the park do not threaten some abstract notion of liberty, but rather strike at the ability of men and women to survive." Nonetheless, Hafetz (2003:1235) rightly interprets many such "challenges to attempts to criminalize behavior associated with homeless people" as "a defensive response to an angry backlash."

This is all sound advice to keep in mind when confronting policies of criminalization, namely that there simultaneously exist acute injustices that need to be remedied as well as larger implications that must not be abandoned in the process. Activists and advocates in many areas experience similar phenomena, being forced into reactive postures regarding arrests and police harassment at the expense of more proactive engagement with the substantive issues uppermost in their minds. How many episodes of political demonstration ultimately degenerate into a battle between police and protesters, while the powerholders and policymakers continue their business as usual, immune from the activists' recriminations? The issue of homelessness actually presents a unique moment in social change praxis to unify both reactive survival aims with proactive policy shifts, since it is precisely the continued existence of street people (which the system wants so badly to preclude) that often seems to represent one of the greatest 'threats' to business as usual. As Talmadge Wright (1997:182) grasps, "existence *is* resistance." Susan Ruddick (1996:64,194) likewise notes that homeless people often resist "simply by their presence;" this is particularly true when they "subvert the meaning of structures not intended for them" by appearing in otherwise-Disneyfied spaces, "ready to confront new, gentrified users of their turf." Moreover, "the presence of the homeless in a gentrifying area or a post-industrial city space . . . can undercut the tenets of the space itself, and its implicit ideology about leisure and wealth" (Ruddick 1996:49). As Peter Marcuse (1988:93) explains, "homelessness is such a danger to the legitimacy of the status quo. Homelessness in the midst of plenty may shock people into the realization that homelessness exists not because the system is failing to work as it should, but because the system is working as it must." In this sense, "people who occupy the margins of society can transform the world in unexpected, even profound ways" (Harter, et al. 2005:324), and an at times "expose the tension between the universality of freedom and the unequal distribution of private property that prevents the enjoyment of freedom" (Kohn 2004:172).

Accordingly, Ruddick (1996:63) suggests resistance strategies centered upon the "tactical control of space;" Wright (2000:53) likewise favors activities through which spatial "hierarchies can be contested." Mitchell (1995:123) also concludes that "social movements must occupy and reconfigure material public spaces in the city," and in a later work (1996a:129) urges that "dissidents of all types must continually assert their presence into public space, if they are ever to be seen and heard" (see generally Ferrell 2001b, for a lively and succinct history of dissident movements and public space). Kohn (2004:184) adds that "if the homeless do not have the opportunity to be visible in public space, if they cannot communicate their needs, then there is no chance that they will convince others to make the social changes necessary to meet these needs." Neil Smith (1992:66) points out that the spatial struggle must simultaneously contemplate its human scale and inherent grounding in the lives and experiences of street people, arguing that "reappropriation of the body, in association with the reappropriation of space" must remain a priority. Thus, for Wright (1997:255), it is possible for the spatial and the social to come together in ways both strategic and subconscious: "The sudden occupation of a stretch of pavement in a public place may be carried out without the conscious intent to redefine the meaning of that space. However, the very act of creating a place to sleep, of survival itself, contributes to the redefinition of that space, especially in the eyes of authorities who wish to maintain a 'proper' version of space as one in which those activities should not and will not be allowed."

Some of these socio-spatial strategies involve activities designed to "increase public visibility" – such as when Mill Avenue's homeless 'slackers' congregate publicly on the busiest downtown street corners – and include micro-actions such as "telling jokes" and "acting crazy" (Wright 1997:199); as Mitchell notes (1996a:157), "to make excluded voices heard, protest requires drama. . . . Being 'unruly' often is a prerequisite for getting heard at all." Tempe's Melee (2000), who I observed using a banana as a mock gun to point at passersby and meowing in a variety of feline languages – captured the essence of this with her comedic-terroristic strategy of social confusion: "I don't fit in with 'normal' people – people are becoming so plastic! – the mood needs to be broken, sometimes with street theater and shock value. . . . I am an entertainer, I am the product of my artistry. It is my purpose to make people think." Hakim Bey (1991) likewise advocates the construction of "temporary autonomous zones" through strategies of "poetic terrorism" built largely around fragmentary, disjointed, bizarre, creative, hilarious, and mildly threatening acts – all done for the purpose of shaking people out of that pervasive state of "cryonic torpor" depicted in Utah Phillips & Ani Difranco's (1996) song, 'Mess With People.' Jeff Ferrell's (1993; 1994; 1995; 1998b) take on the disruptive and transformative power of graffiti is similarly revealing of this fundamentally anarchist agenda of challenging authority through open displays of defiance and perceptual reorientation. Indeed, throughout history people have utilized creative phrasings, colorful demonstrations, and surprising juxtapositions to open up a space for a dialogue that would otherwise have gone unheard or erased. "In a time when corporations control the media, [even] an individual with a cardboard sign can give us something to think about, as long as there remains a public sphere in which to do so" (Amster 2007).

Fig. 4: Openly defiant agitprop in Tempe (circa 2007)

'Shelter from the Storm': The Ecology of Contestation

Another essential project in mobilizing resistance is 'placemaking,' which involves "creating 'safe' spaces in which to gather" (Wright 1997:262), and also embraces the more proactive side of contestation that includes articulating what one is *for* in addition to what one is *against*. Sometimes this takes the form of "establishing encampments" or 'squatting' abandoned spaces – employing tactics that are at once "adaptive and defiant" (Wright 1997:199,266). It also includes examples of homeless people demanding basic services such as "the urgent need for an emergency winter storm shelter in Berkeley" by staging a three-day "Right to Sleep protest" in a public space (Diehl 2005). Challenging prevailing stereotypes of the homeless as "a disabled, laggardly, and incompetent population incapable of collective action" (Snow & Mulcahy 2001:162-3), it is apparent that homeless people often will deploy "strategies enabling individuals to weave together survival and in some cases social transformation" (Harter, et al. 2005:324). The example of 'Justiceville' in Los Angeles exemplified this paradigm of both 'survival and transformation,' as noted in the discussion of 'homeless communities' in Chapter One. As

Ropers (1988:199) observed, "Justiceville was more than an attempt to protect its residents from the elements; it became a real community, with a division of labor and a sense of sharing, caring, and solidarity." Before being mercilessly bulldozed, "Justiceville would come to represent a case study in 'empowerment,' an attempt by the homeless to provide themselves with the shelter, community, and dignity denied them by their social system" (Ropers 1988:199). Picking up on and further extending these themes is the remarkable example of 'Dignity Village' as described in the *Street Spirit* (Tafari 2005):

> The transformation of Dignity Village, the longstanding homeless community in Portland, Oregon, from the shantytown that it became after its fifth sweep, continues unto this day. What was birthed by an act of civil disobedience and protest by homeless people who began a campaign has changed into what we are today. And the zoning of the land on which Dignity stands has changed in its designation from industrial to campground. Dignity Village is now Oregon's first transitional homeless campground.
>
> What guides the transformation of this piece of ground is a vision picked up along the way, along with many good supporters. It is the vision of a green, sustainable urban village where we may live simply and in harmony with our mother Earth and where we may do for ourselves and help ourselves and others.
>
> As our proposal so eloquently states, "Dignity Village is the only place-based community in this town that practices grassroots democracy with an ecological vision. It is the only walkable community not invaded by cars, and it is the most cost-efficient, self-help model for transcending homelessness in the nation."

Touting its multitude of 'green' dwellings including 'strawbale' and 'cob' houses, Dignity Village strives to bring together social and environmental justice as "a model for the future, while helping develop the tools with which to build the model and others like it" (Tafari 2005). In this manner, it fits into a long tradition of grassroots, do-it-yourself 'experiments in living' that sometimes fall under the rubric of 'utopian' or 'anarchist' communities. These experiments suggest that communities constructed upon beliefs such as participatory politics, social welfare, and voluntary mutual aid generally maintain a particular relationship to the earth itself. In many such settings there exists an emphasis on cooperation, simplicity, and reciprocity, as well as the maintenance of an economic safety net in which members have ready access to essentials such as sustenance and shelter (see Ward 1973; Mbah & Igariwey 1997; Bookchin 1991; and Zerzan 1994:17-30, who observes that "food sharing has for some time been considered an integral part of earliest human society," suggesting "the benefits of being part of a society where everything is shared"). As a corollary, there is often a "subsistence perspective" (see von Werlhof 1997; Mies 1993) evident in such endeavors, manifesting in the desire to achieve a reduced impact on the environment arising out of an inherent respect for and symbiosis with the earth, as indicated by the vision of Dignity Village. As Maria Mies (1993:322) observes: "Wherever women and men have envisaged a society in which all . . . could share the 'good life,' where social justice, equality, human dignity, beauty and joy in life were not just utopian dreams never to be realized . . . there has been close to what we call a subsistence perspective. . . . Sustainability is not compatible with the existing profit- and growth-oriented development paradigm." John Clark (1998:18) likewise affirms these tenets:

> "The life of 'simplicity' is in no way the impoverished life of one who seeks escape from the corrupt world and its temptations. Rather it is something much more affirmative: it is the consummate existence of one who has rejected whatever would stunt or distort growth and personal fulfillment. Simplicity is not, however, a quality with implications for personal life alone. It refers also to social institutions which will promote rather than hinder self-realization. A society based on social status, or one glorifying the pursuit of material wealth and permitting economic domination, is inevitably destructive, producing conflict, disorder, envy, and crime."

Homeless communities such as Justiceville and Dignity Village are emblematic of these principles and practices. And yet, as alluded to by the discussion of the 'concentration campus' scheme in Chapter One, such self-organized experiments can be problematic on other levels, as Mitchell (1995:129n.21) astutely observes: "There is a danger in arguing for 'safe havens' . . . especially in the case of homeless people. To the degree that People's Park became an oasis for a homeless counterpublic, was it also possible to ghettoize the social and political production of homelessness to these areas?" As with many revolutionary or anarchist experiments, homeless encampments are likewise vulnerable to forces of enclosure and containment that work against the values and intentions of the undertaking – to wit, the destruction of Justiceville. Still, the lessons learned from these moments of 'revolutionary placemaking' are fundamentally important for movements of all stripes, and are crucial for discerning the potential impact of 'homeless resistance' on the larger society. Because of the relative material scarcity of their lives and their general condition of "no property" status in terms of land rights (see Baron 2004), homeless people can sometimes appear as 'urban nomads' pursuing "the realization of human freedom" by rejecting "the constraints of bourgeois society" and instead becoming "a source of alternative values" (Kohn 2004:178). As such, homeless communities, when they emerge, can invent new forms of both social and ecological relationships, simultaneously challenging the socio-spatial structures inherent in mainstream society and modeling new people-place visions.

All of which, of course, can make them appear 'dangerous' to powerholders and therefore susceptible to the sort of outcome experienced by Justiceville. Thus, for some homeless activists and advocates, this brings the focus back to the tactics of 'temporary autonomy,' which have the advantage of being fluid enough to resist enclosure even as they can also be limited by their fleeting nature. Sometimes these types of strategies are placed under the heading of 'direct action,' which may include protests, demonstrations, civil disobedience, and symbolic occupations. A longstanding example of these values is Food Not Bombs, a leaderless international movement that offers free vegetarian meals made largely of 'reclaimed' food that has been cast aside by mainstream society, and that (according to Wikipedia) "works to call attention to poverty and homelessness in society by sharing food in public places and facilitating gatherings of poor, homeless, and other disenfranchised people." By bringing together homeless people in public places, Food Not Bombs volunteers often incur the wrath of officials in a manner equivalent to the homeless themselves, being subject to regulation and criminalization as recently witnessed in Prescott, Arizona (see Meurer 2008) and Orlando, Florida where a volunteer was arrested (WFTV.com 2007):

> "A man is facing a judge and jury for violating Orlando's ban on feeding the homeless. Eric Montanez, 22, was caught feeding a group in Lake Eola Park earlier this year. . . . Montanez and the group he's involved with, Food Not Bombs, returned to Lake Eola just after sunrise to once again violate the ordinance that has him on trial. Food Not Bombs volunteers served breakfast to about 100 Montanez supporters, most of them homeless. They will serve breakfast, lunch, and dinner during what they're calling a three-day 'ladle-fest,' not a protest. . . . 'We're out here trying to survive from day to day and this gentleman over here is helping us,' said Melvin Moore, a homeless man. . . . 'The law itself should be illegal. Feeding people should not be criminalized. Being poor should not be criminalized,' Montanez said."

At the conclusion of the 'ladle-fest,' Montanez was acquitted by a jury despite clear evidence that he had violated the 'no-feeding' law, implicitly validating the notion that (at least for some members of the larger community) there are higher principles than those contained in municipal ordinances intended to undermine the ability of homeless people to survive. These sorts of 'direct action' strategies – whether of the 'temporary' variety like Food Not Bombs or the more 'permanent' sort exemplified by Dignity Village – indicate new ways of configuring social and material relationships. This, then, is the 'new ecology' of homelessness, born out of mobilizations by homeless people themselves against criminalization and erasure, with the support and encouragement of domiciled advocates. Talmadge Wright (1997:200) describes numerous examples in his book *Out of Place* (subtitled 'Homeless Mobilizations, Subcities, and Contested Landscapes'), including that of "countersurveillance," or the "use of legal tactics and video cameras to document homeless conditions and confrontations with police" in order to "reverse the gaze" of panoptic policies. The National Coalition for the Homeless (2004) specifically insists that "those most affected by injustice must play a leading role in local monitoring projects," and accordingly encourages homeless people to "record civil rights abuses" and to help formulate "solutions to poverty and homelessness." Additional resistance strategies suggested by the NCH (2006) in a pamphlet on 'Homeless Self-Help and Empowerment Projects' include: registering homeless people to vote; forming a 'speakers bureau' in which homeless people share their stories; and starting and/or selling a 'street newspaper' – which can serve to "provide street people with a source of income while also describing the experience of homelessness through poetry and prose and translating this experience into a political program" (Kohn 2004:182).

Another particular example of a 'direct-action placemaking' strategy – one that will help to set the tone for an analysis of the forms of resistance and contestation ensuing in Tempe – that brought a measure of success was a "City Hall sleep-in" in Los Angeles in 1993, as described by Howland (1994:35): "Two-and-a-half months after the sleep-in began, the city council agreed not to enforce the law closing the park between midnight and 5 A.M. In addition, [homeless protester] Ron Taylor says, 'we managed to get two bathrooms opened 24 hours a day. I really and honestly think we gave them a wake-up call.' Taylor encourages people to try similar tactics in other cities."

Taking a Stand . . . Taking a Seat

Back in Tempe, implicitly acting upon Mr. Taylor's advice, some residents were growing determined not to take the city council's adoption of a 'no sitting on the sidewalk' ordinance, um, sitting down. Or more accurately, sitting down was precisely how they would take it: plans were quickly made for a community 'sit-in' on the day the ordinance would take effect, January 18, 1999, Martin Luther King Day. Coincidentally, activists in Philadelphia were staging a similar demonstration that day. One critic there had called the law "part of the 'Disneyfication' of downtown," arguing that it "criminalizes homelessness and violates constitutional rights" (Associated Press 1999). After the event, the media reported that "about 100 protesters bearing signs reading 'The City of Brotherly WHAT?' and chanting 'Stop the war on the poor' staged a rally at City Hall. . . . Protesters of a similar sidewalk ban in downtown Tempe, Ariz., held a sit-in honoring Martin Luther King Jr. The ban carries a fine of up to $500 and 30 days in jail. 'It's not about sitting. It's about one group attacking another,' said protester Luis Fernandez, a 29-year-old researcher" (ACLU 1999). But I'm getting ahead of myself here.

It was apparent to many of us in Tempe that the coincidence of King's legacy converging with our planned protest was more than just a good sign, but also an indicator as to how we might conduct ourselves politically and in what spirit we would approach the issues. It was not with spite in our hearts that we intended to publicly violate the law, but with a sense of solemn duty and celebratory glee. What we hoped was that perhaps a few people would show up in addition to those of us planning the demonstration; that some of the street people we had been talking to would come out; and that maybe the media would be there to help publicize the cause. As it turned out, we underestimated things.

On the appointed day and time, we marched downtown with a few signs, some blank sheets and markers for others to use, water, 'Know Your Rights' pamphlets we'd been giving out that week, and as much of King's wisdom and courage as we could muster. As I said, we were serious of purpose, prepared to be arrested, unsure of who (or indeed if anyone) else would show up, and aware that this was perhaps our one best chance to raise awareness about the law's intent and the impact it would have on all of us as members of a community. For the four of us who made our way down to Mill Avenue that morning, our brothers and sisters of the street were more than a part of that community – they were in many ways its core, one of the real constants in a time of merciless, rampant change. And yet, despite everything that was potentially on the line that day, the mood was light and our spirits were high. The place we had chosen for the demonstration was the infamous Coffee Plantation corner of the Centerpoint complex at Mill Avenue and Sixth Street. The area, perhaps 250 square feet of open brick sidewalk, contained one of the main planters that the street people often congregated around, and was right on the front lines of the ongoing battles between TEAM, the Tempe police, and the transients. Calling ourselves 'Project S.I.T.' (Sidewalk Initiative Team), we agreed that this seemed like the right spot to make our stand by taking a seat.

Now, while we did feel MLK's spirit with us that day, this was not something we approached glibly but with sincere reverence and enough humility to realize that we were a long way from the 'promised land,' both personally and politically. It was clear to us above all that King, like Gandhi before him, had taught to confront authority not out of anger but with respect, to meet one's adversaries – whether they be cops, or merchants, or city officials – in a way that preserves and enhances their dignity and acknowledges their humanity. After all, this is what we were asking from them toward our homeless friends. We also understood that we didn't invent the concept of the sit-in as a political protest strategy, that we were not the first to deploy the sit-in specifically in connection with the issue of homelessness, nor even the first to do so in protest of a sidewalk sitting ordinance. In fact, Palo

Alto was the site of such events back in 1997. One of the organizers there (Christensen 1997) stated that, "this ordinance is wrong and we are deeply offended that it has been adopted in our names. It is wrong to restrict the rights of our fellow human beings without evidence that their actions are creating a threat to the public welfare. It is wrong to adopt punitive measures such as the sit-lie ordinance while allowing positive measures, such as those recommended by the Homelessness Task Force, to languish in the city bureaucracy." A homeless man who participated in the sit-in there told the local media that "the real question is who owns public space – the merchants who pressed for the ban or the people who use the streets?" (in Wildermuth 1997). Back in Tempe, what our small group did know, however, was that there hadn't been anything like this in town for as long as anyone could remember, perhaps even back to the days of the Vietnam war, or at least the 'no-nukes' moment of the early 1980s (cf. Rosenfeld 2000). The feeling of breaking new ground, but in a familiar way, perhaps was what gave us that sense of buoyancy as we arrived at the site of the sit-in.

There was already a crowd when we arrived, including a number of street people, one or two reporters, and police officers positioned across the street at each adjacent corner. By the time the protest officially began, there were perhaps 30 or 40 people gathered around the planter, including a growing throng of media that now included TV camera crews. I had asked Mark Reader, former ASU political science professor, anti-nuclear demonstrator, MLK admirer, and gentle soul, to say a few words to start things off. He spoke with passion about freedom and community and the responsibility of people to "speak truth to power." I spoke next about the sidewalk ordinance and its impact on the rights of everyone, especially the street people, to peaceably assembly in public spaces, invoking King's insight that "injustice anywhere is a threat to justice everywhere," and closing by stating that "one of the highest duties of citizenship is to challenge an unjust law – therefore, I sit on the sidewalk in violation of the ordinance." With that, I sat down, followed by a dozen others, and then a dozen more. Some were drumming; some were making signs; some were already talking to the reporters that had swarmed on us with cameras and microphones from the instant we sat down. Before that day, I had done about 3 interviews total in my life, one TV, one radio, one print. By the time the demonstration broke up about 6 hours later, I had been interviewed more than 20 times, by reporters from the 3 local newspapers, the Associated Press, and every TV and news radio station in town. It was discomfiting, absurd, surreal, almost out-of-body. But it was an opportunity to raise consciousness about Tempe's treatment of both its poorest citizens and its dwindling public spaces.

In addition to the media, many of the bewildered passersby stopped to see what all the noise and commotion was about. Scores took flyers, some took pictures, and a few even sat down and joined the demonstration. The street people who were there, perhaps 15 or 20 different faces throughout the day, seemed to enjoy the spectacle and even the attention. Many of them spoke eloquently to the media and passersby about their experiences and feelings about being singled out for criminal attention. Some expressed sincere feelings of solidarity with the community that they hadn't felt in Tempe before. One told me that he was going to leave Tempe when the sidewalk law took effect, but now was determined to stay and "fight the good fight" (Yogi 1999). A couple arrived in an old van that had 'Fuck the Police' painted on the side – the elderly black man who first stepped out, named Fonzi, also had a button on his lapel that said 'Fuck Fonzi,' which he explained was his way of being an "equal opportunity asshole." A flute had joined the drums that would beat throughout the entire day. One reporter gave me her business card and said to call as soon as someone got arrested. But no one did. The police watched us from a distance all day, but never approached – except a former student of mine who was also an intern with the Tempe police department, there at his superior's bidding to unobtrusively keep an eye on things from the inside. I told him he was welcome to be there – and so he sat with the group for hours.

Obviously, with the intensity of my personal involvement as the main organizer of the protest, and with the tenuous nature of memory apparent when adrenaline is involved, I can only offer the foregoing as my take on the day's events and not necessarily as a literal rendering. But I can provide the media's accounts as a framework for interpreting what one city council member would later tell me was the most significant political event in at least the last decade in Tempe, a day that would open doors of direct action and popular protest that had been stuck for some time, even as things in Tempe had grown progressively regressive. Later that year, thousands of people would gather near the WTO meeting for the 'battle in Seattle' that would have a similar decorking effect on political protests nationally. Here is how the local papers memorialized our microcosmic efforts at strategic sitting:

"Demonstrators crowded the corner of 6th Street and Mill Avenue Monday afternoon, sitting down to protest Tempe's new Sidewalk Sitting Ordinance. Randall Amster, an ASU associate faculty in the School of Justice Studies, said the ordinance is nothing more than a thinly-veiled attempt to sweep away street people, transients, and the homeless from the downtown area. 'When any citizen's rights are trampled upon, all of our rights are diminished,' he said. Mark Reader, a retired ASU political science professor, was one of the nearly 40 people who protested the ban on sidewalk sitting. 'If you don't have the right to sit in a public place, then we've come a long way from freedom,' he said. . . . Tempe police decided not to interfere with Monday's protest. 'It's Martin Luther King Day, we're going to let the protest happen,' said Tempe Police Lt. Mike Ringo. Officers will be enforcing the ordinance in the future, he said."

-- *ASU State Press* (Severson 1999a).

"About 40 people gathered at the northwest corner of Mill Avenue and Sixth Street Monday to protest Tempe's new law that bans sitting on sidewalks. Mostly teenagers and people in their 20s, the protesters carried hand-painted signs with phrases like 'Can the Sidewalk Ban.' Excerpts of Martin Luther King's speeches could be heard over a portable radio as two men banged on bongo drums. 'We hope the sit-in lets the Tempe City Council know we strongly disagree with the ordinance,' said Randall Amster, the protest's organizer. Observing the protest from across Mill Avenue, a plain-clothed Lt. Mike Ringo said Tempe police knew about the demonstration before Monday and had no intention of breaking it up. But they clearly were in violation of the law, he said. 'The police department and the city attorney's office got together and decided to let them protest as long as it didn't get out of hand,' Ringo said. Besides, Mill wasn't too busy Monday, he said, adding no one's public safety appeared in danger to him. 'It's a little congested, but people are getting through,' Ringo said."

-- *East Valley Tribune* (Riordan 1999a)

> "Derek McCarthy sat cross-legged Monday on a brick sidewalk in Tempe, reading a novel, sipping coffee and breaking the law. He was one of two dozen who plopped down on a popular Mill Avenue corner to protest a Tempe law banning sitting on sidewalks. The group sat peacefully to decry the law they call unconstitutional and unfair. Protesters said Martin Luther King Jr. Day was an appropriate time to demonstrate against the ban, which opponents say targets the homeless and takes away personal freedoms. 'There's an irony that we should be gathering today over an issue of sitting and how much of the civil rights movement was built around the act of sitting,' said Mark Reader. Although the group blatantly balked at the new law, police did not hand out any tickets. 'We elected to let them protest, as long as they did so orderly and didn't cause us any problems, and they have done so,' said Lt. Mike Ringo. 'There wasn't reason for us to have any kind of confrontation with those folks.' Tempe Mayor Neil Giuliano said protesters didn't seem to understand the need for the law. 'They have the concept of social justice just all backward,' he said. 'They want the right to sit on the sidewalk and block other people's rights and other people's access. That is not what social justice is about. What we are trying to do in the city is make the sidewalks open and accessible to all citizens,' he said. 'I see this ordinance as a way of just trying to sweep away social problems like homelessness,' said Kristi Wimmer, 25, an ASU justice studies student. 'They are fooling themselves and trying to fool us.'"
>
> -- *Arizona Republic* (Haussler 1999)

After this day of small acts writ large, everything changed. The stakes had been upped in the battle with the city over the remaining downtown public spaces and its treatment of the homeless and transient. The intensive media coverage of and response to the issues would continue for months. Many of the older and younger activists in the community, even those who weren't there on MLK Day, communicated to me how they were energized by the sit-in and the possibilities it presented for political discourse and public debate. Most important was the sense of empowerment experienced by many of the street people, as well as genuine feelings that at least some people in the community really did care. Some of the positive effects for the homeless included the Mayor's State of the City address three weeks later that identified the sidewalk ordinance battle as the impetus for creating the Homeless Task Force that would eventually recommend a more service- than enforcement-oriented approach (see Subramanian 1999). Those of us in S.I.T. had undergone a transformation in the media "from *protestors* to *homeless advocates*," as Wright (1997:239) found in similar actions in the Bay Area of California. Another measurable change was in the "moderating effects on belligerent police practices" (Wright 1997:290), at least for a few months, as the city tried to recover from the public relations black eye it had taken, and as the police tried to figure out how to justify letting people sit down and break the law one day and then try to enforce the ban the next.

Another good sign was how many people really did get what was going on in Tempe, including many of the articles and columns quoted in the previous chapter. Of particular interest were the calls to action issued from many corners, including the *State Press* (Whisler 1999):

> "In a blatant betrayal of the spirit of Dr. King's message, the City Council enacted the sidewalk-sitting ban. With a wink and a smile, they tell us that the ordinance is in the interest of public safety. But some of the facts brought to light at the city council . . . paint a far uglier picture. Before the vote, concerned citizens crowded the council chambers for almost three hours to make their voices heard. They brought to the council's attention that there already existed an ordinance addressing the obstruction of sidewalks. They questioned the removal of benches from downtown. Mostly they expressed their concern for the apparent dehumanization of government policy. . . . The question that remains is: How will we as a community address the blatant disregard for human liberty initiated by our governing body? The courts have refused to act thus far and so the duty lies with us. We have allowed politicians to operate under false motives and hidden agendas for too long. Perhaps this is an opportunity to learn from the past. Through political activism and civil disobedience change can occur. The issue at hand now is not whether we should act, but whether we will. . . . There is a time for change and the time is now. If the cycle of oppression is to repeat itself, then for the sake of humanity, so must the cycle of liberation. We are the agents of change; the responsibility is ours."

To hear such calls, especially from students, made the possibilities for real change in Tempe seem palpable in ways they never had before.

Don't Sit, Don't Stay, Don't Beg: *Sic*-ing the Attack Dogs

But it wasn't all bread and roses, as the inevitable backlash came in prototypical patterns of homeless demonization, as well as in personal attacks on me and those of my 'ilk.' The first salvo was fired by Dan Durrenberger (1999a) of the *Republic*, in a column wonderfully titled 'Non-bathers Shouldn't Set Agenda' that laid out the 'official' position in all its glory, unmasked in its casual brutality and inherent illogic:

> The vagabonds who panhandle the length of Mill Avenue contribute nothing positive to the ambiance of downtown Tempe. The decision to restrict people from sitting and sleeping on Mill's curbs and sidewalks is commendable. It should be applauded. . . .
>
> On Monday, Professor **[sic]** Randall Amster organized a demonstration to denounce Tempe's new sidewalk ordinance. Rather than spending time preparing for the resumption of classes the next day, our faculty associate swooped down from his ivory tower for an event that made a mockery of the day set aside to honor the Rev. Martin Luther King Jr. There he sat on his precious brick sidewalk, an adult surrounded by children, acting as if it were still the 1960s. It was embarassing. . . . There is nothing noble about the creeps who infest parts of downtown. Efforts by guilt-ridden sympathizers to romanticize the lives of these social misfits are misguided.
>
> Contrary to the assertions of its critics, Tempe's ban is designed to promote civility and common courtesy. It sets necessary and minimal standards. It protects the rights of owners to conduct their businesses free from the interference of freeloaders. . . . Those who do not bathe have no right to set the agenda for those who do. Those without jobs have no right to coerce those who work. And the self-indulgent have no right to inject their aberrant eccentricities into the lives of those whose time and talent continue to make downtown Tempe successful. If Tempe's slackers need somewhere to sit, I recommend the front seat of a bus leaving town.

Having never been publicly attacked in such a fashion, I debated how best to respond, if at all. Sensing that the attack was also an invitation to submit my own views for possible publication, I fired off a response (1999a) that the *Republic* ran four days later:

> A number of sources have criticized our invocation of Martin Luther King at the Jan. 18 sit-in. Of course, it was not our choice but the Tempe City Council's to have the ordinance go into effect on MLK Day. This was a coincidence of circumstance and history, and represents no small irony that while Tempe was celebrating MLK's life and works, it criminalized sit-ins, which were utilized by MLK and others in the civil rights struggle of the 1950s and 1960s. King understood the inherent interconnection of humankind, that when anyone is oppressed – particularly the "least of these, my brethren" – we all share in that oppression. Intimated by his statement that "injustice anywhere is a threat to justice everywhere," I firmly believe King would support our struggle to ensure the rights of the homeless and the transient, in his belief that "any man's suffering diminishes me."
>
> Without dignifying Mr. Durrenberger's personal attacks on me, I feel compelled to respond to this unwarranted pillory of my actions. . . . The brick sidewalk in question was not mine, but belongs to the public at large, and in my view that includes the homeless and transients. The purpose of the demonstration was to preserve the public nature of our downtown sidewalks, not to claim some right of ownership or control, as have the Tempe City Council and the commercial interests that dominate Mill Avenue with 'public behavior' ordinances such as the sitting ban. . . .
>
> On Jan. 8, Mr. Durrenberger's column was titled, 'Tempe is a study in diversity.' Apparently, such calls for celebrating diversity don't extend to the homeless, the transient, 'slackers,' the unemployed, or 'non-bathers,' but only those deemed 'serious' or respectable by Mr. Durrenberger according to his own standards of social desirability.
>
> Perhaps this successful vice president of a local public-relations firm ought to step down from *his* 'ivory tower.' The thin air up there seems to be affecting his heart.

Even as we were making preparations for another sit-in, the mainstream media, existing somewhere in that narrow space between neo-liberal and neo-conservative paradigms, was prepared to counter-punch my column and character, this time from the right in Doug MacEachern's (1999a) jocular *Tribune* column, 'Sit-in for Sidewalk Slackers Salutes Society's Simpletons' (I am not making this stuff up!):

> Where, exactly, a handful of punky, transgressive white kids with a penchant for splicing every fleshy outcropping with metal rings spent their idle hours really didn't matter a whole lot to me. But that was before Randall Amster, Arizona State University instructor and smarmy, Berkeley-esque '60s holdover, took up their cause. Now I care ever so deeply for the cause of removing the bottoms of these filthy cretins from the good concrete of Tempe.
>
> Now, Amster – smarmy, retro, Summer-of-Love lovin' Amster – has informed the Tempe city attorneys of his intent to conduct a sit-in on Saturday on behalf of the oppressed slacker community. Why Saturday? Because Saturday is the 51st anniversary of the assassination of Mohandas Gandhi! Besides invoking Gandhi, Amster also has raised the name of Martin Luther King on behalf of the shiftless, stinky, money-begging slackers. Gandhi and MLK would, no doubt, weep.
>
> DTC director Rod Keeling makes a perfectly reasonable case why packs of idle slackers shouldn't be permitted to lounge in the paths of elderly shoppers: "How can we have a successful public space unless we have some expectation of civility among the people we meet there?"
>
> But that's precisely what drives the campus lefties: unalloyed contempt for bourgeois notions of civility and community and the hypocritical Eurocentric rules that prop them up. We've known for a long time now that Mill Avenue slackers annoy regular people.

Well, at least Doug got that last part right. But to call a guy 'smarmy' twice in one column, that's just cold! Luckily, not everyone in the media was as unkind as the Dan-Doug one-two combination. In fact, some in the press really did get the point, as evidenced by this *Salt Lake Tribune* editorial (1999), titled 'In the Spirit of Dr. King':

> "Many celebrate the birthday of slain civil rights leader Martin Luther King Jr. as nothing more than a paid holiday. Not so for a small group of Arizona activists, who used the day last week for a sit-in to protest a Tempe ordinance that bans sitting or lying on sidewalks. The activists chose the nation's newest holiday to make their point: that the Tempe ordinance unfairly targets street people, transients, and the homeless. . . . The connection of their cause with that of King, who championed civil rights, as well as Gandhi's ideas of passive civil disobedience, is admirable. It is what the holiday is supposed to be about. . . . Arizona's SIT activists have a better grasp of what a national holiday honoring King should mean than those who think it should just be another paid day of idleness."

Emboldened by such sentiments, we went ahead with the second sit-in, less than two weeks after the first. Things were calmer the second time around; the day had a more lilting quality than the frenetic force of the first, as reported in the *State Press* (Severson 1999b):

> "For the second time in two weeks, Tempe police watched as 30 ASU students and Tempe residents broke the law Saturday afternoon by sitting on downtown Mill Avenue sidewalks. Randall Amster said he thought that Saturday's event was 'more mellow' than the first one. Randall added that it was peaceful and that is what was important. 'By keeping this issue before the conscience of the community, we hope to demonstrate to the city of Tempe that there is significant public sentiment for eliminating this unjust ordinance.' Yogi, a 22-year-old homeless Tempe man, also took a seat in protest. 'It's not fair to say this way of living is wrong. A public sidewalk is for everyone. I believe the city should have talked to us, the people the law is targeted toward, before passing the law,' he said. 'Something could have been worked out.' Project S.I.T. chose to voice its opposition in the empty lot of Seventh Street and Mill Avenue in remembrance of what was there before. The corner 'was home to three public benches, and homeless individuals in the downtown area often assembled there,' Amster said."

The *Republic*'s coverage of the event (Trujillo 1999) further noted:

> "In the '60s, protesters staged sit-ins to fight racial discrimination, gender inequality and war. Saturday, they sat cross-legged, holding signs to protest a ban on sitting in Tempe. Although the group actively broke the law Saturday, two police officers rode by on bicycles without issuing tickets. . . . Oliver Gatz, 26, a homeless man who frequently sleeps in vacant lots in Tempe and sits on the sidewalks, smiled as he watched the crowd grow to 30 strong. 'They could be sitting at the Coffee Plantation complaining about it,' said Gatz, whose right arm bears the tattoo, 'Food not bombs,' 'but they're over here doing something about it.'"

By now this first wave of direct action, centered upon the 'tactical control of space' and 'empowerment of the homeless,' was drawing to a close. The town was buzzing about slackers, sidewalks, sit-ins, and such. The homeless community was as vocal and visible as they'd ever been. I was getting calls for interviews daily, including from national sources such as Court TV and *Mother Jones* magazine (who later that year would name ASU one of the nation's top 10 activist campuses on the basis of S.I.T.'s exploits). Tempe seemed to be feeling the pressure, but nothing was being done, either good or bad, regarding the homeless situation or the sidewalk ordinance itself. Citations were not being issued under the law, although some of the homeless were beginning to notice that police officers would approach them under the guise of the ordinance, constituting what is known as a 'contact,' which could at times lead to searches and ID checks. But by and large, the city seemed to be in a holding pattern, a sleeping giant unsure of what its next move would be. In the meantime, though, the Dan & Doug show was gearing up for a final round of *ad hominem* assaults, directed once again at yours truly in particular, and the slackers in general.

> Doug (MacEachern 1999b): "On Saturday, allegedly 'compassionate' activists in Tempe threw a sit-in on the sidewalks of downtown Mill Avenue, protesting an ordinance forbidding such sitting. Slackers panhandle aggressively. They can be rude, obnoxious even. In many respects, they're like a lot of college professors, only more exotic. . . . It is a tradition of post-Vietnam Era liberalism to anoint certain,

> selected behaviors once denigrated as 'transgressive' and elevate them to 'community' status. . . . Not only do liberal activists make no effort to excuse the behavior of their newfound chosen 'communities,' they celebrate them. Celebrating these kids, romanticizing them and assigning them rights they neither deserve nor require, encourages the wretches to remain precisely where they are. It is welfare state-ism in miniature, wherein all that matters is that Amster, et al, feel the afterglow of their morally superior compassion."
>
> Dan (Durrenberger 1999b): "You remember Randall Amster. He is the self-appointed champion of Tempe's socially flaccid sit-and-spit crowd. They sit on sidewalks and spit in the eye of visitors, the taxpaying public and downtown business owners. . . . What drives a fellow like Randall Amster? It is the overwhelming desire to be someone important. Thus, the challenge. How to become that important someone. Simple. You invent a cause and exploit those dumb enough to climb aboard your bandwagon. Over the years, the leaders of odd religious cults have performed similar mischief. That is what this nonsense is all about. Amsterites are consumed with the propagation of a spurious form of social religion hidden behind a trumped-up veil of social justice. The philosophy celebrates losers and denigrates winners. . . . Tempe's ban on sidewalk sitting is not an issue of civil rights, free speech or assembly. Nor is it an issue of academic freedom. These silly behaviors are nothing more than desperate struggles to satisfy grieving egos. . . . Abandoning the curb and sitting in a chair is the first step out of life's gutter."

Okay Dan, I will if you will. But there was more important work to be done than fret over such shenanigans. My response to Dan, Doug, the DTC, et al., would soon come in the courtroom.

Legal Rights: The Laurels of Litigation

While all of the direct-action drama was unfolding in Tempe, I was simultaneously challenging the ordinance in federal court. Being a law school graduate and having practiced for a short time in the early 1990s, and with my strong interest in spatial issues and sense of kindredness with the street people, I realized that I was uniquely situated to bring such a challenge. I also knew that First Amendment cases were among the thorniest and most difficult to get into court with, as well as being keenly aware that I had never even argued a motion in court before, let alone a federal district court. But here was a chance to do something productive and positive with the legal skills that I had long since abandoned during my process of 'political awakening' (see Hibberd 2000; Steckner 2001a; Ferrell 2001b). So on the Friday before the first sit-in, I went to the federal courthouse in Phoenix and filed an emergency motion for a temporary restraining order (TRO) against enforcement of the ordinance. The judge who heard the motion listened intently and asked many pointed questions, but ultimately ruled that while we were "close to making out a case," there was not enough before her to warrant granting the extraordinary remedy of a TRO at that point. Thus, while a fuller exposition of the case would later be heard by another federal judge, we were on our own in terms of risking arrest at the first sit-in. Although not immediately successful in terms of legal results at that point, I still felt positive about the potential of the case and sensed that it would turn out to be an important component in the overall struggle to overturn the law in particular and the city's draconian policies toward the street people in general.

A bit of legal context is in order here. Almost two decades ago, Richard Ropers (1988:215) opined that "the problem of homelessness may be the leading human rights issue for the United States." More recently, the two leading national homeless rights organizations (NCH/NLCHP 2006:18) argued that "laws and practices that criminalize homelessness . . . violate international human rights law," including basic rights such as freedom of movement, equal protection and non-discrimination, and prohibitions against 'status crimes.' In advocating specifically for the civil rights of homeless people, the National Coalition for the Homeless (NCH) and the Bringing America Home campaign, have focused upon issues including the proliferation of hate crimes, the imposition of fines and criminal sanctions, police harassment and brutality, profiling and selective enforcement of laws, spatial exclusion orders, 'bum-proof' benches, lack of available shelter spaces, and the infringement of the right to vote. Homeless newspapers such as *Street Spirit* often publish 'know your rights' information, including an article detailing 'The Legal Rights of Homeless People in Berkeley' (James & Neumann 2005), which offered counsel regarding trespass laws, sleeping in parks, panhandling, vending newspapers, recovering confiscated property, and properly managing animals such as dogs. In order to ensure the protection of homeless peoples' human and civil rights, the NCH (2004) urges "using the legal system to fight unconstitutional ordinances that criminalize life-sustaining activities."

As noted above, however, such efforts often assume a defensive posture that arguably "does nothing to address the root causes of homelessness," to such an extent that leading civil rights groups such as the NCH "themselves recognize that anti-criminalization lawsuits . . . do not create affordable housing or accessible services" (Hafetz 2003:1239). Still, legal challenges to oppressive policies "have resulted not only in providing immediate relief for many of the homeless, but also in increasing the attention . . . to the plight of the homeless," comprising both "an advocacy tool and an instrument to gain immediate relief" (Ropers 1988:190,198). As scholars of 'legal geography' have observed, "law as an instrument of change, domination or resistance, and a means through which justice might be given practical realization, has, in innumerable ways, shaped . . . the basic terms and experience of social life" (Delaney, et al. 2001:xv). More directly, as Hafetz (2003:1240,1261) explains:

> "Legal advocacy also has fostered effective organizing approaches, raising awareness of and sympathy for homeless people (and helping mobilize public sentiment against anti-homeless ordinances). While such litigation may establish only negative rights, it has helped lead some governments to initiate programs designed to assist homeless people. . . . Legal advocacy also can play an important role in shaping the public's attitudes about homelessness and deepening its understanding of this complex problem. It can foster political change by pressuring policymakers to act. Certainly, lawyers have helped focus public attention on the issues, including by opposing efforts by cities to criminalize homelessness."

Positive examples of such efforts include (among many that could be cited here) a homeless legal clinic at Arizona State University staffed by almost 100 law students (Hermann 2005), and a group of 20 lawyers who provide *pro bono* legal services to the homeless (Lewis 1995):

> "When called upon . . . the attorneys will advocate through the courts for homeless individuals and families to assure that their rights are not violated. . . . [A local service provider

> said,] 'since there is no mechanism in place to protect human and civil rights of the homeless, something we've asked for for 10 years now, and since they say, "If you want something done do it yourself," we've put together a program' to address the gaps in care for the homeless. . . . 'They wouldn't be in the political position they're in if they had active legal voices.'"

With all of this in mind, back in Tempe it would be mid-February of 1999 by the time the case was heard by the court again, this time on my motion for a preliminary injunction against the ordinance. Having by then participated in two well-reported sit-ins and planning others in the near future, I was able to get legal 'standing' to maintain the challenge by violating the law and therefore being personally at risk of arrest. I argued that the law was discriminatory in both intent and function, and that my First Amendment rights as a protester were infringed by a tenuous 'permit application' for sit-ins that the city had produced and delivered to me. In all cases I refused to sign a permit, in the belief that one could not be required to validate the very law that was being challenged, and that in any event it would be unconstitutional to require a person to obtain a permit from the same entity that they were protesting against, in this case the city of Tempe. The judge heard oral argument for over one hour on the motion, asking many detailed and difficult questions of both sides. Near the beginning of the hearing, he admitted that he was not inclined to grant the motion, but by the end he had heard enough at least to order further briefing from both sides on certain key issues including standing, whether sitting was 'expression' for purposes of the First Amendment, and whether the permit requirement was constitutional. After submitting the briefs, it would be a matter of months before the judge rendered a decision. In the meantime, we had another small sit-in in March, and a larger 'peace vigil' and sit-in in April, both times with street people participating and without interference from the police.

When the judge's ruling came down in early May of 1999, it set off a flurry of media reports, and changed the balance of power in terms of the legal and political contest. Here is how the decision was reported by the Freedom Forum, a national First Amendment center based out of Vanderbilt University in Tennessee (Ciarimboli 1999):

> "A federal judge has placed a temporary halt on an Arizona city's efforts to enforce a highly controversial sidewalk sitting

> ban, allowing weary citizens to rest on Tempe's walkways – at least for now. U.S. District Judge Stephen McNamee granted Arizona-based Project S.I.T. a preliminary injunction, forbidding enforcement of the law until the court decides whether it violates the First Amendment. In its request for an injunction, S.I.T. attacked the law's permit-application policy, which requires potential sit-in demonstrators to provide the name of a responsible party and the date, hours and location of the demonstration. In approving the injunction, McNamee cited the U.S. Supreme Court's 1960 decision in *Talley v. California*, in which the court concluded: 'The requirement that those desiring to exercise free speech rights identify themselves and supply the names, addresses, and telephone numbers of sponsoring or responsible persons has a "chilling effect" on free speech, and is unconstitutional.' McNamee also cited a 1981 decision by the 9th U.S. Circuit Court of Appeals, which stated that 'persons desiring to exercise their free speech rights may not be required to give advance notice to the state.' Sitting bans similar to Tempe's have been implemented in over 20 cities across the United States.

The local media also rang in, with this *Tribune* column (Dunn 1999b):

> "News of the injunction was received rather indifferently by many local businesses. Several store owners and managers said they didn't care to comment. Calls to Rod Keeling of the DTC went unreturned. 'I haven't noticed a difference either way,' said Steve Neilsen, co-owner of Slices restaurant on Sixth Street. 'That's pretty cool,' said Dylan Levine, when informed of the preliminary injunction. Levine, who said he hails from 'everywhere,' was perched atop a trash receptacle at the corner of Sixth Street and Mill Avenue. He said that although he sometimes enjoys sitting on the sidewalk, he had no immediate plans to do so. 'I'll spread the word though,' he pledged. Tempe assistant city attorney Marlene Maerowitz is confident the sidewalk-sitting ban will survive constitutional scrutiny. She said it's already a winner in the court of public opinion. 'If we didn't have to legislate against this type of behavior it would be great,' Maerowitz said. 'Unfortunately there are lots of people who don't engage in proper, civil,

> acceptable social behavior. This wouldn't be happening if people could behave appropriately and conform to what is considered socially acceptable.' Proper. Acceptable. Appropriate. Conform. Put them all together and you get 'Blah.' With the preliminary injunction in place, now is the time to protest the homogenization of Tempe. Get on your butts and do something about it."

In an editorial criticizing the judge's decision (Arizona Republic 1999), it was still noted that the law "in fact did burden the rights of Tempe's slacker-citizens to lounge like slugs on city sidewalks. The ordinance is the famous 'anti-slacker' law. It was created with urban layabouts in mind. And, no bones about it, the law's intention was to control young panhandlers, whose habit was to stretch out on the community's sidewalks as if it were their living room." The *Republic* of course found such aims perfectly reasonable and even desirable – and the Constitution be damned, as I (1999b) pointed out in response:

> Tempe [should] not have allowed the push of homogenization to lead to the adoption of a supposedly neutral ordinance whose expressed intention is, as you infer, to remove and eradicate "young panhandlers" from the downtown area. This is blatant discrimination, and the ordinance has properly been challenged on that basis.
>
> In a bygone day, Mill Avenue was the historic center of Tempe's public discourse, and although commerce was among the values and activities encouraged there, it wasn't the only one. We all know that the immediate future of downtown Tempe has already been decided in favor of commercialization and continuing development. The question is whether there will still be a space for spontaneous expression, political speech, musicmaking, just 'being' – indeed, diversity itself.
>
> Tempe apparently has been sacrificed on the altar of crass commercialism. Et tu, editors?

Following the preliminary injunction, I filed a motion for summary judgment and the entry of a permanent injunction, on the basis that the judge had basically ruled that the permit requirement was unconstitutional. It would be almost 10 months before the judge ruled, granting the motion and 'permanently' rendering Tempe's sidewalk ordinance unenforceable (*Amster v. Tempe*, CV-99-00072-SMM). As reported in the *Tribune* (Riordan 2000), the judge's decision "means Tempe police cannot ask those lounging on downtown sidewalks to move – unless they are on the private sidewalk areas now owned by the Centerpoint retail complex at Sixth Street and Mill Avenue." A subsequent editorial (East Valley Tribune 2000), however, lamented that "a judge's scrapping of Tempe's sidewalk-sitting ban is a disappointment for downtown business owners and responsible citizens hoping to reclaim public spaces from panhandlers." The editorial did note that, "instead of slamming the door on Tempe's professional apologists for ne'er do wells, such as ASU's Randall Amster, city officials should invite them to submit constructive suggestions of their own. . . . The Tempe City Council's challenge now is to find, with help from the community, that delicate balance between rights and responsibility." The city declined the offer to include homeless advocates and the homeless in its deliberations, choosing instead to dig its heels in and file an appeal to the U.S. Court of Appeals for the Ninth Circuit. It would take almost a year and a half for the appeal to be resolved, during which time the injunction remained firmly in place.

In the interim, news of the small victory we had attained in Tempe began to spread. Activists and homeless advocates in cities such as Philadelphia reached out to share stories, experiences, and strategies. National advocates including the NLCHP (National Law Center on Homelessness and Poverty) and NCH (National Coalition for the Homeless) forwarded expressions of congratulations and solidarity. Back home, as the Tempe Homeless Task Force was formed and a 'needs assessment' study commissioned, some of us in S.I.T. began to branch out into different realms and focus on other social justice issues. In addition to continuing with my interviews and outreach on Mill Avenue, I became deeply involved in a growing grassroots campaign to save Tempe Butte (one of the last remaining downtown open spaces and frequent site of homeless 'urban camping') from being dynamited and developed with high-end retail and residential components (see Hibberd 2000). Legal interest in the sidewalk case itself remained high, resulting in a number of law review articles on the subject (e.g., Leckerman 2001), including one inspired specifically by and focusing upon the Tempe ordinance and lawsuit (Houck 2000). Both articles concluded that sidewalk sitting bans were unconstitutional and endorsed challenges to their enforcement.

Legal Wrongs: The Limits of Litigation

During the course of the legal battle, I was guided by principles divined by others who had previously engaged in such contests. The aim would be to "expose and reverse an institutional anti-homeless policy" and to "enjoin the law enforcement strategy" that supported it (Waxman 1994). Other foundational tenets would be "the empowerment of homeless people" (Rosenthal 1996:203) that comes with counteracting portrayals that "serve to dehumanize the homeless," and to this end we would "strive to give the homeless a human face, showing them as people deserving of rights and dignity" (Waxman 1994). "Ultimately," as Gregg Barak (1991:152) concurs, "we are talking about the right to human dignity" (cf. Samuel 1999). Of course, pursuing legal remedies is not without risk, as suggested by Madeleine Stoner's (1995:173) chapter on 'The Limitations of Judicial Advocacy,' Barak's (1991:145) observation of "the dialectics of legal repression and liberation," and Talmadge Wright's (1997:293) important admonition:

> "The problem with litigation, when practiced in isolation from direct action, is that 'working for the homeless' takes precedence over 'working with the homeless.' It serves to maintain distance from a marginalized 'Other,' to maintain the social relations that reproduce systemic inequalities and to reinforce a lack of trust between advocates and the homeless."

These caveats include the critique from some legal circles that sees "the attorney-client model of representation as a form of domination that inhibits the growth of genuine class-consciousness among poor people and blunts fertile possibilities for social change" (Hafetz 2003:1243), and begins to explain in part the NCH's (2004:11) insistence that homeless people must "play a leading role" in "organizing for change." While not unmindful of these limitations inherent in the legal system, the Tempe case was something of a unique situation in that there was no actual 'lawyer' litigating the suit; I was representing myself as someone whose rights were infringed by the sidewalk law, even though the rights of the homeless were obviously uppermost in my mind. This is one of those legal wrinkles that makes it difficult at times to challenge an unjust law, since it isn't easy to get standing to maintain a suit nor do vulnerable people often feel empowered to put themselves on the line in order to do so. Sometimes, those of us with more secure domains and support systems should in fact be the ones to stand up publicly and 'take the heat' over controversial actions, as long as the people most immediately affected by the challenged policy or law are fully empowered to decide for themselves how (or even if) they want to participate. In other words, to maintain an artificial 'rule' that *only* people of a certain class ought to be able to organize can be restrictive in its own right, and can serve to undermine the very autonomy that it ostensibly seeks to promote.

Having said that, the extra-legal strategies (e.g., sit-ins, sleep-ins, demonstrations, encampments, etc.) that I have detailed here are fully informed by the belief that "it is necessary to bring the often abstract pursuits of attorneys back down, quite literally, to the cold concrete – to face the miseries that mock all pretensions of a just society" (Blasi 1987:180), and have been guided by the notion that "it is essential that activists continue to challenge restrictive-rights discourse not just in the courts, but also in the street, where a more positive vision of a just society can be fought for" (Mitchell 1996b:172). As Ferrell (2001a:176) counsels, "resistance to injustice must emerge, not just in courtrooms and political campaigns, but in the streets and spaces, in the everyday cultural politics, of the city. At a minimum, gutter punks and street activists throw alternative identities up against enforced uniformity, offer moments of autonomous pleasure in the face of orchestrated entertainment, celebrate a sort of shambling marginality in counterpoint to an emerging economy and aesthetics of middle class consumer life. Beyond this . . . they also succeed in organizing eclectic communities of difference, and effective political resistance, inside the spaces they share." The sidewalk campaign in Tempe was built on these premises, that legal advocacy had a role to play but ultimately the vision of a more just world would manifest outside the courtroom.

One last issue that deserves brief mention here is the very nature of 'right' themselves as a sought-after goal of many efforts aimed at producing social change. Historically speaking, rights as a political concept were actually demanded by the bourgeoisie to protect their domains of property and privilege. While later being picked up on by working-class people, resulting in a liberalization of rights discourse in the U.S., it remains the case that rights – civil, human, or both – sometimes can run the risk of validating the very system that created oppression in the first place. As Don Mitchell (1996b:171) expounds, "the language of rights, particularly public rights, is itself detrimental to progressive causes [since rights] reify certain relations of power."

Blomley (1994:24-5) likewise observes that rights discourse can reinforce "hegemonic power relations," and inquires: "What does it mean, for example, that many oppositional groups speak 'rights-talk,' appealing to equity, liberty, and justice, if that language carries with it certain associations that may well be hostile to the aims of such movements?" Among the legal community, 'critical legal studies' advocates have similarly argued that "in establishing 'rights' for their clients, public interest lawyers were winning only pyrrhic victories because the system itself ultimately reinforced alienation and powerlessness among the poor" (Hafetz 2003:1241-2).

Perhaps it was my keen awareness of all of these limitations of the law as an agent of social change (see, e.g., Bachmann 2001; Anleu 2000; Rosenberg 1993; Fox 1991) – something that I intuitively understood as an 'anarchist lawyer' (see Hibberd 2000) and as one who had seen first hand the myriad ways in which the law creates and protects relationships premised upon hierarchy, property, and control – that eased the impact of what would transpire with the lawsuit. The Ninth Circuit Court of Appeals decided to hold the oral argument on appeal at a special session of the court, in the great auditorium at the ASU College of Law (such sessions are rare, but not unheard of in cases of particular import or interest) (cf. Steckner 2001a). The argument was well attended by law students, friends of S.I.T., and members of the Tempe community. As is their wont, the judges grilled both sides without necessarily revealing how they were leaning in the case. I recall feeling somewhat anxious about the whole spectacle of it all, but also remained confident that the facts, the law, and the equities were on our side and would tip the scales of justice in our favor.

After the argument but before the court rendered its decision, the *Tribune* ran an editorial (2001a: 'Too Broad a Law') arguing that "Tempe's ordinance as it is before the court encroaches on every American's right of free speech, which we all have regardless of how we look or smell, or whether we're standing or sitting on public property." Six weeks later, however, the court's ruling came down, as described in the two major local papers:

> Tempe's ban on sitting on downtown sidewalks was upheld as constitutional, a federal court ruled Tuesday. A three-judge panel of the 9th Circuit Court of Appeals, reversing a lower court decision, said Tempe does not violate First Amendment rights when it requires a permit to sit or lie on sidewalks. . . .

> The sidewalk ordinance goes into effect immediately, said Marlene Pontrelli, deputy city attorney. "We believe the court has upheld the law as we have previously interpreted it," she said.
>
> Randall Amster, who believes the ban unfairly targets the homeless and so-called slackers, said, "It was not the decision I was hoping for." But he noted that the legal battle raised awareness about the homeless and led to peaceful sit-ins on Mill Avenue. "The spark of social activism that got lit in this case is important," he said. "Even a legal loss doesn't mean the whole thing's a loss."
>
> -- *Arizona Republic* (Steckner 2001b)

> Taking up space on a piece of sidewalk doesn't deserve First Amendment protection, a federal appellate court ruled Tuesday. Randall Amster, an associate professor [sic] of justice studies, said the fight for sidewalk rights isn't over. "There may be a couple of legal arguments that still need to be reviewed," he said.
>
> Tempe has never enforced the ordinance, as Amster organized several sit-ins without interference.
>
> The appellate court's reversal of the ruling made supporters of the ordinance happy at Tempe City Hall.
>
> Jason, a 20-year-old who declined to give his last name, said he is frequently challenged by downtown shop clerks who don't want him around. He lashed out at the ordinance while sitting on a brick planter on Mill Avenue, eating chow mien with his fingers. "It's a public sidewalk," Jason said. "They don't need to be arresting or ticketing anybody for it."
>
> -- *East Valley Tribune* (Templar 2001b)

Following the appellate ruling, the *Tribune* repeated its call to 'Find Middle Ground to Sit On' (2001b), asserting that "a reasonable law could forbid sitting so close to shop entrances as to obstruct clear evacuation paths in case of fire, deny customers unfettered access to shops and cafes, or block sidewalk strollers. But banning it elsewhere actually could backfire on merchants by restricting the free-form pedestrian traffic along Mill Avenue that makes it lucrative to set up shop there." Once again, the paper urged that the city, merchants, and advocates should "work out a compromise allowing free association but doesn't impede customers or passersby, both vital ingredients to a thriving commercial district." The city, however, chose not to seek 'middle ground' but instead prepared to begin enforcing the ordinance. Hearing reports that folks were being hassled downtown, I went and sat down on the sidewalk and was confronted by private security guards from TEAM almost immediately. What I reminded the guards of that evening, and what I pointed out to the city as well, was that until the district court judge vacated his injunction, the prohibition on enforcement remained in place and that any attempt to enforce the law before then would place them in contempt of court. Over six months later, on December 20, 2001, the district judge did finally dismiss the case and vacated the injunction *sua sponte* (on his own initiative and without requesting input from the parties). After contemplating the options remaining in the case (including petitioning to the U.S. Supreme Court for review of the Ninth Circuit's decision), I decided to end the legal contest and begin exploring alternatives with community members for continuing the challenge to the sidewalk ordinance in particular and the Disneyfication of Tempe in general.

For starters, there was consideration given to strategies to employ when the city began to enforce the ordinance. During the course of the litigation, the city bound itself to an absurd policy under which every permit application for sitting on the sidewalk would be immediately granted without question. I pointed out that this meant an individual could secure a permit for a year-long open-ended demonstration that includes anyone who states they are protesting the ordinance – effectively creating an exception certain to swallow the rule, rendering the law meaningless. The district court appreciated the inanity of this eventuality and issued the injunction; the appellate court overturned the injunction but explicitly affirmed that the city was bound to this *pro forma* policy (see *Amster v. Tempe*, 248 F.3d 1198 (9th Cir. 2001)). Thus, as a possible tool for defeating enforcement, one could secure a permit for a permanent and ongoing demonstration against the ordinance whose protections would extend to anyone who self-identified as a protester. Other plans considered then included more sit-ins; a 'squat-in' or a 'stand-in' (it is illegal only if one's posterior touches the ground, so squatting or standing avoids the prohibition); advocating a boycott of Mill Avenue businesses; and using informational pickets and chamber-packing tactics to increase the pressure on the city council to repeal or modify the law. Many local homeless outreach entities, street people, and sundry activist groups expressed the energy and desire to participate in such events – mettle that would be tested, as the *State Press* (Davis 2002) reported:

> "Police are beginning to enforce a controversial 1998 sidewalk-sitting ordinance. The ordinance, which was tied up in legal proceedings after being challenged by Randall Amster, an ASU graduate student, was deemed constitutional by the 9th U.S. Circuit Court of Appeals. The time has passed for the ordinance to be appealed to the Supreme Court, allowing police to actively begin enforcing the ordinance. 'We are currently making policy about it,' [Tempe police Sgt. Noah] Johnson said. 'We will give two warnings before we consider making an arrest.'"

Nonetheless, despite the legal loss and the impending enforcement of the ordinance, the overall impact and legacy of S.I.T. seemed positive by and large, as Don Mitchell (2003:231-32) affirmed:

> "One of the most interesting current interventions into the 'order' of public space – the campaign to secure the city – is Tempe, Arizona's 'Project S.I.T.' Project S.I.T. was created 'to study, analyze, and challenge sidewalk ordinances and other public behavior laws that aim selectively at homeless/street people and their right to exist in public places.' Project members engage in civil disobedience (staging sit-ins on Tempe and other Arizona sidewalks, thereby updating that old tradition of disobedience that runs through the labor activists of the first part of the 20th century and the civil rights and student activists of the 1950s and 1960s), legal action, education, and outreach. Project S.I.T. won an important victory in early 2000 when it secured a court decision overturning Tempe's 'anti-sitting' law. An appellate court later reversed that decision, but the case is still unsettled, as a new round of appeals has been filed. Project S.I.T.'s aim, like that of lawyers for homeless people . . . is not really (or not only) to secure the right to sit on a sidewalk or to sleep in a park, which as we have seen is a pretty narrow right indeed. Rather, it is to contest two related issues: the privatization of public space and the lack of decent affordable housing. Project S.I.T. members have found that many of the apparently public

sidewalks of downtown Tempe have been deeded to developers and business owners. With private, rather than public, property rules in effect, therefore, people can be removed for entirely arbitrary reasons, that is, without cause. Project S.I.T. is devoted to exposing this wholesale transfer of the public realm into private hands and to reversing it – to asserting a right to the city for all and not just for the cappuccinoed few. Simultaneously, the Project continually highlights the fact that there is not a single homeless shelter in the city of Tempe. In such a circumstance, the enforcement of no-sitting and no-sleeping laws is simply perverse; it quite fundamentally denies the right of some people to *inhabit* the city. Project S.I.T. is working to implement a more just vision of order on the streets of Tempe."

Contested Realms: The Struggle Continues

Following the work of S.I.T., what would ensue in terms of community action and social protest against criminalization in Tempe exceeded my hopes and expectations when the legal challenge was discontinued and S.I.T. dispersed in mid-2002. By late 2003, under banners such as 'It Shouldn't Be Illegal to Be Homeless' and 'Stop the War Against the Homeless,' a group of local activists, street people, and members of the college community called the Free to Camp Coalition (geocities.com/freetocampcoalition) launched an aggressive and colorful campaign aimed at Tempe's homeless policies in general and the urban camping ordinance in particular. An initial protest event took place on Mill Avenue on November 15th, as reported in the local media (Welch 2003): "Protesters marched peacefully Saturday night through downtown Tempe in opposition to an ordinance that bans sleeping on city property. . . . Elizabeth Venable, who organized the demonstration, said the law unfairly targets the homeless. She added that the problem is compounded because Tempe lacks an appropriate number of homeless shelters." The article noted that this event was part of what would become "an ongoing effort to repeal the ordinance," and so two weeks later another demonstration was held (Christopherson 2003):

> More than 50 protesters chanted, "Neil is a creep! Let people sleep!" and other slogans as paraded up and down Mill

> Avenue on Saturday night to protest Tempe's Urban Camping Ordinance. ASU postgraduate Elizabeth Venable, who coordinated the protest, said she wanted to "deal explicitly" with the criminalization of homelessness.
>
> "People aren't addressing the political issues and the ways the state punishes [the homeless] or the ways people become homeless," she said. . . . "Sitting doesn't hurt anyone and sleeping doesn't hurt anyone, and they're basic things that people need to do to stay alive," Venable said. "The message that [the homeless] are getting is that [they] shouldn't be able to stay alive. Like they're not worthy of living."
>
> The protesters continued to the entrance of retail clothing store Abercrombie & Fitch, where they sat and chanted, "We don't want a yuppie nation!" and "Shelters, not jails!" ASU nursing junior Anna Mitchell, who was working at Abercrombie & Fitch Saturday night, said she sympathized with the protesters' message. "I think [the Urban Camping Ordinance] isn't really fair to the people because they don't have any other option," she said.
>
> Protester Kevin Lyons, 25, said he's lived on the streets of Tempe for the past 11 months. "This ain't no free country. It's a free country for people with money," he said, adding that he "has no life" as a result of the ordinance. "I can't sleep at night," he said.
>
> By the end of the protest, several people had joined the protesters spontaneously. "This seemed more important than doing anything recreational," said [one]. "I think it's wrong to take away anyone's freedom because it's basically a form of discrimination." [Another] said it's tough for homeless people in Tempe because there isn't a shelter nearby and shelters in neighboring cities are often full.

On January 15, 2004, the Coalition presented a petition to the Tempe City Council calling for the repeal of the urban camping law, as described by the *Arizona Republic* (Rau 2004a):

> More than 1000 students, professors, activists and homeless have signed a petition against Tempe's urban camping ordinance. Dozens showed up to present the petition to City Council last week.

> "The last decade has seen a marked increase in the persecution of the homeless in Tempe," said Elizabeth Venable of the Free to Camp Coalition. In 2003, Tempe police handed out 23 misdemeanors to violators of this ordinance. Serena Turley argued that it is cheaper to house the homeless than it is to put them in jail.
>
> Tempe homeless coordinator Theresa James said she doesn't see a shelter in Tempe's near future. She said the city helps fund shelters in other communities, and pulling that money to open a Tempe shelter won't fix the problem.
>
> James said Tempe could improve the way it deals with the homeless, but she said it should be done in a way that doesn't hurt the rest of the community. "If we allow homeless youth to camp out downtown, it disrupts the business owners," she said. "You have to think of it from all perspectives."

Recently speaking to James (2008) about the current situation in Tempe, she noted the urban camping law is still being enforced but the sidewalk sitting ordinance hardly is, if at all; she further observed, however, that in general things are "getting better" for the homeless in Tempe, that there is "a dialogue happening," and that there has indeed been a gradual but perceptible "shift away from criminalization toward services," as evidenced by homeless outreach efforts such as the mobile 'HOPE' and the quarterly service fair, 'Project Homeless Connect.' Still, some things don't change all that much over time, as a final item from the coverage of Free to Camp's petition action before the Council indicates (Keim 2004a): "Rod Keeling, executive director of Tempe's business coalition, the Downtown Tempe Community, was the only person at the meeting to speak in favor of the ordinance."

Back at it again the following month, the Coalition escalated the stakes with a march and sleep-in along Mill Avenue on a busy Saturday night. The throng of activists and the homeless snaked its way through downtown in an impressive and multi-faceted action (Davis 2004):

> More than 100 homeless advocates marched up and down Mill Avenue in downtown Tempe on Saturday night in a unified call for a homeless shelter in the city. The activists stopped on several street corners and sat on sidewalks with a mock shelter in protest of city ordinances they say are designed to keep the homeless out of downtown Tempe.

Many civic and student organizations, including the Free to Camp Coalition, East Valley Food Not Bombs, and Local to Global Justice, as well as homeless people in Tempe, hoped to alert people to the fact that there is no homeless shelter in Tempe. Chants such as, 'Being homeless is not a crime,' 'We need shelter,' and 'Now's the time!' rang out as curious onlookers passed by. Tempe police and private security guards kept a close eye on the rally but left the protesters alone.

Randall Smith marched with a sign saying, 'Stop the War Against the Homeless,' while others read, 'Public space for all,' and 'Homelessness is not a crime.'

Tim Coomer, 32, who is homeless, also marched in support with a sign that stated, '*I AM home*.' 'The no-camping ordinance has put a lot of people on the run into Phoenix,' Coomer said. 'A lot have been arrested for essential actions required to live. We have a right to life, as well as several other things that have been taken away from us.'

Fig. 5: Protest against anti-homeless policies in Tempe, 2004

Appropriately, the *State Press* (Keim 2004b) explicitly connected the dots back to the days of S.I.T., observing: "Some activists refuse to stand for Tempe's treatment of the homeless any longer. Demonstrators periodically sat or 'slept' on the sidewalk, violating Tempe's sidewalk sitting ordinance. A few security guards and Tempe police officers stood near protesters when they sat along Mill Avenue, but did not stop the demonstration." While I am pleased to note that I was among the demonstrators that evening who continued the tradition of taking a stand by taking a seat, I am even more heartened to report that the continuing struggle to bring sanity to Tempe's policies, to bring respect to its homeless residents, and to bring democratic vigor to its dwindling downtown public spaces had been passed on to very good hands. The combination of these 'placemaking' and 'empowerment' efforts with the outreach work of Homeless Coordinator Theresa James, as well as the 2004 election of former council member Hugh Hallman (the most outspoken official critic of the sidewalk ordinance) as mayor, could indeed indicate that the political landscape in Tempe has shifted, with possibilities for meaningful transformation at least tangible.

The Final Frontier: Lost (and Found) in Space

Of course, reality tends to intrude on such prospects. Mayor Hallman has been less vocal than Councilman Hallman was about the rights of homeless people, but at least hasn't shown the sort of overt animus that characterized the previous mayor's tenure. And it is still the case that ordinances such as 'urban camping' are enforced in a city that lacks shelters. On the positive side, the Ninth Circuit recently ruled that Los Angeles' version of the 'no sitting' law was unconstitutionally 'cruel and unusual' (*Jones v. City of Los Angeles*, 444 F.3d 1118 (2006)). Most importantly, homeless people in Tempe seem to be more confident and situated. As Wright (1997:324) concludes: "Collective empowerment must be the focus of the continuing struggle to end homelessness and achieve social justice. The celebration of democratic self-realization and self-management without the necessary public and cultural spaces that allow that to occur merely reinforces systemic inequities required by the reproduction of capital." Accordingly, we must work to carve out and maintain small spaces for resistance, and at the same time continually move toward a strategy of "linking local struggles together on a global basis" (Wright 1997:324). This is a prescription not only for contesting policies of homeless demonization and spatial colonization, but also for creating a world of social justice and environmental harmony – places where this work seeks to arrive.

CHAPTER SEVEN

CITIES OF THE FUTURE

Localizing the Global, Globalizing the Local

As indicated throughout the many paths this work has taken, I have sought to explore and analyze the patterns of interconnection among five particular spheres: (i) the lived experiences of homeless people, (ii) the impetus of development and gentrification; (iii) the material and ideological erosion of public space; (iv) the enactment of anti-homeless ordinances and regulations; and (v) emerging forces of resistance to these trends. While it is clear that these spheres are related, it is not always as obvious how and in what direction. For instance, resistance is often a response to criminalization, but it is also proactively present in the daily lives of homeless people. Similarly, homelessness is often taken to be caused primarily by economic and structural factors, yet it has also been argued that homeless people are the cause of economic problems and a significant threat to business interests; thus, homelessness is at times viewed as a consequence of deep crises in capitalism, while at other times as a cause of such crises. In effect, this conundrum points out the distinction between correlation and causation, and suggests avenues for further research and investigation, which this conclusion chapter seeks to initiate by looking at the 'big picture' of globalization as well as the smaller snapshots of the salient issues is a variety of locales from around the world.

The Spatiality of Globalization and Resistance

> "There is no single moment within the social process devoid of the capacity for transformative activity – a new imaginary; a new discourse arising out of some peculiar hybrid of others; new rituals or institutional configurations; new modes of social relating; new material practices and bodily experiences; new political power relations arising out of their internalized contradictions. Each and every one of these moments is full to the brim with transformative potentialities."
>
> -- David Harvey (1996:105)

Capitalism as a political, economic, and social system is often defended as reflective of 'human nature;' as being an expression of the 'natural order' of things; or simply along the lines that it 'works.' All of these rationales are specious, tautological and, ultimately, self-fulfilling. Things work until they don't, and human nature tends to become what the dominant system dictates it to be, especially when people are in large measure forced to abide its tenets in order to gain access to food, clothing, and shelter. The 'natural order' argument might be the least persuasive, first since nature's own processes tend to belie this assessment, and second since none of us is sufficiently gifted with insight to make final pronouncements about the 'way things are supposed to be' to such an extent that we may seek to impose our view on others. Simply put, capitalism may well have played an important role historically speaking, but to accept it as the highest evolution of human processes is at best nostalgic and at worst irresponsible. As a species, I believe that we can, should, and eventually will do better.

In order to move the dialogue forward, however, it is necessary to have a deeper sense of how things came to where they are at this point, picking up in particular where the previous chapter left us in terms of resistance strategies in the face of seemingly inevitable development(s). Indeed, in the ongoing dialogue centered on capitalism, neoliberalism, and globalization, there is a ubiquitous unspoken grounding that often assumes the inevitability of a "global mode of regulation" characterized by "technocratic networks" and "U.S.-style libertarianism" (Brown 1997). Conceptual limitations of the universal-versus-particular variety also pervade, sometimes colorfully animated as 'McWorld versus Jihad' (see Chew & Denemark 1996:50-2). Such allusions suggest the presence of a 'global-versus-local' dialectic that potential resistance movements must confront, and a tendency of movements to either factionalize or become coopted in attempting to impact 'the system,' as Andre Gunder Frank (in Amin, et al. 1990:167) has observed:

> "Very few social movements are antisystemic in their attempt, and still less in their success, to destroy the system and to replace it by another one or none at all. There is overwhelming historical evidence that social movements are not antisystemic in this sense. Indeed, social movements often achieve a measure of success by institutionalizing their demands or even themselves within the system. . . . Moreover, their effects are often unintended, so that not infrequently these effects are incorporated if not coopted by the system, which ends up being invigorated and reenforced by movements, which were formally anti-systemic but did not turn out to be antisystemic."

In a world that seemingly accepts the constitutive and hegemonic inevitability of global capital and neoliberalism (cf. Massey 2000:281-3), it often appears that movements fail to accomplish meaningful transformation because they "tend to focus on restricted issue spaces rather than more comprehensive programs of dissent" (Brown 1997:256). Such movements might instead seek to engage the system both locally and globally, particularly and universally, from within and without – in the belief that "the universal and particular are not only juxtaposed but interwoven and implicated in each other," yielding an inescapable and potentially transformative "global-local nexus" (Slater 1997:258). Immanuel Wallerstein (in Amin, et al. 1990:47,53) likewise makes the point that "it is not the case that some movements are 'universalistic' and others 'particularistic.' All existing movements are in some 'ghetto,'" yet are simultaneously framed by a "world order" that requires a "global strategy." As David Harvey (1990:238-39) further observes, all resistance movements, "no matter how well articulated," are still "subject to the power of capital over the co-ordination of universal fragmented space and the march of capitalism's global historical time that lies outside of the purview of any one of them." Todd May (1994:25) similarly notes that for Horkheimer and Adorno, "every resistance is effectively stifled: not by being suppressed, but by being rendered yet another spectacle in the parade of culture. Resistance that cannot be appropriated is merely left outside the system, a testament of its own absurdity." Finally, Magnusson (1996:92): "Capitalism tends to reshape resistances to fit the spaces it provides for them;" and Massey (2000:281): "Every attempt at radical otherness [is] so quickly commercialized and sold or used to sell." However you choose to say it, there is a strong sense that any attempt at *resistance* must first come up against processes of cooptation (Ferrell & Sanders 1995:16) and our individual lifelines of reliance on the very system being challenged (cf. Guattari 1996), with the awareness that we are all parts of and pawns in the same totalizing 'reality.' A passage by Elizabeth Garsonnin (in Mander 1991:138) provides a sense of this pervasive psychological and cultural moment of 'enclosure':

> "I can really identify with the young people today; how trapped they must feel. The natural world is almost gone, and it's being replaced by this awful hard-edged, commercial creation, with techno-humans running it. They're already in Antarctica. They're in all the jungles. They're tagging all the animals. Their satellites are photographing everything. They know what's in the ground and what's on the land. Soon they'll be on Venus and Mars. And they're inside human cells. Where is there left for the mind to flee? They've even invaded the subjective spaces, the fantasy world. As an artist I feel as if the sources of creation are being wiped out and paved over. It makes the only viable art protest art, but I hate that. It means they already have us confined; we can only react to them. I am so sad."

What many are trying to cope with today is the assertion of the Critical Theorists (among others) that "there is no outside to capitalism" (Sharp, et al. 2000:15), that "capitalism covers the whole of social space; it is unitary in its colonization of the lifeworld" (see May 1994:26,31), constituting what Debord (1983:17) has called a "present phase of total occupation of social life by the accumulated results of the economy." As Pierre Clastres (1994:50) has observed:

> "What does western civilization contain that makes it infinitely more ethnocidal than all other forms of society? It is its system of economic production, precisely a space of the unlimited, a space without a locus in that it constantly pushes back boundaries, an infinite space of permanently forging

> ahead. What differentiates the West is capitalism, as the impossibility of remaining within a frontier, as the passing beyond of all frontiers; it is capitalism as a system of production for which nothing is impossible, unless it is not being an end in itself: whether liberal, private as in Western Europe, or planned, of the State, as in Eastern Europe. Industrial society, the most formidable machine of production, is for that very reason the most terrifying machine of destruction. Races, societies, individuals; space, nature, seas, forests, subsoils: everything is useful, everything must be used, everything must be productive, with productivity pushed to its maximum rate of intensity."

Insights such as this suggest that it is useful to invoke the concept of *hegemony* when speaking of 'the system' and the pervasive, relentless nature of late capitalism. Nonetheless, despite appearing unassailable, it is equally apparent that "no hegemony is ever total," but is instead "a process rather than a thing," and there is in fact no modality of power that does not admit the possibility of contestation (Comaroff 1992:29; see also Foucault 1977 and Sharp, et al. 2000, on *power* as the inherent link between domination and resistance). Thus, while "in its hegemonic dimensions, any culture does present itself as relatively coherent, systemic, consensual, [and] authoritative," it must be noted that "there are always countervailing forces: dialects that diverge, styles that do not conform, alternative moralities and world maps" (Comaroff 1992:29-30). These 'countervailing forces' often appear as "open power struggles," sometimes as "parody," and even as "mundane activity of indeterminate intention and consequence" (Comaroff 1992:30) – with the salient point being that they do in fact appear. We must, in other words, always account for the presence of particular *forms of living*, "the locus of agency" – which, as Harvey notes, is omnipresent: "So who and where are the agents of social change? Again, the simplest answer is everyone, everywhere. Everyone who lives, acts, and talks is implicated" (1996:105-6). The homeless and the domiciled alike carry this burden, and share this innate power.

In the end, even if we are asked to concede the apparent hegemony and cultural logic of corporate globalization and its pervasive set of signs and signifiers, there are still strategies of subversion and resistance available that are both constitutive of identity and transformative of culture; indeed, it is precisely the massification of cultural forms that simultaneously prohibits and invites contestation. As Harvey (1996:106) notes, "because of [internal] contradictions, there are innumerable leverage points within the system that can be seized upon by dissident groups or individuals to try to redirect social change down this or that path. There are always weak links." The question then becomes how to actualize those 'weak links' and at what level they are best engaged. Is it the dedicated individual that is best situated to manifest contestation, or does it require a collective effort or even a national focus to bring about a tangible change? Perhaps it will take an explicitly global movement to nudge the dialogue forward in a meaningful way. Despite incessant debates about the perceived primacy of one or the other of these particular avenues, it is more likely the case that it will take people working at every level to get it done.

'Scales' and the Weight of the World

> "You're better off being homeless than being me."
>
> -- Britney Spears (1/21/08)

An important framework for unpacking the processes of globalization and the potentialities of resistance involves what are sometimes called 'scales' of analysis. As Neil Smith (1992:66) opines, there are sequential and overlapping levels from which to consider social phenomena, in geographic scales of "body, home, community, urban, region, nation, [and] global." Smith has identified the body scale as the foundation for "any revolutionary 'project' today, whether utopian or realistic" (1992:66), whereas the global scale is viewed as "primarily a construct of the circulation of capital" (1992:76). In subsequent work, Smith (1996:xvii) further explores the "link between different spatial scales," mirroring what Burawoy (2000:2) has referred to as the attempt to "link up the local to the global," and reflected more broadly in the view that capitalism and its attendant values and crises are "reflected in the dynamic reorganization of social spaces at all scales of reference from the micro-architectural to the global" (Delaney, et al. 2001:xvi). Thus, when considering *scales*, we are simultaneously looking at physical, cultural, and environmental phenomena, comprising a nascent *ecological* perspective on capitalism and all that it represents. And in terms of issues specifically relevant to this study, Smith (1996:75) concludes that "gentrification . . . is closely connected with . . . 'globalization.'" Once again, however, while the connection is clear, the matter of direction requires further explication.

In one sense, it is apparent that "the process of gentrification is quintessentially international. It is taking place . . . in cities throughout most of the Western advanced capitalist world" (Smith & Williams 1986:17). This could be read to imply that globalization is partly a cobbling together of local gentrification schemes, or that gentrification is a local manifestation of processes that are fundamentally global. Then again, perhaps the precise direction of the relationship or its dominant pole of origin is beside the point, since the nexus between the local and global is more dialectical than dichotomous in any event, more mutually reflexive than mutually exclusive (cf. Soja 2000:218). Indeed, it may also be that the presence of a third 'variable' is the point of implicit connection between gentrification and globalization, as Smith (1984:ix) alludes to in his early work: "Deindustrialization and regional decline, gentrification and extrametropolitan growth, the industrialization of the Third World and a new international division of labor, intensified nationalism and a new geopolitics of war – these are not separate developments but symptoms of a much deeper transformation in the geography of capitalism." In this view, it might be said that capital is both localizing and globalizing itself simultaneously and in mutually reinforcing ways.

Fast-forwarding closer to the present, it has by now become clear that "we are all being globalized" (Bauman 1999). Of course, depending upon one's relative socio-political location, this can either be very profitable and entertaining, or economically devastating and dehumanizing, or some proportional combination thereof. This is not merely a First World versus Third World situation, however, since some people living in First World countries suffer the negative consequences of globalization as starkly as many in the Third World do. While factors of race and gender are intimately connected to these issues, it is equally apparent that class figures prominently as well – a point evidenced quite dramatically in the polarized experiences of urban *flaneurs*, tourists, consumers, merchants, and developers on the one hand, and those of the urban homeless, street people, vagabonds, 'gutter punks,' and 'crusty' kids on the other. Indeed, as Zygmunt Bauman (1999:93,97-8) has appropriately discerned:

> "What is acclaimed today as 'globalization' is geared to the tourists' dreams and desires. Its second effect – a *side*-effect, but an unavoidable one – is the transformation of many others into vagabonds. Vagabonds are travellers refused the right to turn into tourists. They are allowed neither to stay put (there is no site guaranteeing permanence, the end to undesirable mobility) nor search for a better place to be. . . . *A world without vagabonds is the utopia of the society of tourists.* Much of the politics in the society of tourists – like the obsession with 'law and order,' the criminalization of poverty, recurrent sponger-bashing, etc. – can be explained as an ongoing, stubborn effort to lift social reality, against all odds, to the level of that utopia. . . . And so, paradoxically, the tourist's life is all the more bearable, even enjoyable, for being haunted with a uniformly nightmarish alternative of the vagabond's existence. In an equally paradoxical sense, the tourists have vested interest in rendering that alternative as dreadful and execrable as possible. . . . Were there no vagabonds, the tourists would need to invent them."

Still, despite the rapid pace of development and the expansion of processes of criminalization and marginalization, it remains the case that "so far, we've only glimpsed the leading edge of this emerging 'Fantasy City' but there is every indication that by the next millennium this will have become a global trend . . . the globalizing, nondescript city" (Hannigan 1998:1,199). As such trends are becoming increasingly obvious and as the rate of change continues to increase as well, it is appropriate to inquire: "Are we prepared to overlook the cultural diversity in the community in favor of pre-packaged corporate entertainment destinations? Will there be room for leisure activities other than those which can be branded, licensed, franchised and rolled out on a global scale? And finally, are we prepared to designate our inner cities no-go zones except for the heavily fortified themed attractions which welcome a constant flow of tourists embarked on leisure safaris into the depths of the postmodern metropolis?" (Hannigan 1998:200). Whereas the responses to these queries offered by business interests and their customers have come to dominate local politics and influence development decisions, the contentions of the homeless, poor, and displaced have been largely ignored.

In the eyes of many observers, we therefore appear to have reached a state of affairs that, as indicated above, essentially signals "the triumph of capitalism," in all of its full implications and harsh realities, as Edward Soja (2000:216) unabashedly lays bare:

> "[N]eoliberalism has forged a new synthesis or hybrid that effectively rationalizes, celebrates, and promotes the globalization process and the increasing globality of industrial production, commercial trade, financial integration, and information flow. It has brought to the fore a new global class of economic and political entrepreneurs who operate not only transnationally but also at the national, regional, metropolitan, and local scales to foster those conditions that facilitate the freedoms of global capitalism: increasing privatization of the public sphere, deregulation in every economic sector, the breakdown of all barriers to trade and the free flow of capital, attacks on the welfare state and labor unions, and other efforts to reshape the power of established political and territorial authorities to control both the globality of production and the production of globality."

As Don Mitchell (2003:164) has further explained, "what is at work is the implementation, at the urban scale, of a regulatory regime – and its ideological justification – appropriate to the globalizing neoliberal political economy."

All of these globalized processes of privatization, capital accumulation, control of production, ideological hegemony, and spatio-political dominance are of course intimately connected to issues of homelessness, sanitization, and criminalization. In fact, it might be said that homelessness is an issue that touches all of the scales from the body to the globe and back again, presenting an important and instructive moment for perceiving connections between local experiences and global regimes – akin to what Burawoy (2000:4) calls "the lived experience of globalization." By focusing the inquiry at three junctures of the scale in particular – homelessness as the *body*, gentrification as the *urban*, and neoliberal economics as the *global* – it is possible to gain new insights into familiar queries. In so doing, it will be useful to undertake the analysis from two related but conceptually distinct perspectives: the point where global forces and trends localize, and the moment where local processes become global phenomena. As such, these points are necessarily somewhat abstract and perhaps oversimplified to a degree, but are nonetheless saved by the fact that they are offered here partly as conclusions to this volume, but more so as suggestions for open-ended avenues of future action, investigation, and dialogue.

Localizing the Global

> "Capital shapes and controls the urban ecology. Ultimately the same forces that built an urban space can destroy it. . . ."
>
> -- Fitzpatrick & LaGory (2000:68)

The first moment to consider is where global forces find expression in localities, communities, and/or individuals. In a manner, "the idea is to dig up local traces of the huge shakeup we call 'globalization,'" guided by the understanding that "this new 'globalization' does not represent a new shattering of the integrity of the local; our 'locals' were already globally connected, expansive, reflexive" (Gowan 2000:78-9). In fact, "local politics has long been subject to influences originating in the global economy," to such extent that "globalization is bringing about a massive homogenization" that finds concrete expression in "urban regimes" that comprise "the formal and informal 'arrangements' by which public bodies and private interests function together to be able to make and carry out governing decisions" (Leo 1996:77-8). Cities around the world have been impacted by "development norms that have become global. Or, to put it another way, norms and practices based in the global economy have a homogenizing effect on local . . . political cultures" (Leo 1996:83). As Knox (1995:8) likewise concludes, "cities throughout the developed world have recently entered a new phase [which] has its roots in the dynamics of capitalism and, in particular, the globalization of the capitalist economy, the increasing dominance of big conglomerate corporations." In more succinct fashion, Tempe's Free to Camp Coalition captured these sentiments with an apt slogan: 'Mill Avenue: Our Own Little Piece of Corporate Globalization.'

As Neil Smith's prolific writings have further indicated, *gentrification* is often the name given to these global processes of homogenization and corporate dominance when they crystallize in particular urban spaces. As we have also seen, gentrification is inherently exclusionary, particularly from the perspective of street people. Hence, while it is clear that "gentrification and homelessness in the new city are a microcosm of a new global order etched by the rapacity of capital" (Smith 1992:91), it is also evident that the "trend to super-segregation" is likewise a "global phenomenon" (Passaro 1996:82; see also Hetzler, et al. 2006). Moreover, in the sense of how local conditions are created by global forces, it appears that "as the economy has globalized, large sectors of the urban poor have become increasingly underemployed and the poorest have gotten even poorer. The marginalization of the poor, along with a steady rise in the cost of housing, coupled with a decline in the supply of low-income housing, have led to a situation in which a larger segment of the urban poor are at risk for becoming homeless" (Fitzpatrick & LaGory 2000:136). In this light, we begin to perceive that homelessness is strongly influenced by global forces, as are the economic policies that further exacerbate the already-tenuous plight of the impoverished. As an anti-gentrification flyer from New York's Lower East Side bluntly asserted: 'This is the domestic face of the New World Order!' (in Passaro 1996:100). Indeed, this visage often appears as the local face of global hegemony through the relentlessly exclusionary and increasingly brutal regimes imposed by business interests and endorsed by city councils.

An additional perspective on these phenomena can be found in the pervasive push of *privatization* both locally and worldwide. This aspect may well be the underlying hallmark of globalization, found everywhere from the water in Cochabamba to the sidewalks in Tempe. As Peterson (2006:356) recently observed, "privatized public space, exemplified by the 'elimination and/or intensified surveillance of urban public spaces' and the 'creation of new privatized spaces of elite/corporate consumption' . . . is by now a defining measure of neoliberalism and its expression in the neoliberal city." Blomley (2004:30-1) further connects the dots of how global processes become embedded in local communities through downtown redevelopment schemes, urban housing markets, gentrification, and privatization: "Self-consciously radical, neoliberalism is, in part, a language of property – a return to central axioms of eighteenth-century liberalism, which places private property as the foundation for the individual self-interest, which when exercised through the free market, is to lead to optimal social good. The city, moreover, provides a space in which neoliberalism is particularly intense." All of this has yielded a world where "the intensification of urban social control measures stems from the ascendance of neoliberal global capitalism and the related transformation of urban economies, [which] has led many cities to compete with each other to create the most hospitable environment for corporate investment and headquarters, luxury-living facilities, tourism and retail operations" (Beckett & Herbert 2007:18). While many studies have shown that such processes are evident across the U.S., there is potential for further investigation to amplify the global nature of these phenomena, as indicated in a recent report (UN News 2005):

> "The growing *privatization* of property [is] among the driving forces behind the 1.6 billion inadequately housed people across the world, including an estimated 100 million who are completely homeless, a United Nations human rights monitor said today. Miloon Kothari, Special Rapporteur on the right to adequate housing, said inequality in global land ownership was a rising trend, and cited recent figures which showed that a mere 2.5 per cent of landowners controlled nearly three-quarters of all private land. The main concern was a phenomenon of 'urban apartheid' taking place across the world, partly due to an urban gentrification process . . . and a colossal gap in the supply of formal-sector housing. . . . He also noted a trend across the globe towards reducing public housing expenditures and subsidies, pointing to, as an example, a $28 billion drop between 1976 and 2002 in the budget authority for federal housing assistance in the United States. Mr. Kothari said there was also a lack of legal provisions to enable communities to inhabit or own land as well as a growing tendency to criminalize the homeless and the landless. His annual report contained recommendations concerning the need for States to apply diligently their human rights obligations and to control land speculation. . . ."

In the end, it appears that issues such as homelessness, gentrification, and privatization are local matters with global origins and implications. As the capitalist system globalizes, it simultaneously localizes in concrete municipal regulations, development norms, and enforcement regimes. The net effect is a global order composed of homogeneous local terrains, linked literally through technologies of communication and conveyance, materially through shared economic schemes, and ideologically through values of 'civility' and consumption. In this way, every locale in the network moves toward and eventually becomes a microcosm of the whole, reproducing the overall theme in spatially-bounded packages known in the plural sense as 'cities' – but with mass-marketing and generic urban development, might just as well be taken together and uniformly referred to as The (Global) City. Of course, differences do exist between cities, even among those in geographic proximity, and this is not to say that every city has become a generic 'fantasy land' or a diabolical and overdeveloped 'dystopia.' The analysis here is meant to suggest rather that there is a dominant and demonstrable trend emerging, one that has been imposing an inevitable linearization of development norms and regimes of spatial and social control. Thus, while perhaps *no* city is yet a fully realized generic fantasy/dystopia, to some extent this is the direction that *every* city in the global system is inexorably moving.

Globalizing the Local

Indeed, it might even be said that this is the direction cities have *always* been moving, perhaps constituting the true nature of their purpose and design as "corporations indistinguishable as a legal matter from any other commercial corporation" (Frug 2001:162). (This may partly explain why BIDs – quasi-governmental yet privately-held 'business improvement districts' – have proliferated in cities around the world, as noted in Chapter Two). As Magnusson (1996:23) observes:

> "Municipalities had been conceived originally as corporations belonging to the local business class, with a mission to promote their cities within the global economy. . . . Under conditions of globalization, such an effort was likely to connect a city with its counterparts elsewhere in the world. Thus, the boundaries that contained the municipality politically were always breaking down. People engaged in municipal politics were drawn into wider fields of activity in which sovereignty was at best irrelevant and at worst an obstacle to effective action. . . . The institutional weight of the state grounds the municipal authorities in questions of land use and local administration. Nevertheless, urban politics takes people beyond these questions, especially when it is invested with the hopes and aspirations of vital social movements."

In addition to lending support to the idea of a 'global city,' this view also suggests that such processes work in both directions, and that global forces from 'above' can also be impacted and influenced by local movements from 'below.' This opens up a space for and the possibility of "the proliferation of groups that constitute themselves in particular communities as nodes within international networks" (Magnusson 1996:93). In other words, while global networks (literal and figurative) are often used to impose and maintain regimes of consumption and control, they can also be utilized by oppositional movements grounded in local actions to impact the entire system.

In fact, sometimes the most globally significant movements are those that are most intensely grounded in local or regional concerns (the Zapatistas in Chiapas, Mexico for example); as Magnusson (1996:93) notes, "global reach depends on local rootedness." For homeless activists and advocates, this means that while homelessness "is a deep structural crisis in modern capitalism," it is also an issue that can be raised and perhaps remedied through "widespread oppositional social movements among the very poor" (Wagner 1997:66). In a sense, then, the struggles of, by, and on behalf of homeless individuals and communities are always already struggles against gentrification, criminalization, and globalization. The more that local nodes of resistance to homeless sweeps, demomization campaigns, and development explosions occur, the greater the pressure brought to bear on the entire system, not just its local branch office. Homeless struggles for spatial justice and social dignity don't simply help transform local arrangements, but they also comprise a challenge that resonates throughout all of "the scales of the city – from the body, through the region and the nation, to the globe" (Pile & Keith 1997:13).

Nonetheless, a bit of caution is in order, since, as with the anti-globalization movement in North America, "it is premature to call this dramatic intervention from the streets a 'counter-hegemonic globalization'" (Burawoy 2000:350). In addition, there is always a larger frame to consider that seems to be both immune to and yet impacted by local upheavals (Fitzpatrick & LaGory 2000:7): "[E]xperts generally agree that the single most important global environmental influence . . . is the process of urbanization itself. . . . [I]f world urbanization trends continue, it is estimated that roughly 25 years from now more than two-thirds of the world will be urban. The impact on the ecosystem of such an event would be catastrophic, with dramatic increases in pollution, consumption of nonrenewable resources and irretrievable losses of millions of known and unknown animal and plant species." Still, perhaps because the stakes are so high, "the rolling out of neoliberalization has been met by sustained and creative opposition," including an "urban resistance [that] has also increasingly focused on the 'concrete life-worlds of people'" (Blomley 2004:31). Such moments raise the prospect of "the proliferation of transnational social movements, propelled by imaginations of a global dimension" (Burawoy 2000:350), even as they remain true to the everyday experiences of people confronting local issues and concerns.

Indeed, for many so-called 'anti-globalization activists,' the global dimension of their work is consciously cultivated and in many ways necessitated by the fact that meetings of entities such as the World Trade Organization (WTO), International Monetary Fund (IMF), and World Bank that are often targeted for protest constantly change locations and lack a specific center of operation. For the homeless, the opposite is often true, since their struggles for survival and socio-spatial justice are intensely local and rarely overtly conscious of the global frame. And yet, there is an inherent quality among many street people and homeless communities that implies a sense of the macrocosmic picture, in that "they assert values and life-ways drawn from the past as both critique and shield against the alien landscape of the new, that landscape we attempt to contain and describe within the encompassing hot signifier, 'globalization'" (Gowan 2000:81). In the end, as Jeff Ferrell (2001a:177) has observed, "along Mill Avenue, across the United States, and around the world, the lessons are the same" – authority persists, but so does resistance. The macro-structures that impose values and landscapes on local communities are simultaneously susceptible to being impacted, transformed, or even perhaps dismantled by local movements, especially as these movements proliferate and begin to link strategically and in solidarity. This serves as a source of hope and inspiration for activism and scholarship focusing upon themes including homelessness, public space, globalization, and resistance. It also suggests the utility of new avenues of outreach and research that could deepen the analysis by exploring similar processes in a global context, thereby fostering the links between individuals and local communities that are contesting the forces of what has been termed "a form of postmodern colonialism" (Silbey 2001:264). To facilitate this nascent process of creating what might be called 'interconnected mobilizations,' I offer these brief vignettes from around the world.

Cases and Places: The Global Ecology of Homelessness

Homelessness is a global phenomenon, even more so in light of worldwide forces of privatization, urbanization, and corporatism. The dismantling of social safety nets (often at the behest of neoliberalism), rising housing costs, and lower real wages have all contributed to a growing number of people becoming impoverished and, in many cases, homeless. The United Nations Human Rights Commission has looked at these issues in a global context, as reported in *Third World Economics* (Raghavan 2002): "At the global level, the number of humanity's homeless or precariously sheltered persons continues to grow in step with indicators of economic inequality. To understand why this is occurring while global economic integration is creating new wealth as never before seen requires a better understanding of how and why processes of economic globalization are apparently not leading to the fulfillment of economic, social and cultural rights." This in-depth article about the consequences of globalization continues:

> "The increased competition among cities to attract capital and businesses for generating employment and sources of revenue has led to widening inequalities between cities, 'with consequent discrepancies in level of essential services provided to citizens.' In large cities, the growing competition for central spaces has also initiated gentrification and the creation of new ghettos of exclusion. In economically neglected cities and rural areas, local authorities continue to face difficult challenges with limited revenues to deal with unemployment, increased demand for social security and the need to upgrade public services. In the urban housing sector, reliance on market mechanisms has tended to result in neglect of the poor. The continued deterioration of conditions, particularly with respect to housing and related services, faced by the majority of the urban and rural poor around the world has caused tremendous concerns over unfettered globalization. . . . Privatization of essential services is an[other] aspect that warrants close attention when assessing the impact of globalization on the right to adequate housing."

Picking up on these themes, presented here are snapshots of policies and forces similar to those I have described in Tempe and other cities in the U.S. A great deal of exceptional research and commentary has been generated around these issues in recent years, with a global perspective beginning to emerge as suggested by the passage quoted above. What remains to be achieved is a systematic comparative study of various locales around the world; while such an undertaking is beyond the scope of this volume, my intention here is to suggest points of reference for further investigation. Some of what follows is amazingly concordant with what we have already seen in U.S. cities – for example, the distribution of literature by local business interests in Sweden "which urged people not to give alms to beggars" (Sahlin 2006:17) on the grounds that it does more harm than good, mirroring a discursive tactic utilized almost verbatim by the local BIDs in Tempe and Phoenix. Other details in these narratives are unique to the particular places and cultures in which they occur, although similarities may still exist – such as the relative rarity of encounters with homeless people in New Zealand juxtaposed with a municipal regulation there that is "extraordinarily sweeping, covering all manner of begging in all areas of public space at all times" (Laurenson & Collins 2007:656).

Canada: Squeezing Out the Squeegees

The first stop is our neighbor to the north, where some of the most apt ethno-geographies of street life and its spatial regulation have been generated in recent years. Of particular interest there has been the first province-wide anti-homeless regulation, passed in Ontario under the moniker of the 'Safe Streets Act.' An edited volume called *Disorderly People: Law and the Politics of Exclusion in Ontario* (Hermer & Mosher 2002:13-6) took up this issue and connected it to larger themes:

> "By their very nature, homeless people have no choice but to 'hang around' in public space, attempting to negotiate . . . spaces where they can survive and carry out subsistence activities. . . . It is one of the ironies of the *Safe Streets Act* . . . that, despite the government portrayal of squeegee kids as lazy, work-shy troublemakers, the law that they used to target them nevertheless constructs them as commercial solicitors. . . . This [and other] legislation has created new forms of regulation and surveillance, involving newly empowered agents, new powers of arrest and search, and harsher modes of punishment. And just as significant is how this legislation has

> . . . enabled a moral climate where the identification and scapegoating of 'disorderly' individuals has become a central role of government. . . . Indeed, the underlying logic that has been installed in this politics of exclusion is the forging of an unquestioned linkage between the existence and control of disorderly people and the securing of safety and security."

A subsequent essay in this volume (Mosher 2002:51) further explores themes of purification, privatization, regulation, and exclusion, concluding that "the presence of panhandlers and squeegee workers on our streets serves a deeply important function. Their presence, at least for many, spurs important questions about why and how so many people could be so destitute; about how existing policies and practices might be contributing to this; about how others (oneself included) benefit from existing arrangements; and about the nature of our obligation to strangers in need." Another essay (Ruddick 2002:56) considers how homeless people often mobilize "by being politically active, . . . by organizing themselves in social groups, by developing social networks, [and] by actively creating alternative forms of living."

Looking at anti-panhandling laws that have proliferated in Canadian cities, Collins and Blomley (2003:42) observe that such laws "may be interpreted as signaling a growing mistrust of the ideal of a truly inclusive public space and the hegemony of those private interests that assert that if cities are to compete in a global economy, they must 'purify' the urban landscape. Thus, just as the privatization of public space (for example, through public-private redevelopment partnerships and private policing and surveillance) is being lauded by urban governments, its use by the homeless and destitute for the purpose of seeking small, seemingly private transactions is being prohibited." A subsequent study of homeless 'social exclusion' in Canada (Gaetz 2004:447) completes the loop by concluding that "repressive enforcement measures meant to contain street youth delinquency are routinely enacted in the name of community and public safety. Street youth are regularly 'moved on' from public spaces; the police are called on by politicians at various levels of government to 'crack down' on squeegeeing and panhandling; and the visible presence of street youth is depicted by the media as having a negative impact on business." From Tempe to Toronto, the song remains the same.

Australia and New Zealand: The Trend Down Under

Moving from north to south, similar processes and practices have been noted, such as this take on matters in Brisbane, Australia (quoted in Lloyd & Auld 2003:340), where "'"exclusion from community space (where ownership is not in public hands) occurs not in response to illegal activity but as a response to behaviour that is seen as annoying, "anti-social," or simply involves people congregating or "hanging around." Those most often excluded from such spaces are young people, particularly homeless. . .'" (see also Malone 2002, on 'Youth Culture and Spatial Exclusion" in Australia). Further touching upon nearly every theme explored thus far, an entire issue of the Australian publication *Parity* from February 2006 looks at "Public Space and Homelessness," and includes chapters focusing on 'Neo-Liberal Ideology;' developing a 'Human Rights Framework;' the 'Privatisation of Public Space;' the use of 'Public Space for Fun and Profit;' the ways in which people are 'Excluded from Private and Public Spaces;' processes of 'Criminalising People in Public Space in Australia' as well as 'The Increasing Regulation of Young People in Public Space' and 'The Impact of Fines' on homeless people; and concludes with a call for 'Taking Back the Commons.' No rest for the weary down under.

Across the Tasman Sea, scholars in New Zealand have looked at concomitant emerging trends there. While some of these issues appear to be in an earlier stage of development, cities including Auckland, Nelson, and Wellington have in recent years "responded to the presence of homeless people in their jurisdictions, in part through adopting punitive regulations" including blanket restrictions on begging, prohibitions on public consumption of alcohol and sleeping in vehicles, and the issuance of citations for trespassing (Laurenson & Collins 2006:188), as well as prohibitions on camping in public space and squeegeeing (Laurenson & Collins 2007:657). And yet, coexisting with these punitive measures are also government-sponsored outreach programs (Laurenson & Collins 2007:660): "The fact that all three local authorities are working with service providers to address homelessness suggests a clear departure from the municipal focus on punitive regulation so clearly documented in the literature." As the authors of two recent in-depth, comparative studies ultimately conclude (Laurenson & Collins 2007:665):

> "Recent geographical research on homelessness policy has focussed, understandably, on discriminatory regulations, as part of a broader critique of urban neoliberalism and the ways in which urban space can be reworked for the benefit of capital and social elites. However, this does not mean that cities and local authorities are not also engaging in supportive, non-regulatory approaches. By identifying and discussing the non-punitive approaches to homelessness that have been adopted in New Zealand, the current research acknowledges that local authorities can and do successfully implement supportive measures to improve the position of homeless people. This approach should be encouraged and promoted alongside criticisms of anti-homeless regulations."

Similarly, as noted throughout the chapters in this work, Tempe has seen a gradual but discernable shift toward more non-punitive outreach efforts, as confirmed in a recent interview with Homeless Coordinator Theresa James (2008). While not necessarily solving larger issues such as the privatization of space and police profiling of people who appear 'out of place,' these efforts merit mention as potentially positive steps.

Europe: Regulating the Roofless

Across continental Europe similar themes emerge, perhaps more so in recent years due to the increased interconnection among national economies. Still, there are unique aspects to be found, including the subtle yet revealing terminological shifts in Latvia where homeless people are referred to as 'roofless' and public space is classified by whether it is 'open air' or 'covered with roof' (Trapenciere 2006). In recent years there, "a new category of roofless persons have appeared," namely "people who have been evicted from their apartments as a result of debts . . . or who have been evicted from denationalized buildings" (Trapenciere 2006). In Latvia, alcohol use in public spaces is prohibited, as is begging, transgressions for which people must "be taken to the police." Politicians there "emphasize the individual responsibility" perspective on homelessness, and there appears to be increasing public antipathy reflected in "strong stereotypes" based largely on appearance or odor, as a homeless woman there reflected: "Nobody likes us. The social workers are so unpolite and rude. Even in the church they try to keep away from you when you try to talk to them. The people have become so merciless" (Trapenciere 2006).

The Swedish case is even more complex, and in many ways more reminiscent of processes observed across North America. Phenomena documented there include the exclusion of homeless people from city centers; the "subtle removal of public benches in a gentrified area;" anti-begging and anti-camping laws; the nightly closure of "central blocks" of an urban area; the "interaction of city renewal, public-private partnerships, and zero tolerance in urban policing;" and the ultimate use of practices of "border control . . . to keep [an] area 'clean,'" as well as "discipline . . . to organise and control people spatially" (Sahlin 2006). In addition to curtailing the mobility and survival activities of homeless people through the use of legislation, urban design features such as 'defensible space,' and the invocation of standards of proper public 'decorum,' of particular interest are the emerging trends of privatization there, as Sahlin (2006) details:

> "Many [public-private] partnerships explicitly target the appearance of the downtown area or the 'city core,' with the sometimes less outspoken aim to attract certain kinds of people and deter others. . . . Typically, these neo-corporative organisations nowadays provide very little information and hardly any controversial news for non-members on their websites. But with their focus on profit and commerce, there are all reasons to suspect that they are not fond of homeless people in the centre, and that the goal to promote 'safety' implies exclusion of people who are blamed for causing insecurity, if not crime. . . . In this kind of partnership . . . important employers and property owners . . . gain an influence over municipal rules, norms, decisions and priorities that many residents would find undue and at odds with the principles of democracy. . . . As an element in the privatisation of public control, private security companies have partly replaced . . . the police. . . . This neo-corporatism might lead to – and speed up – a gradual displacement of the definitions of places, behaviour and legitimate control: public space becomes private, private security guards replace public police, legal behaviour becomes improper, begging is redefined as molestation, and local crime prevention councils turn into informal guardians of the new private order and profit."

A final example from the continent is Jurgen von Mahs' (2005) comparative study of homelessness in Germany and the U.S., with a specific focus on Berlin and Los Angeles. Noting at the outset that "the German system is more generous, inclusive, comprehensive, and less fragmented than that of the United States" (2005:929), it is still the case that "the numbers and characteristics of each city's corresponding homeless populations are surprisingly similar" (2005:932), explained by the author as follows (2005:941): "Although Germany has de jure maintained its welfare state at the national scale, administrations at the local scale have de facto begun to implement policies that increasingly resemble U.S. policy approaches. More specifically, there is evidence that homeless people in Germany are, similar to those in the United States, affected by serious welfare state deficiencies, displaced and criminalized by institutions of public order and safety, and contained in inhospitable urban areas, and in this way become increasingly socially and spatially excluded over time and with increasing durations of homelessness." In this sense, we begin to perceive the impact of global regulatory norms on both urban spaces and homeless people alike.

The UK: New Wrinkles on an Old Face

In many ways, the United Kingdom is the progenitor of the forces documented and discussed here. Half a millennium of vagrancy laws, poor laws, and enclosures of the commons have led seamlessly to the omnipresence of CCTV (closed-circuit surveillance cameras) in public places and a 'tough on crime' sensibility that transcends political ideologies. Recent moves include 'zero tolerance policing' that borrows heavily (although at times unspokenly) from 'broken windows' policies and reflects a "creeping militarization of the police" (Atkinson 2003:1839); "the removal of those people who tarnish [the] image" of central shopping districts (2003:1838); and a novel practice in Glasgow whereby "beggars [were] constantly moved on, arrested or even marched to the nearest charity collection point where they were forced to hand over all of their money" (2003:1838). As in other locales, such emerging strategies are often attributed to factors including "footloose capital investment" and "the restructuring of welfare regimes," with the net effect being that the desire for "attractive urban spaces . . . may drive responses that clear or bar undesirable users" as a policy-driven "form of street-level city image manipulation" intended to draw greater "capital investment" (2003:1840). Also noted is an interesting twist called 'diverted giving' which "was set up to encourage sympathetic passers-by with collection points to help beggars through local agencies rather than giving to them directly and thereby supporting drug and alcohol habits" (2003:1838). Interestingly, the city of Tempe (at the behest of the DTC) is considering a proposal to place signs on parking-type meters encouraging people who want to give alms to homeless people to place the monies there instead of giving directly to someone on the street, with the pledge that funds collected in this manner will be used to support legitimate service providers and not to sustain destructive lifestyles (James 2008). Sensing the potential impact of BIDs such as the DTC on policies across the Atlantic, Atkinson (2003:1840) concludes that "[i]nterest in public spaces is growing and recent proposals for US-style [BIDs] by the UK government continue a trend which appears to be privatising public spaces to make them cleaner and safer. However, BIDs have been criticised for setting up private police forces that have been used to exclude groups such as the homeless."

An even more sinister innovation than 'diverted giving' and BIDs are ASBOs, or 'anti-social behavior orders,' which have "the potential not only to further constrict the rapidly diminishing public space available to the homeless, but to overtly criminalize poverty and homelessness" (Winford 2006). These court orders can be obtained by "police forces, local councils, housing trusts, and 'registered social landlords'" for any behavior deemed "likely to cause harassment, alarm, or distress;" the alleged behavior need not in itself be criminal, but once cemented in a court order, violations are punishable by up to five years in prison (Winford 2006). Not surprisingly, poor people are especially vulnerable and are often evicted under such orders, which generally serve to limit certain behaviors (e.g., drinking or cursing) for some duration in a particular place; equally apparent is that "ASBOs disproportionately impact homeless people," as Winford describes:

> "[O]ne homeless man has been banned from being drunk or buying or consuming alcohol anywhere in England and Wales. A homeless woman was given an order banning her from begging or sleeping in Reading town centre for two years. A 36 year old homeless man was given an order forbidding him from sleeping on Manchester's streets or asking 'earnestly and humbly' for change. . . . A homeless man in Birmingham, forbidden from begging, breached his order and was jailed for

> two years. Having served eight months he was released but soon breached the order again and was jailed for three years, a total of five years for what is . . . a non-criminal offense."

As with many policies in the U.S., Winford concludes that "ASBOs by no means address the causes of homelessness. As a new basis for eviction from housing, they contribute to the problem of homelessness. But they go further than this, effectively criminalizing homelessness."

Latin America: Whose Space?

In all of these brief international examples, it is of course impossible to summarize events on an entire continent in a few paragraphs. Still, trends do seem to emerge at least regionally if not nationally, and there are global forces at work that tend to create similar outcomes in far-flung locales. For instance, a 2004 conference took up the broadly-construed question of 'The End of Public Space in the Latin American City?' and asked participants to discuss whether public spaces "are being eroded or reshaped by neo-liberalism, by the progressive withdrawal of the state from traditional arenas of social policy, . . . by changes to consumption patterns, planning policies or globalisation." One of the presenters looked at the impact of privatization and fragmentation on Mexico City, observing that it "encapsulates what we might call the 'yin/yang' of globalization – it houses both the best and the worst of our global future. Its elite neighborhoods are among the most impressively designed urban communities in the Americas; [yet] its poverty is severe" (Herzog 2004:6). Duly noting this growing sense of polarization, the presenter noted that "examples of commodified tourism spaces abound," but still "there are many qualities that continue to make Mexican public space unique," including: Mexico's cultural affection for the past; a tendency toward 'greening' its public spaces; the widespread performance of daily rituals in urban public space; the longstanding acceptance and use of public space as a site of political protest; and the strong embrace of art in public space, including murals (2004:7). Thus, "while public space in Mexico City (and other large cities in Mexico) is compromised by globalizing influences such as privatization and commodification," there are still a plethora of "culturally unique practices that allow Mexican urban space to retain some of its dynamic qualities" (2004:8).

Turning to the situation in South America, another presenter noted that "several revitalization projects have been implemented in Brazilian major cities, most with a cultural and recreational bias," including one in particular that combined "historic preservation with cultural and economic revitalization [through] an alliance of city planners and local retailers against gentrification and displacement" (del Rio 2004:14). Another unique example cited was a 1995 initiative "to integrate squatter settlements into the surrounding neighborhoods . . . by providing the communities with physical upgrading of public spaces, complementary social projects, and distribution of land titles" (2004:14). In the end, a hopeful assessment was offered (2004:15): "While most of the contradictions of a global and free-economy are certainly present in Brazilian cities, our studies also reveal that a number of government-sponsored projects are producing urban areas that are more livable, attractive, and responsive to communities. While private space becomes more entrenched and sometimes expands over the public realm, public space in Brazil seems to be alive and well."

Back in Mexico, however, a look at so-called 'street children' – youths who "generate income by begging, mugging, washing windshields and doing other odd jobs" and "take shelter in out-of-sight or disregarded spaces such as abandoned buildings, accessible rooftops, or subway ventilation tunnels" – painted a less rosy picture (Magazine 2004:25). In this instance, the influence of neoliberalism has been to leave the city government strapped to the point of being unable to manage its public spaces, leading to the "abandonment of public space to the likes of street children as the flipside to privatized security in middle- and upper-class gated communities," and constituting a resultant "loss of public space, although not to privatization but to neglect" (2004:26-7). In what seems a fairly unsympathetic take on children who due to larger cultural and economic forces wind up living on the streets, the presenter noted their "disheveled appearance, as well as their odors" and how these "detract from the intended attractiveness of parks and other public spaces" as well as how "their presence constitutes an apparent and real threat to the security of certain citizens, at times restricting their movements in and use of public spaces" (2004:27). Paralleling the views of American scholars such as Robert Ellickson (1996), these sorts of analyses at least possess the virtue of reflecting a diversity of perspectives that illuminate important issues. Indeed, if we are interesting in deconstructing the potential hegemony of globalization, multiplicity would seem to be a desirable attribute.

South Africa: Out in the Cold, Yet Cleaning Up Cape Town

From promise to challenge, and vice versa, the South African experience is uniquely disturbing. Following the dismantling of the apartheid regime, many suddenly found themselves homeless, with the *New York Times* reporting an estimate of 8 million over a decade ago (Daley 1996). The article described vast shanty towns, court-ordered evictions, and modest shacks being burned. An estimated quarter million homeless people were living in downtown Johannesburg alone, squatting in parking lots and near garbage dumps. Many had hoped to secure small plots for building more stable shacks, but as of 1996 even these meager opportunities had not yet developed, indicating a profound human rights crisis across the newly-emerging nation. Not being especially familiar with the intricacies of this region, I was hopeful that the passage of almost twelve years might have brought improvement, however an article from 2007 (IRIN) said otherwise:

> "An unusually severe blast of winter weather has swept across South Africa, killing at least 17 people through exposure and highlighting the country's ongoing and chronic housing shortages. South Africa's several million strong homeless population was particularly hard hit as temperatures plunged to record lows. The government has been on a furious building spree during the dozen years since the fall of apartheid, but the housing shortfall still stands at an estimated 2.5 million homes. According to the Centre on Housing Rights and Evictions, 7.5 million South Africans lack access to adequate housing and secure tenure in South Africa. 'We have 14 shelters and house about 1500 people per night,' said Hassan Khan, director of the Haven Night Shelters. 'We are under a tremendous amount of pressure to care for the many who need it, especially during the winter months when sleeping on the streets is no longer an option.' Khan said his group was working closely with both [governmental] authorities to find a long-term solution to South Africa's almost overwhelming housing woes. 'I would have to say the problem is getting worse,' Khan said. 'If people give a little bit of money to children on the streets, they are actually increasing the problem because they are making it possible for someone to continue living on the streets, but that is no solution. We need to get these people off the streets for good.'"

In the face of this mass hardship, it was surprising to find a different set of concerns down on the coast in Cape Town, where an October 2005 article from CapeTownMagazine.com described how the "inner city is set for an extensive facelift" under the guidance of the Cape Town Partnership (CTP), whose director noted that "security and cleanliness are key issues." This revealing article goes on to note that "the CTP and the city are discussing the future of the Grand Parade, Cape Town's oldest public space;" that the "CTP has employed homeless people living on the Parade as cleaners;" and that "the deployment of four security guards, housed in a prefabricated kiosk on the Parade, had been successful in deterring crime." Although these are themes familiar in many U.S. cities, in Cape Town the director of the CTP also mentioned the priority that locals have in the development process, as well as the desire to create affordable housing as part of the overall plan. However, a subsequent scholarly investigation (Spocter 2007) analyzed "the closure of urban public space in Cape Town" through forces of "citizen-driven privatisation," noting that such practices have had a long pedigree that pre-dates the end of apartheid.

Japan: Lost in Transition

And so we complete this global circuit of telltale vignettes by arriving in Asia – Japan, in fact, where a society of apparent abundance (and in many ways a model for the global economy) confronts new issues:

> "Japan's homeless population barely exceeded 1000 during the economic heydays of the 1980s. Today, after a decade of slow growth and recession, more than 25,000 people are living on the streets, with thousands more teetering on the brink. Japan's homeless problem remains tiny compared with other countries – homeless Americans, for example, number more than 2 million – but it is a hot issue on this prosperous island nation of 130 million simply because it is now too obvious to ignore. The economic miracle has turned to a morass, and the evidence is sky blue. That's the color of the tarpaulins once seen primarily at building sites but now in widespread use as makeshift tents for the homeless. Hide Nakajima once ran the presses for a Kyoto printing company. Three years ago the company downsized. Nakajima lost his job. Now 39, Nakajima lives beneath one of the many bridges spanning

> Kyoto's Kamo River. His self-made home is a simple, wood-frame box – 4 feet high and covering an area the size of a single bed. The exterior, like the dozens of other homes along the river, is wrapped in a blue tarp. Some suggest Japan's burgeoning homeless population symbolizes a more profound problem. They say that in Japan's post-war haste to rebuild, traditional values like honor, respect, teamwork and taking care of the less fortunate were either ignored or forgotten. 'People are cold,' says Nakajima. 'Because we have no home they think we're lazy and don't want to work. I used to think the same thing, though'" (Donison 2002).

In keeping with their reputation as efficient innovators, a recent online article (Alter 2006) observed: "The homeless are everywhere, even in tidy Japan, where many have developed ingenious houses that quickly fold away and can be easily rebuilt after police raids. Some of them are quite elegant, with tatami mats and bonsai shrubs. Architect Kyohei Sakaguchi has been studying and documenting them. 'These homes embody simplicity, functionality and are at one with their environment. . . . I don't want to idealize the situation homeless people find themselves in,' he said. 'But in a world where most of us live in mass-produced, concrete boxes, Zero Yen Houses are precious works of art. They deserve to be recognized.'" Along these lines, a documentary filmmaker from Germany further added (in Verena 2007): "I am always amazed that such blue villages can exist without people coming and disturbing them, destroying their houses, stealing from their gathered goods and accepting that public space is used for 'alternative housing' in such a peaceful way. Well, obviously there are official clearings and people do get pushed away, which is a very sensitive issue, but still I am always impressed that they manage to stay for quite a while and obviously build something up!" At the end of the day, however, familiar themes of regulation and resistance emerge:

> "The Osaka Municipal Government is today removing homeless communities from two of its parks in preparation for the World Rose Convention. Around a third of Japan's 25,000 homeless are based in Osaka, and these evictions are meeting mass resistance. 'We cannot tolerate such violent acts,' about 100 people shouted as the city government started dismantling the tents. Many homeless people in Japan live in stable tent

> communities in the parks of its larger cities. However, Japan has increasingly been attempting to remove its homeless park communities from view permanently. The parks are the refuge of people displaced by the brutal economy of Japan. The homeless receive no help from government or political parties, and are not eligible for social welfare. The winter here is incredibly severe, and the tent cities and soup kitchens that the homeless themselves organise have been attacked by the city authorities. [As one homeless resident observed:] 'The homeless struggle in Osaka is under severe attack [and] the street demonstration was very heavily contained by many police, but still we resist. We understand the limitations of fighting our struggle so that we the dispossessed can fit into the brutal economic system. We want our whole lives as ours, not workfare, not welfare. We want an entire change from this capitalist system'" (libcom.org 2006).

Cities of the Present . . . and the Future?

This seems like an appropriately defiant note to conclude on, having by now at least glimpsed an emerging worldwide trend that reads as such: the workings of the global economy contribute to the creation of homeless people; financially-strapped cities compete to draw capital investment; urban development norms of 'safety' and 'order' are established to make public spaces more attractive for retail and upscale tenancies; homeless people are seen as disorderly and unsafe, and thus are regulated and sought to be removed from view; once-public spaces in urban centers are privatized to allow a greater degree of surveillance, control, and exclusionary authority; and yet against all odds homeless people and their advocates often fight back! This albeit oversimplified narrative nonetheless does serve as a crudely approximate snapshot of city life from Melbourne to Mexico City, from Stockholm to Seattle, and from Tokyo to Tempe. The question, of course, then becomes what the future will hold, both worldwide and in local communities where global norms are simultaneously created and reflected. In-depth investigations of current conditions might lead us to predict 'more of the same,' but that would be a very linear rendering and, in any event, would reflect a profound failure of the imagination. Critical research can reflect the past and present, but the future has yet to be written.

REFERENCES

ACLU (American Civil Liberties Union). 1997. "Boulder Considers Amending Sidewalk Ordinance," 12/4/97.

----------. 1999. "The City of Brotherly WHAT?" *Freedom Network*, 1/19/99.

Adler, Patricia A., and Peter. 1994. "Observational Techniques," in Denzin & Lincoln (eds.), *Qualitative Research*.

Alter, Lloyd. 2006. "Housing Built by Japanese Homeless an Art Form," *Design & Architecture*, 3/18/06.

Altheide, David L. 1996. *Qualitative Media Analysis*. Newbury Park: Sage.

----------, and John M. Johnson. 1994. "Criteria for Assessing Interpretive Validity in Qualitative Research," in Denzin & Lincoln (eds.), *Qualitative Research*.

Amin, Samir, et al. 1990. *Transforming the Revolution: Social Movements and the World System*. NY: Monthly Review.

Amole, Tustin. 1998. "Loitering Law Would Be No Idle Threat," *Denver Rocky Mountain News*, 8/17/98.

Amster, Randall. 1998. "Taking a Stand to Keep Sitting Legal," *ASU State Press*, 9/3/98.

----------. 1999a. "Criminalizing Social Gaffes Doesn't Sit Well," *Arizona Republic*, 1/26/99.

----------. 1999b. "Stand is Unworthy on Tempe Slackers," *Arizona Republic*, 6/2/99.

----------. 1999c. "Town Lake is for the Birds," *ASU State Press*, 9/8/99.

----------. 1999d. "Sleepless in Tempe? Try the City Jail," *ASU State Press*, 11/30/99.

----------. 1999e. "Ethnography at the Margins: Vagabonds, Transients, and the Specter of Resistance," *Humboldt Journal of Social Relations*, v25/n1.

----------. 1999f. "A Holiday Lesson from Roland of Lazarus," *Arizona Republic*, 12/19/99.

----------. 2000a. "Nirvana?! Don't Look for It in Downtown Tempe," *Arizona Republic*, 3/15/00.

----------. 2000b. "Tempe Destroying Its Public Spaces," *Arizona Republic*, 4/5/00.

----------. 2007. "Prison Protester Epitomizes Value of Free Speech," *Prescott Daily Courier*, 10/15/07.

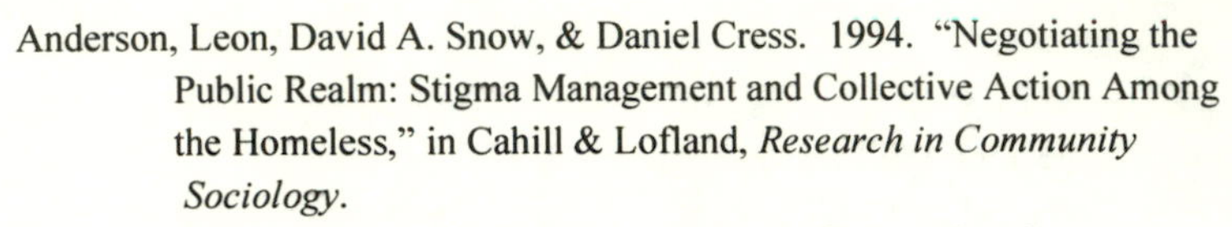
Anderson, Leon, David A. Snow, & Daniel Cress. 1994. "Negotiating the Public Realm: Stigma Management and Collective Action Among the Homeless," in Cahill & Lofland, *Research in Community Sociology*.

Anleu, Sharyn L. Roach. 2000. *Law and Social Change*. CA: Sage.

Arizona Republic (editorial). 1998a. "Ambience of the Sidewalks: Rules Threaten Artistic Tempe," 11/8/98.

----------. 1998b. "Ordinance is Not the Right Answer to Mill Slackers," 12/16/98.

----------. 1999. "Sidewalk is for Pedestrians, Too," 5/18/99.

----------. 2000. "Is Full-service 'Campus' a Solution for Homeless?" 4/22/00.

----------. 2001. "Give Hope to the Homeless," 12/10/01.

----------. 2002. "A Symbolic Lift for Homeless," 11/22/02.

----------. 2003. "Campus for Dignity," 8/22/03.

----------. 2004. "Homeless Struggle in Tempe," 12/18/04.

Arnold, Kathleen Ryder. 1998. *Homelessness, Citizenship, and Identity.* UCLA (doctoral dissertation).

----------. 2004. *Homelessness, Citizenship, and Identity: The Uncanniness of Late Modernity*. NY: SUNY Press.

Arrigo, Bruce A. 1998. "Shattered Lives and Shelter Lies? Anatomy of Research Deviance in Homeless Programming and Policy," in Ferrell & Hamm (eds.), *Ethnography at the Edge*.

Arrington, Vanessa. 1996. "Law Does Not Sit Well for Some in Seattle," *Palo Alto Weekly*, 7/19/96.

ASA News. 2004. "Exposure to the Homeless Increases Sympathetic Public Attitudes," *American Sociological Association*, 3/22/04.

Associated Press. 1999. "Civil Libertarians Sue Philadelphia Over New 'Sidewalk Behavior' Law," 1/20/99.

ASU State Press (editorial). 1999. "Ordinance Attacks Homeless," 1/19/99.

----------. 2000a. "Tempe Ignores its Homeless Population," 4/17/00.

----------. 2000b. "Yuppieland: Tempe's Newest Theme Park," 4/26/00.

----------. 2000c. "City, DTC Ignore Homeless Problem," 10/23/00.

----------. 2004. "Little Hope for Tempe Homeless," 2/23/04.

Atkinson, Rowland. 2003. "Domestication by *Cappuccino* or a Revenge on Urban Space? Control and Empowerment in the Management of Public Spaces," *Urban Studies*, v40/n9.

Bachler, Aaron. 2000. "Downtown Plan for Tempe Caters to Corporate Greed," *Arizona Republic*, 9/12/00.

Bachmann, Steve. 2001. *Lawyers, Law, and Social Change.* Bloomington, IN: Unlimited Publishing.

Baker, Donald E. 1990. "'Anti-Homeless' Legislation: Unconstitutional Efforts to Punish the Homeless," *University of Miami Law Review*, v45/p417.

Barajas, Victor. 1999. "Tempe's Got the Hookup," *Arizona Republic*, 8/19/99.

Barak, Gregg. 1991. *Gimme Shelter: A Social History of Homelessness in Contemporary America*. NY: Praeger.

Barber, Marsha. 1998. "No Shoes, No Shirt – No Rights?" *Asheville Mountain Xpress*, 11/18/98.

Barclay, Harold. 1990. *People Without Government: An Anthropology of Anarchy*. Seattle: Left Bank Books.

Baron, Jane B. 2004. "Homelessness as a Property Problem," *The Urban Lawyer*, v36/n2.

Baudelaire, Charles. 1974. *Selected Poems* (G. Wagner, trans.). NY: Grove.

Bauman, Zygmunt. 1993. *Postmodern Ethics*. Cambridge, MA: Blackwell.

----------. 1995. "The Stranger Revisited – and Revisiting," in *Life in Fragments: Essays in Postmodern Morality*, MA: Blackwell.

----------. 1996. "From Pilgrim to Tourist – or a Short History of Identity," in S. Hall & P. DuGay (eds.), *Questions of Cultural Identity*, UK: Sage.

----------. 1999. *Globalization: The Human Consequences*. NY: Columbia University Press.

----------. 2000. "Social Issues of Law and Order," *British Journal of Criminology*, v40/p205.

Baumohl, Jim (ed.). 1996. *Homelessness in America*. US: Oryx Press.

Beaver, Michelle. 2000a. "Mill Avenue Development Sends Mom and Pop Shops Packing, Creates Upscale 'Urban Flavor,'" *ASU State Press*, 8/25/00.

----------. 2000b. "Service Group Aids Tempe's Homeless Youths," *ASU State Press*, 10/23/00.

Becker, Howard S. 1970. *Sociological Work: Method and Substance*. Chicago, IL: Aldine.

Beckett, Katherine, and Steve Herbert. 2007. "Dealing with Disorder: Social Control in the Post-Industrial City," unpublished manuscript.

Berkley, Blair J., and John R. Thayer. 2000. "Policing Entertainment Districts," *Policing: An International Journal of Police Strategies & Management*, v23/n4.

Bey, Hakim. 1991. *T.A.Z.: The Temporary Autonomous Zone, Ontological Anarchy, Poetic Terrorism*. NY: Autonomedia.

"Bill." 2000. Interview on Mill Avenue. 4/24/00.

Black, Donald. 1976. *The Behavior of Law*. NY: Academic Press.

Bland, Karina. 1998. "Street Kids Get Lifeline," *Arizona Republic*, 10/22/98.

Blasi, Gary L. 1987. "Litigation on Behalf of the Homeless: Systematic Approaches," in *The Rights of the Homeless*, Practicing Law Institute, H4-5023.

----------. 2007. *Policing Our Way Out of Homelessness? The First Year of the Safer Cities Initiative on Skid Row*, report, 9/24/07.

Blomley, Nicholas K. 1994. *Law, Space, and the Geographies of Power.* NY: Guilford.

----------. 2004. *Unsettling the City: Urban Land and the Politics of Property.* NY: Routledge.

----------. 2006. "Editorial: Homelessness and the Delusions of Property," *Transactions of the Institute of British Geographers*, v31/n1.

"Blossom." 1998. Interview on ASU Campus. 4/20/98.

Blumer, Herbert. 1969. *Symbolic Interactionism: Perspective and Method.* Englewood, NJ: Prentice Hall.

Blythe, Anne. 1998. "Downtown Problems Could Get New Fixes," *Chapel Hill News*, 9/27/98.

Bookchin, Murray. 1991. *The Ecology of Freedom: The Emergence and Dissolution of Hierarchy.* NY: Black Rose.

Borchard, Kurt. 2005. *The Word on the Street: Homeless Men in Las Vegas.* Las Vegas, NV: University of Nevada Press.

Boxall, Bettina. 2001. "Downtown Denizens Try Liberal Town's Patience," *Los Angeles Times*, 2/11/01.

Brinegar, Sarah J. 2000. "Response to Homelessness in Tempe, Arizona: Public Opinion and Government Policy," *Urban Geography*, v21/n6.

Brown, Kristen. 1999. "Outlawing Homelessness," *National Housing Institute, Shelterforce Online*, July/August.

Brown, Thomas Ford. 1997. "Ideological Hegemony and Global Governance," *Journal of World-Systems Research*, v3.

Burawoy, Michael, et al. (eds.). 1991. *Ethnography Unbound: Power and Resistance in the Modern Metropolis.* LA: University of Calif. Press.

----------. 2000. *Global Ethnography: Forces, Connections, and Imaginations in a Postmodern World.* LA: University of California Press.

Burch, Claire. 1998. "Tales of Young Urban Squatters," *Street Spirit*, v4/n8.

Buric-Adam, Mirsada. 2004. "City Police Suspend Nine of Their Own," *Prescott Daily Courier*, 2/18/04.

Cahill, Spencer E., & Lyn H. Lofland. 1994. *Research in Community Sociology: The Community of the Streets.* CT: JAI.

CapeTownMagazine.com. 2005. "Cape Town Inner City is Set for an Extensive Facelift," 10/5/05.

Capra, Fritjof. 1991. *The Tao of Physics* (3d ed.). Boston, MA: Shambala.

Carlson, Coralie. 2004. "Key West Running Out of Room for the Homeless," *Arizona Republic*, 3/8/04.

Carr, Stephen, et al. 1992. *Public Space*. NY: Cambridge University Press.

Cart, Julie. 2001. Interview at Salvation Army. 2/23/01.

Chew, Sing C., and Robert A. Denemark (eds.). 1996. *The Underdevelopment of Development: Essays in Honor of Andre Gunder Frank.* UK: Sage.

Christensen, Ellen. 1997. "A Sit-in Against Sit-lie," *Palo Alto Weekly*, 4/23/97.

Christopherson, Jesse. 2003. "Homeless, Others Protest City's 'No Camping' Ordinance," *ASU Web Devil*, 12/1/03.

Ciarimboli, Erin. 1999. "Federal Judge Halts Enforcement of Sidewalk Sitting Ban," *Freedom Forum*, 6/3/99.

Clark, John. 1998. "The Tao of Anarchy," *Fifth Estate*, v33/n1, Summer.

Clastres, Pierre. 1994. *Archeology of Violence.* Brooklyn, NY: Semiotext(e).

Clifford, James. 1988. *The Predicament of Culture: Twentieth Century Ethnography, Literature, and Art.* Cambridge, MA: Harvard.

Cohn, Ari. 2007. "Homeless Count Conducted in Quest for $20M from U.S.," *East Valley Tribune*, 3/19/07.

Collins, Damian, and Nicholas Blomley. 2003. "Private Needs and Public Space: Politics, Poverty, and Anti-Panhandling By-Laws in Canadian Cities," in *New Perspectives on the Public-Private Divide* (Law Commission of Canada, ed.), Vancouver: UBC Press.

Comaroff, John and Jean. 1992. *Ethnography and the Historical Imagination.* San Francisco: Westview .

Conner, Roger L. 1999. "Disorder Laws and the Courts: Review of Recent Developments," communityinterest.org/publications/rcreport.htm.

Cox, Anthony A. 2000. "Downtown Changes Sanitize Tempe," *Arizona Republic*, 1/25/00.

CPTED. 2001. www.tempe.gov/tdsi/Planning/CPTED/cpted1.htm.

Crawford, Margaret. 1995. "Contesting the Public Realm: Struggles Over Public Space in Los Angeles," *Journal of Architectural Education*, v49/n1.

Daley, Suzanne. 1996. "South Africa Losing Battle to House Homeless," *New York Times*, 5/3/96.

Daniels, Wes. 1997. "'Derelicts,' Recurring Misfortune, Economic Hard Times and Lifestyle Choices: Judicial Images of Homeless Litigants and Implications for Legal Advocates," *Buffalo Law Review*, v45.

"Dante." 2000. Interview on Mill Avenue. 4/17/00.

Davis, Kristina. 2002. "Police to Target Panhandlers, Sidewalk Sitters," *ASU State Press*, 2/20/02.

----------. 2004. "Homeless Advocates Call for Shelter," *EV Tribune*, 2/22/04.

Davis, Mike. 1990. *City of Quartz: Excavating the Future in Los Angeles.* NY: Verso.

----------. 1991. "A Logic Like Hell's: Being Homeless in Los Angeles," *UCLA Law Review*, v39/p325.

----------. 1992. "Fortress Los Angeles: The Militarization of Urban Space," in Sorkin (ed.), *Variations on a Theme Park.*

----------. 1998. *Ecology of Fear: Los Angeles and the Imagination of Disaster*. NY: Metropolitan.

Debord, Guy. 1983. *Society of the Spectacle.* Detroit, MI: Black & Red.

Dehavenon, Anna Lou (ed.). 1996. *There's No Place Like Home: Anthropological Perspectives on Housing and Homelessness in the United States.* CT: Bergin & Garvey.

Delaney, David, Richard T. Ford, and Nicholas Blomley. 2001. "Preface: Where is Law?" in N. Blomley, D. Delaney, & R.T. Ford (eds.), *The Legal Geographies Reader: Law, Power, and Space*, UK: Blackwell.

del Rio, Vicente. 2004. "Urban Design and the Future of Public Space in the Brazilian City," in Jones & Ward (eds.), *Conference Proceedings: The End of Public Space in the Latin American City?*, University of Texas at Austin.

Denzin, Norman K., and Yvonna S. Lincoln (eds.). 1994. *Handbook of Qualitative Research.* CA: Sage.

Diaz, Elvia. 2000. "Tempe Eyes Homeless Center," *Arizona Republic*, 9/5/00.

----------. 2001a. "A Step in Helping Homeless," *Arizona Republic*, 3/19/01.

----------. 2001b. "Council to Consider Shelter for Homeless," *Arizona Republic*, 10/18/01.

Diehl, Michael. 2005. "Berkeley Protesters Demand Shelter from the Storm," *Street Spirit*, March.

Diesing, Paul. 1991. *How Does Social Science Work?: Reflections on Practice.* Pittsburgh, PA: Univ. of Pittsburgh Press.

Donison, Les. 2002. "Japanese Introduced to Homelessness," *Pittsburgh Post-Gazette*, 8/5/02.

Doolen, Dina. 1999. "Most Vagabonds Well-behaved, Say Three Who Live on the Streets," *Tucson Citizen*, 9/14/99.

Drucker, Susan J., and Gary Gumpert (eds.). 1997. *Voices in the Street: Explorations in Gender, Media, and Public Space*. Cresskill, NJ: Hampton Press.

DTC (Downtown Tempe Community, Inc.). 1998. "Daytime Security Program Update," *Board of Directors,* 11/98.

----------. 1999. "Offering a Helping Hand," *Downtowner*, v3/n1.

----------. 2000a. "T.E.A.M. Helps Tempe Grow," *Downtowner*, v4/n1.

----------. 2000b. "Everywhere They're Needed," *Downtowner*, v4/n4.

----------. 2000c. "Downtown Tempe *Is* Fantasy Land," *Downtowner*, v4/n6.

----------. 2001a. "State of the Downtown," *Downtowner*, v5/n3.

----------. 2001b. "Giving the Downtown a Face Lift," *Downtowner*, v5/n3.

----------. 2002a. "Police Crackdown on Aggressive Panhandling," *Downtowner*, February.

----------. 2002b. "Businesses May Aid in Aggressive Panhandling Arrests," *DTC Insider*, February.

Duff, Audrey. 1999. "This Ain't No KOA," *The Austin Chronicle*, v15/n24.

Duneier, Mitchell. 1999. *Sidewalk*. NY: Farrar, Strauss & Giroux.

Dunn, Dan. 1999a. "Sidewalk-sitting Ban About Our Uneasiness, Not Security," *East Valley Tribune*, 1/23/99.

----------. 1999b. "Park Yourself on Tempe's Sidewalks While You Can," *East Valley Tribune*, 5/5/99.

Durrenberger, Dan. 1999a. "Non-bathers Shouldn't Set Agenda," *Arizona Republic*, 1/22/99.

----------. 1999b. "ASU Activist Driven by Ego," *Arizona Republic*, 2/5/99.

----------. 1999c. "Tempe's Homeless Nearly Invisible, Always Present," *Arizona Republic*, 12/10/99.

----------. 2000. "In Search of Urban Nirvana," *Arizona Republic*, 3/3/00.

----------. 2005. "Tempe On Way to Its Potential," *Arizona Republic*, 3/11/05.

East Valley Tribune (editorial). 2000. "Find a Way to Curb Slackers," 2/3/00.

----------. 2001a. "Too Broad a Law," 4/2/01.

----------. 2001b. "Find Middle Ground to Sit On," 5/19/01.

Eaton-Robb, Pat. 2007. "Homeless Families on the Rise, with No End in Sight," *Associated Press*, 10/8/07.

Einstein, Albert. 1954. *Ideas and Opinions*. NY: Bonanza.

Ellickson, Robert C. 1996. "Controlling Chronic Misconduct in City Spaces: Of Panhandlers, Skid Rows, and Public-Space Zoning," *Yale Law Journal*, v105/p1165.

Emerson, Ralph Waldo. 1969. *Selected Prose and Poetry* (2d ed.). NY: Holt, Rinehart, and Winston.

Enright, Robert. 1998. "'Incorporated' a Word that Tells All About DTC," *Arizona Republic*, 3/22/98.

Fabyankovic, Janet. 2000. "Alternatives to Homeless Criminalization," *Law and Order: The Magazine for Police Management*, v48/n8.

Faith, Bill. 1999. "Criminalizing Homeless is No Solution," *Columbus Dispatch*, 12/25/99.

Farrell, Chad. 2005. "Sharing Neighborhoods: Order & Disorder in Homeless-Domiciled Encounters," *American Behavioral Scientist*, v48/n8.

Fernandez, Luis A. 2008. *Policing Dissent: Social Control and the Anti-Globalization Movement.* NJ: Rutgers University Press.

Ferrell, Jeff. 1993. *Crimes of Style: Urban Graffiti and the Politics of Criminality.* NY: Garland.

----------. 1994. "Confronting the Agenda of Authority: Critical Criminology, Anarchism, and Urban Graffiti," in G. Barak (ed.), *Varieties of Criminology*, London: Praeger.

----------. 1995. "Urban Graffiti: Crime, Control, and Resistance," *Youth & Society*, v27/n1/p73.

----------. 1997. "Criminological *Verstehen*: Inside the Immediacy of Crime," *Justice Quarterly*, v14/n1.

----------. 1998a. "Youth, Crime, and Cultural Space," *Social Justice*, v24/n4/p21.

----------. 1998b. "Freight Train Graffiti: Subculture, Crime, Dislocation," *Justice Quarterly*, v15/n4.

----------. 1999. "Anarchist Criminology and Social Justice," in B. Arrigo (ed.), *Social Justice/Criminal Justice: The Maturation of Critical Theory in Law, Crime and Deviance*, NY: West.

----------. 2001a. "Remapping the City: Public Identity, Cultural Space, and Social Justice," *Contemporary Justice Review*, v4/n2.

----------. 2001b. *Tearing Down the Streets: Adventures in Urban Anarchy.* NY: Palgrave.

----------. 2006. *Empire of Scrounge: Inside the Urban Underground of Dumpster Diving, Trash Picking, and Street Scavenging.* NY: New York University Press.

----------, and Clinton R. Sanders (eds.). 1995. *Cultural Criminology.* MA: Northeastern University Press.

----------, and Mark S. Hamm (eds.). 1998. *Ethnography at the Edge: Crime, Deviance, and Field Research.* MA: Northeastern University Press.

Finberg, Kathy. 1998a. "Proposed Anti-Slacker Measure is Anti-Tempe," *Arizona Republic*, 11/17/98.

----------. 1998b. "Downtown Tempe on Upswing," *Arizona Republic*, 12/1/98.

Fiscus, Chris. 2000. "Upscale Living Coming to Downtown Tempe," *Arizona Republic*, 4/25/00.

Fitzpatrick, Kevin, and Mark LaGory. 2000. *Unhealthy Places: The Ecology of Risk in the Urban Landscape*. NY: Routledge.

Fitzpatrick, Tom. 1993. "Sidewalk Stories," *Phoenix New Times*, 5/19/93.

Flashes. 1998. "Finally, a Solution," *Phoenix New Times*, 11/19/98.

Foscarinis, Maria. 1996. "Downward Spiral: Homelessness and Its Criminalization," *Yale Law & Policy Review*, v14/p1.

----------, and Richard Herz. 1995. "The Criminalization of Homelessness: An Overview of Litigation Strategies," *Clearinghouse Review*, v29/n8-9.

----------, Kelly Cunningham-Bowers, and Kristen E. Brown. 1999. "Out of Sight – Out of Mind? The Continuing Trend Toward the Criminalization of Homelessness," *Georgetown Journal on Poverty Law & Policy*, v6/p145.

Foucault, Michel. 1977. *Discipline and Punish: The Birth of the Prison.* NY: Vintage.

----------. 1988. "The Political Technology of Individuals," in *Technologies of the Self*, MA: University of Massachusetts Press.

Fox, Dennis. 1991. "Law Against Social Change," dennisfox.net.

Frug, Gerald. 2001. "A Legal History of Cities," in N. Blomley, D. Delaney, & R.T. Ford (eds.), *The Legal Geographies Reader: Law, Power, and Space*, UK: Blackwell.

Gaetz, Stephen. 2004. "Safe Streets for Whom? Homeless Youth, Social Exclusion, and Criminal Victimization," *Canadian Journal of Criminology and Criminal Justice*, v46/n4.

Galindo, Steve. 2000. "California Copy Replaces Old Mill Avenue," *ASU State Press*, 3/22/00.

Garfinkel, Harold. 1987. *Studies in Ethnomethodology.* UK: Blackwell.

Gately, Edward. 2000. "Tempe's Lap of Luxury," *East Valley Tribune*, 4/9/00.

Gaura, Maria Alicia. 1994. "Santa Cruz Eases Panhandler Law," *San Francisco Chronicle*, 7/28/94.

Gilstrap, Peter. 1995. "Mill Rats," *Phoenix New Times*, 12/7/95.

Glaser, Gary. 1987. *Justiceville.* Berkeley, CA: University of California Extension Media (VHS).

Goffman, Erving. 1963. *Behavior in Public Places: Notes on the Social Organization of Gatherings*. NY: Free Press.

----------. 1971. *Relations in Public: Microstudies of the Public Order.* NY: Basic Books.

Goldberg, David Theo (ed.). 1995. *Ethical Theory and Social Issues.* Fort Worth, TX: Harcourt Brace.

Goodman, Peter S. 1996. "Berkeley is Set to Curb Sidewalk Sitters," *Washington Post*, 12/7/96.

Gowan, Teresa. 2000. "Excavating 'Globalization' from Street Level: Homeless Men Recycle Their Pasts," in Burawoy et al. (eds.), *Global Ethnography.*

Graeber, David. 2004. *Fragments of an Anarchist Anthropology.* UK: Prickly Paradigm Press.

Guattari, Felix. 1996. *Soft Subversions* (S. Lotringer, ed.). NY: Semiotext(e).

Hafetz, Jonathan L. 2003. "Homeless Legal Advocacy: New Challenges and Directions for the Future," *Fordham Urban Law Journal*, v30.

"Half-pint." 2000. Interview on Mill Avenue. 4/29/00.

Hannigan, John. 1998. *Fantasy City: Pleasure and Profit in the Postmodern Metropolis*. NY: Routledge.

Harcourt, Bernard E. 2001. *Illusion of Order: The False Promise of Broken Windows Policing*. Cambridge, MA: Harvard University Press.

Harris, Timothy. 2008. "Stop the Sweeps. Stop the Lies. Fight Back!" *Real Change*, 1/2/08.

Harter, Lynn M., Charlene Berquist, B. Scott Titsworth, David Novak, and Tod Brokaw. 2005. "The Structuring of Invisibility Among the Hidden Homeless: The Politics of Space, Stigma, and Identity Construction," *Journal of Applied Communication Research*, v33/n4.

Harvey, David. 1973. *Social Justice and the City*. US: Edward Arnold.

----------. 1990. *The Condition of Postmodernity: An Enquiry into the Origins of Cultural Change*. Cambridge, MA: Blackwell.

----------. 1996. *Justice, Nature, and the Geography of Difference*. Blackwell.

----------. 2006. "The Political Economy of Public Space," in S. Low & N. Smith (eds.), *The Politics of Public Space*, NY: Routledge.

Haussler, Alexa. 1999. "Tempe Sit-in Protests New Law," *Arizona Republic*, 1/19/99.

Heath, Cole. 2007. "Homeless Court is Year Old," *Arizona Republic*, 2/24/07.

Herman, Marc. 1997. "Down and Out," *Santa Cruz MetroActive*, 11/13/97.

Hermann, William. 2000a. "Neighbors Fear Homeless Presence," *Arizona Republic*, 1/17/00.

----------. 2000b. "New Homeless 'Campus' Gains Community Support," *Arizona Republic*, 4/15/00.

----------. 2005. "Ready for New Life," *Arizona Republic*, 4/14/05.

----------. 2007a. "Project HOPE is Assisting Tempe's Homeless," *Arizona Republic*, 1/27/07.

----------. 2007b. "HOPE for the Homeless: Tempe Program Reaches '1 Person at a Time,'" *Arizona Republic*, 8/2/07.

Hermer, Joe, and Janet Mosher (eds.). 2002. *Disorderly People: Law and the Politics of Exclusion in Ontario*. Nova Scotia: Fernwood.

Herzog, Lawrence A. 2004. "Globalization and the Crisis of Public Space: The Example of Mexico," in Jones & Ward (eds.), *Conference Proceedings: The End of Public Space in the Latin American City?*, University of Texas at Austin.

Hesse, Herman. 1951. *Siddhartha*. NY: New Directions.

----------. 1972. *Steppenwolf*. NY: Bantam.

Hetherington, Kevin. 1997. *The Badlands of Modernity: Heterotopia and Social Ordering*. NY: Routledge.

Hetzler, Olivia, Veronica E. Medina, and David Overfelt. 2006. "Gentrification, Displacement, and New Urbanism: The Next Racial Project," *Sociation Today*, v4/n2.

Hibberd, James. 2000. "Anarchy How? Can an Anarchist with a Law Degree Break the Rules of Modern Activism and Still Save Tempe Butte?" *Phoenix New Times*, 5/11/00.

Hil, Richard, and Judith Bessant. 1999. "Spaced Out? Young People's Agency, Resistance, and Public Space," *Urban Policy and Research*, v17/n1.

Holstein, James A., and Jaber Gubrium. 1995. *The Active Interview*. CA: Sage.

Holthouse, David. 1998a. "Meet the Crusties: Spanging, Squatting and Looking for Hot Dog Jesus with Tempe's Street Kids," *Phoenix New Times*, 2/26/98.

----------. 1998b. "Crusty Crackdown: Tempe City Council Primed to Pass New 'Sidewalk Squatting' Law," *Phoenix New Times*, 10/22/98.

HomeBase Youth Services. 2001. Caseworker interviews and outreach ride-along. 6/13/01.

Homeless Task Force. 2000a. "Homeless Task Force Report" (draft), *Tempe Community Council*, 8/3/00.

----------. 2000b. "Homeless Task Force Report" (volume 1), *Tempe Community Council*, 9/21/00.

Hopper, Kim, Ezra Susser, and Sarah Conover. 1985. "Economies of Makeshift: Deindustrialization and Homelessness in New York City," in *The Rights of the Homeless*, Practicing Law Institute, 1987.

Houck, Beth Waldock. 2000. "Spinning the Wheel After *Roulette*: How (and why) to Overturn a Sidewalk Sitting Ban," *Arizona State Law Journal*, v32/n4/p1451.

Howland, George. 1994. "The New Outlaws: Cities Make Homelessness a Crime," *The Progressive*, May.

Huth, Mary Jo, and Talmadge Wright (eds.). 1997. *International Critical Perspectives on Homelessness*. CT: Praeger.

Huxley, Aldous. 1954. *The Doors of Perception.* NY: Harper & Row.

IRIN. 2007. "South Africa: Winter Chill Nips Homeless on the Streets," *Reuters AlertNet*, 5/24/07.

Irwin, Megan. 2006. "The Devil Went Down to Phoenix . . . Will It Be Any Better than Tempe?" *Phoenix New Times*, 11/23/06.

IWW (Industrial Workers of the World). 1994. "The Criminalization of Poverty in Santa Cruz: Managing Social Dissent" (pamphlet).

Jackson, Chuck. 1998. "A Little More Civility in Order in Houston's Public Places," *Houston Chronicle*, 12/20/98.

Jacobs, Art. 1997. "Tempe Spin Doctors Didn't Note Enormous, Negative Cost of DTC," *Arizona Republic*, 8/23/97.

----------. 1998. "Taxpayers Doing Too Much for Downtown Tempe," *Arizona Republic*, 2/4/98.

James, Karla, and Osha Neumann. 2005. "The Legal Rights of Homeless People in Berkeley," *Street Spirit*, May.

James, Theresa. 2008. Telephone interview. 1/16/08.

"Jocko." 2000. Interview on Mill Avenue. 4/24/00.

Jones, Melissa L. 1999. "Ambassador to Homeless," *Arizona Republic*, 4/5/99.

Jones, Trevor, and Tim Newburn. 1999. "Policing Public and Private Space in Late Modern Britain," in P. Carlen & R. Morgan (eds.), *Crime Unlimited? Questions for the 21st Century*, UK: MacMillan.

Jorgenson, Danny L. 1989. *Participant Observation: A Methodology for Human Studies*. CA: Sage.

Kanter, Rosabeth Moss. 1972. *Commitment and Community: Communes and Utopias in Sociological Perspective.* MA: Harvard University Press.

"Katy." 2000. Interview on Mill Avenue. 4/29/00.

Kawash, Samira. 1998. "The Homeless Body," *Public Culture*, v10/n2.

Keeling, Rod. 1998a. "Downtown Tempe Gives Their Side," *ASU State Press*, 9/4/98.

----------. 1998b. "Time to Sweep Slackers Off Mill Ave.," *Arizona Republic*, 11/6/98.

Keim, Amanda. 2004a. "Coalition Petitions Council to Repeal Camping Ordinance: ASU Students Part of Effort to Decriminalize Camping," *ASU State Press*, 1/24/04.

----------. 2004b. "Activists Hold Sit-in on Mill Avenue," *ASU State Press*, 2/23/04.

Kelling, George L. 1999. *'Broken Windows' and Police Discretion.* Washington, D.C.: NIJ Research.

----------, and Catherine M. Coles. 1996. *Fixing Broken Windows: Restoring Order and Reducing Crime in Our Communities*. NY: Martin Kessler/Free Press.

"Kevin." 1999. Interview at the Salvation Army. 12/16/99.

----------. 2000. Interview on Mill Avenue. 4/29/00.

Khanh, Truong Phuoc. 2002. "Homeless Refuge," *San Jose Mercury News*, 12/12/02.

Knox, Paul. 1995. *Urban Social Geography: An Introduction.* US: Longman Scientific & Technical.

Koch, Andrew M. 1993. "Poststructuralism and the Epistemological Basis of Anarchism," in *Philosophy of the Social Sciences*, v23/n3.

Kohn, Margaret. 2004. *Brave New Neighborhoods: T he Privatization of Public Space*. NY: Routledge.

Koskela, Hille. 2000. "'The Gaze Without Eyes': Video-Surveillance and the Changing Nature of Urban Space," *Progress in Human Geography*, v24/n2.

Kress, June B. 1995. "Homeless Fatigue Syndrome: The Backlash Against the Crime of Homelessness in the 1990s," *Social Justice*, v21/n3.

Kressel, Shirley. 2000. "Privatizing the Public Realm," *The Progress Report*.

Kristeva, Julia. 1991. *Strangers to Ourselves*. NY: Columbia University Press.

Kropotkin, Peter. 1968 [1927]. *Kropotkin's Revolutionary Pamphlets*. NY: Benjamin Blom.

----------. 1972 [1914]. *Mutual Aid: A Factor of Evolution*. NY: NYU Press.

----------. 1993 [1912]. *Fields, Factories and Workshops*. UK: Transaction.

Kulp, Cyndy. 2000. "Panhandling Begs for Solutions," *Denver Post*, 1/16/00.

Lauderdale, Pat. 2003. *A Political Analysis of Deviance* (2d ed.). CA: de Sitter.

Laurenson, Penelope, and Damian Collins. 2006. "Towards Inclusion: Local Government, Public Space and Homelessness in New Zealand," *New Zealand Geographer*, v62.

----------. 2007. "Beyond Punitive Regulation? New Zealand Local Governments' Responses to Homelessness," *Antipode*, v39/n4.

Lauria, Mickey (ed.). 1996. *Reconstructing Urban Regime Theory: Regulating Urban Politics in a Global Economy*. CA: Sage.

Lebow, Edward. 2001. "Not So Private Lives," *Phoenix New Times*, 9/13/01.

Leckerman, Jason. 2001. "City of Brotherly Love? Using the Fourteenth Amendment to Strike Down an Anti-homeless Ordinance in Philadelphia," *University of Pennsylvania Journal of Constitutional Law*, v3/p540.

Lee, Barrett A., and Townsand Price-Spratlen. 2004. "The Geography of Homelessness in American Communities: Concentration or Dispersion?" *City & Community*, v3/n1.

Lee, Barrett A., Chad R. Farrell, and Bruce G. Link. 2004. "Revisiting the Contact Hypothesis: The Case of Public Exposure to Homelessness," *American Sociological Review*, v69/n1.

Lees, Loretta. 2003. "The Ambivalence of Diversity and the Politics of Urban Renaissance: The Case of Youth in Downtown Portland, Maine," *International Journal of Urban and Regional Research*, v27/n3.

Lefebvre, Henri. 1996. *Writings on Cities*. Cambridge, MA: Blackwell.

Legge, James (trans.). 1962. *The Texts of Taoism*. NY: Dover.

Lelchuk, Ilene. 2001. "S.F. Stung By Accusations of Callousness," *San Francisco Chronicle*, 8/23/01.

Leo, Christopher. 1996. "City Politics in an Era of Globalization," in Lauria (ed.), *Urban Regime Theory*.

"Leon." 2000. Interview on Mill Avenue. 4/24/00.

Lewis, Nancy. 1995. "20 Attorneys Agree to Serve the Homeless," *Virginia Beach Beacon*, 4/2/95.

Ley, Shawn. 2000. "Bonus Report: Tempe's Sidewalks Sold," KNXV, 1/13/00.

libcom.org. 2006. "Japan: Osaka's Homeless Resist Evictions," 1/30/06.

Linoff, Vic. 1998. "Giuliano Off Target Defending Rio Salado," *Arizona Republic*, 6/7/98.

Liskow, Samantha. 1999. "Civil(ity) War: Does Houston have to Get Tougher on Street People?" *Houston Press*, 7/22/99.

Lloyd, Kathleen, and Christopher Auld. 2003. "Leisure, Public Space and Quality of Life in the Urban Environment," *Urban Policy and Research*, v21/n4.

Lofland, Lyn H. 1973. *A World of Strangers: Order and Action in Urban Public Space*. NY: Basic.

----------. 1998. *The Public Realm: Exploring the City's Quintessential Social Territory*. NY: Aldine.

Loukaitou-Sideris, Anastasia, Evelyn Blumenberg, and Renia Ehrenfeucht. 2005. "Sidewalk Democracy: Municipalities and the Regulation of Public Space," in E.B. Joseph & T. Szwold (eds.), *Regulating Place: Standards and the Shaping of Urban America*, NY: Routledge.

Lydersen, Kari. 2000. "In Many Cities, Being Homeless is Against the Law," *In These Times*, 6/12/00.

MacDonald, Heather. 2007. "The Reclamation of Skid Row," *City Journal*, Autumn.

MacEachern, Doug. 1999a. "Sit-in for Sidewalk Slackers Salutes Society's Simpletons," *East Valley Tribune*, 1/28/99.

----------. 1999b. "Compassionate Activists Help Slackers Stay in Fantasy World," *East Valley Tribune*, 2/1/99.

Maerowitz, Marlene Pontrelli. 1997. "Homeless Aren't Tempe's Responsibility," *Arizona Republic*, 10/18/97.

----------. 1998. "Walking Only on Sidewalks is the Point," *Arizona Republic*, 12/12/98.

Magazine, Roger. 2004. "Street Children, Public Space and State Indifference in Mexico City," in Jones & Ward (eds.), *Conference Proceedings: The End of Public Space in the Latin American City?*, UT-Austin.

Magnusson, Warren. 1996. *The Search for Political Space: Globalization, Social Movements, and the Urban Political Experience*. Toronto: University of Toronto Press.

Malone, Karen. 2002. "Street Life: Youth, Culture and Competing Uses of Public Space," *Environment & Urbanization*, v14/n2.

Mander, Jerry. 1991. *In the Absence of the Sacred: The Failure of Technology and the Survival of the Indian Nations.* San Francisco: Sierra Club.

Marcuse, Peter. 1988. "Neutralizing Homelessness," *Socialist Review*, v18.

Massey, Doreen. 1994. *Space, Place, and Gender.* UK: Polity Press.

----------. 1999. "Philosophy and Politics of Spatiality: Some Considerations," *Hettner Lecture in Heidelberg, Germany.*

----------. 2000. "Entanglements of Power: Reflections," in Sharp, et al. (eds.), *Entanglements of Power.*

May, Jon. 2000. "Of Nomads and Vagrants: Single Homelessness and Narratives of Home as Place," *Environment and Planning D: Society and Space*, v18/p737.

May, Todd. 1989. "Is Post-structuralist Political Theory Anarchist?" *Philosophy and Social Criticism*, v15/n2.

----------. 1994. *The Political Philosophy of Poststructuralist Anarchism.* PA: University of Pennsylvania Press.

Mbah, Sam, and I.E. Igariwey. 1997. *African Anarchism: The History of a Movement.* Tucson, AZ: See Sharp.

McCarthy, John D., and Clark McPhail. 2006. "Places of Protest: The Public Forum in Principle and Practice," *Mobilization: An International Quarterly*, v11/n2.

McCloy, Mike. 2001. "Proposed Campus for Homeless Raises Ire of Downtown Residents," *Arizona Republic*, 6/21/01.

McConkey, Robert C. 1996. "'Camping Ordinances' and the Homeless: Constitutional and Moral Issues Raised By Ordinances Prohibiting Sleeping in Public Areas," *Cumberland Law Review*, v26/p633.

McIntyre, Meghan. 1999. "Mill Avenue Homeless Cause Problem for City," *ASU Student Press*, 6/18/99.

Mealer, Bryan. 1999. "Safety First: Are the Homeless Targeted in the Name of Crime Prevention?" *Austin Chronicle*, v18/n31.

"Melee." 2000. Interview on Mill Avenue. 4/19/00.

Meserve, David. 2001. "Ordinance 1320: The Two-word Solution," *Arcata Eye*, 3/13/01.

Meurer, Derek. 2008. "Local Activist Group, Courthouse Security Disagree," *Prescott Daily Courier*, 1/6/08.

Mies, Maria, and Vandana Shiva. 1993. *Ecofeminism.* London: Zed.

Miller, Henry. 1991. *On the Fringe: The Dispossessed in America.* Lexington.

Millich, Nancy. 1994. "Compassion Fatigue and the First Amendment: Are the Homeless Constitutional Castaways?" *U.C.-Davis Law Review*, v27.

Mitchell, Don. 1995. "The End of Public Space? People's Park, Definitions of the Public and Democracy," *Annals of the Association of the American Geographer*, v85/n1/p108.

----------. 1996a. "Introduction: Public Space and the City," *Urban Geography*, v17/n2/p127.

----------. 1996b. "Political Violence, Order, and the Legal Construction of Public Space: Power and the Public Forum Doctrine," *Urban Geography*, v17/n2/p152.

----------. 1997a. "The Annihilation of Space by Law: The Roots and Implications of Anti-Homeless Laws in the United States," *Antipode*, v29/n3/p303.

----------. 1997b. "Power, Tactics, and the Political Geography of Policing: Comments on Steve Herbert's *Policing Space*," *Urban Geography*, v18/n5.

----------. 1998a. "Anti-Homeless Laws and Public Space: Begging and the First Amendment," *Urban Geography*, v19/n1.

----------. 1998b. "Anti-Homeless Laws and Public Space: Further Issues," *Urban Geography*, v19/n2.

----------. 2001. "Postmodern Geographical Praxis? The Postmodern Impulse and the War Against the Homeless in the Post-Justice City," in C. Minca (ed.), *Postmodern Geography: Theory and Praxis*, Blackwell.

----------. 2003. *The Right to the City: Social Justice and the Fight for Public Space*. NY: Guilford.

----------, and Lynn A. Staeheli. 2006. "Clean and Safe? Property Redevelopment, Public Space, and Homelessness in Downtown San Diego," in S. Low & N. Smith (eds.), *The Politics of Public Space*, NY: Routledge.

Morris, Brian. 1998. "Anthropology and Anarchism," *Anarchy: A Journal of Desire Armed*, v16/n1 (#45).

Morris, Ruth, and Colleen Heffren. 1988. *Street People Speak.* NY: Mosaic.

Mosher, Janet. 2002. "The Shrinking of the Public and Private Spaces of the Poor," in J. Hermer & J. Mosher (eds.), *Disorderly People*.

Moss, J. Jennings. 1999. "Increasingly, Homeless Seen as Blight," *ABCNews.com*, 11/24/99.

Munzer, Stephen R. 1997. "Ellickson on 'Chronic Misconduct' in Urban Spaces: Of Panhandlers, Bench Squatters, and Day Laborers," *Harvard Civil Rights-Civil Liberties Law Rev.*, v32/p1.

Navarro, Bruno. 2000. "Homeless Gripe, City Fences Fall," *Arizona Republic*, 10/21/00.

Naymik, Mark. 1998. "Street People," *Philadelphia City Paper*, 5/14/98.

NCH (National Coalition on Homelessness). 1997. "The Criminalization of Homelessness: U.S. Cities Ban Homeless Activity," *Safety Network*.

----------. 2003. "As Homelessness Increases, Number of Laws Targeting Homeless People Rise," nationalhomeless.org.

----------. 2004. *Illegal to be Homeless: The Criminalization of Homelessness in the United States*, nationalhomeless.org.

----------. 2006. "Homeless Self-Help and Empowerment Projects," nationalhomeless.org.

---------- and NLCHP. 2002. *Illegal to be Homeless: The Criminalization of Homelessness in the United States*, nationalhomeless.org.

---------- and NLCHP. 2006. *A Dream Denied: The Criminalization of Homelessness in U.S. Cities*, nationalhomeless.org.

Nelson, Gary. 2001. "Sidewalk Sprawlers Deserve the Road," *East Valley Tribune*, 5/19/01.

Nelson, Katie. 2006. "5 Homeless Center Sites Proposed," *Arizona Republic*, 6/1/06.

Newman, Oscar. 1973. *Defensible Space: Crime Prevention Through Urban Design*. NY: Collier.

Nietzsche, Friedrich. 1996. *Human, All Too Human: A Book for Free Spirits*. NB: University of Nebraska Press.

Nieves, Evelyn. 1998. "Fed Up, Berkeley Takes Aim at Homeless Youths," *New York Times*, 11/3/98.

----------. 2002. "In Famously Tolerant City, Impatience with Homeless," *New York Times*, 1/18/02.

Niman, Michael I. 1997. *People of the Rainbow: A Nomadic Utopia*. Knoxville, TN: University of Tennessee Press.

NLCHP (National Law Center on Homelessness and Poverty). 1999. *Out of Sight – Out of Mind?: A Report on Anti-Homeless Laws, Litigation and Alternatives in 50 United States Cities*. Washington, D.C.

----------, and NCH. 2007. *Feeding Intolerance: Prohibitions on Sharing Food with People Experiencing Homelessness*. Washington, D.C.

"Nona." 2001. Interview on Mill Avenue. 5/16/01.

Noonan, Dennis. 1996. "Cultural Cleansing: Is There Solution for Homeless Camp?" *Tucson Weekly*, 3/21/96.

Norse, Robert. 2001. "City Council's Underhanded Attack on Camp Paradise," *Street Spirit*, v7/n11.

----------, and Becky Johnson. 2002. "Camp Paradise Faces Exile," *Street Spirit*, v8/n1.

Norval, Aletta F. 1994. "Social Ambiguity and the Crisis of Apartheid," in E. Laclau (ed.), *The Making of Political Identities*, NY: Verso.

O'Brien, Keith. 2001. "Undue Process," *New Orleans Times-Picayune*, 10/7/01.

O'Leary, Zina. 2004. *The Essential Guide to Doing Research.* CA:Sage.

O'Malley, Michael. 1999. "Holiday Crackdown Sweeps Up City's Homeless," *Plain Dealer*, 12/1/99.

Palmer, Lucia M. 1993. "Anarchy and the Condition of Contemporary Humanism," *History of European Ideas*, v16/n4.

Palo Alto Weekly (editorial). 1997a. "Caution: Sit-lie Zone Ahead," 3/19/97.

----------. 1997b. "Debate is Latest in History About How Police Should Regulate Street People," 5/21/97.

Parenti, Christian. 2000. "Discipline in Playland: Policing the Themepark City," in *Lockdown America*, NY: Verso.

Passaro, Joanne. 1996. "Imagined Immunities: Policing Public Space and Reinscribing a Gendered Private Realm," in *The Unequal Homeless: Men on the Streets, Women in Their Place*, NY: Routledge.

Pela, Robrt L. 2004. "Don't Park It: Homeless for the Holidays," *Phoenix New Times*, 12/16/04.

----------. 2006. "Phoenix *Means* Well," *Phoenix New Times*, 1/26/06.

Peterson, Marina. 2006. "Patrolling the Plaza: Privatized Public Space and the Neoliberal State in Downtown Los Angeles," *Urban Anthropology*, v35/n4.

Petrie, Bob. 1994a. "Group Hopes to Bring Music to City Streets," *Arizona Republic*, 7/11/94.

----------. 1994b. "Marketing of Tempe Assessed," *Arizona Republic*, 8/5/94.

----------. 1997. "Downtown Tempe Group Holds Its Own, Seeks Funds for Renewal," *ArizonaRepublic*, 8/20/97.

----------. 1998a. "Tempe Police Hope Proposed Law Won't Sit Well With Transients," *Arizona Republic*, 8/27/98.

----------. 1998b. "Sides Squaring Off on Restricting Youths in Tempe Public Areas," *Arizona Republic*, 12/6/98.

----------. 1998c. "Tempe Set to Ban Sidewalk Sitting," *Arizona Republic*, 12/17/98.

----------. 1999. "Tempe Cruising Crackdown," *Arizona Republic*, 4/3/99.

----------. 2002. "Tempe's Welcome Mat," *Arizona Republic*, 7/19/02.

Phillips, Utah, and Ani Difranco. 1996. *The Past Didn't Go Anywhere.* Buffalo, NY: Righteous Babe Records.

Phipps, Brion Inness. 2007. "Nowhere to Nap: How Service Providers and Homeless Adult Males View the Influence Criminalizing Survival Activities has on Support Service Use, an Exploratory Study," Smith College School for Social Work (Master's thesis).

Pile, Steve, and Michael Keith (eds.). 1997. *Geographies of Resistance*. NY: Routledge.

"Piper." 2000. Interview on Mill Avenue. 4/24/00.

Porter, William. 1997a. "Tempe Searches for Way to Keep Downtown Distinctive," *Arizona Republic*, 3/28/97.

----------. 1997b. "Tempe on Brink of Redevelopment Explosion," *Arizona Republic*, 6/11/97.

Prendergast, Kim. 1998a. "City Proposal Would Eliminate 'Mill Rats,'" *ASU State Press*, 8/28/98.

----------. 1998b. "Cameras Have Locals Saying 'Cheese' on Mill," *ASU State Press*, 9/9/98.

----------. 1999. "DTC-sponsored Cards Ask for Donations Rather than Handouts," *ASU State Press*, 2/5/99.

Pressley, Sue Ann. 1996. "Homeless Are Run Out of Town," *London Guardian*, 1/2/96.

Quinn, Daniel. 1996. *The Story of B.* NY: Bantam.

Raghavan, Chakravarthi. 2002. "Homeless, Precariously Sheltered, Continue to Grow in Number," *Third World Economics*, 3/16/02.

Rau, Alia Beard. 2003a. "'They Just Don't Want Kids on Mill,'" *Arizona Republic*, 3/1/03.

----------. 2003b. "Tempe 'Romancing' Retailers, Downtown Prospects," *Arizona Republic*, 3/3/03.

----------. 2003c. "High on Lofts in Tempe," *Arizona Republic*, 5/26/03.

----------. 2003d. "Tempe's All-America Honor," *Arizona Republic*, 6/17/03.

----------. 2004. "Homeless Get Support: Urban Camping Ban Challenged," *Arizona Republic*, 1/24/04.

Raybaud, Antoine. 1993. "Nomadism Between the Archaic and the Modern," *Yale French Studies*, n82/p146.

Reed, Sean Michael, and Elizabeth Venable. 2001. "Tempe Development Plan: Hello Yuppies, Goodbye Homeless," *ASU State Press*, 7/10/01.

Riordan, Nikki. 1998. "Tempe Cements Ban on Sidewalk Sitting," *East Valley Tribune*, 12/18/98.

----------. 1999a. "Foes Stage Sit-in Over Tempe Sidewalk Ban," *East Valley Tribune*, 1/19/99.

----------. 1999b. "New School of Thought," *East Valley Tribune*, 1/29/99.

----------. 2000. "Sidewalk Ordinance Gets Boot," *East Valley Tribune*, 2/1/00.

Robb, Robert. 2004. "Mayoral-race Fistfight Blurs Tempe Issues," *Arizona Republic*, 3/3/04.

Robb, Ross. 1998. "Letters Wrong, DTC No Enemy of the Taxpayer," *Arizona Republic*, 2/11/98.

Rocky Mountain News (editorial). 2000. "Too Much Crackdown," 5/18/00.

Romano, Angela. 1998. "City May Privatize Sidewalks to Check Panhandlers," *Arizona Wildcat*, 9/18/98.

Ropers, Richard H. 1988. *The Invisible Homeless: A New Urban Ecology*. NY: Human Sciences.

Rose, Jaimee. 2000. "Mall Avenue Tied Up in Chains," *Arizona Republic*, 4/21/00.

Rosenberg, Gerald N. 1991. *The Hollow Hope: Can Courts Bring About Social Change?* IL: University of Chicago.

Rosenfeld, Dave. 2000. "Tempe Takes Positive Step in Dealing With Homeless," *ASU State Press*, 9/29/00.

Rosenthal, Rob. 1996. "Dilemmas of Local Antihomelessness Movements," in Baumohl (ed.), *Homelessness in America.*

Rousseau, Jean-Jacques. 1973 [1750-62]. *The Social Contract and The Discourses*. UK: Everyman's.

Routledge, Paul. 1997. "A Spatiality of Resistances: Theory and Practice in Nepal's Revolution of 1990," in Pile & Keith (eds.), *Geographies of Resistance*.

Ruddick, Susan M. 1990. "Heterotopias of the Homeless: Strategies and Tactics of Placemaking in Los Angeles," *Strategies: A Journal of Theory, Culture, and Politics*, v3/p184.

----------. 1996. *Young and Homeless in Hollywood: Mapping Social Identities*. NY: Routledge.

----------. 2002. "Metamorphosis Revisited: Restricting Discourses of Citizenship," in J. Hermer & J. Mosher (eds.), *Disorderly People*.

Sahlin, Ingrid. 2006. "Urban Definitions of Places and Behaviour," *European Observatory on Homelessness*, November.

Salt Lake Tribune (editorial). 1999. "In the Spirit of Dr. King," 1/25/99.

Sarlat, Rick. 1998. "City Council Becomes Battleground Over Sidewalk Bill," *Philadelphia Tribune*, 6/5/98.

Schakel, Patrick. 1998. "Tempe to Decide on Sidewalk Law," *East Valley Tribune*, 10/29/98.

Severson, Carrie. 1999a. "ACLU Protests Sidewalk-sitting Ban," *ASU State Press*, 1/19/99.

----------. 1999b. "Project S.I.T. Sits Down to Protest New Tempe Law," *ASU State Press*, 2/1/99.

Shaffer, Gwen. 1998. "Street Sweeper," *Philadelphia City Paper*, 6/11/98.

Sharp, Joanne P., Paul Routledge, et al. (eds.). 2000. *Entanglements of Power: Geographies of Domination/Resistance*. NY: Routledge.

Sibley, David. 1995. *Geographies of Exclusion: Society and Difference in the West*. UK: Routledge.

Silbey, Susan S. 2001. "'Let Them Eat Cake': Globalization, Postmodern Colonialism, and the Possibilities of Justice," in N. Blomley, D. Delaney, & R.T. Ford (eds.), *The Legal Geographies Reader: Law, Power, and Space*, UK: Blackwell.

Simon, Harry. 1992. "Towns Without Pity: A Constitutional and Historical Analysis of Official Efforts to Drive Homeless Persons from American Cities," *Tulane Law Review*, v66.

----------. 1995. "The Criminalization of Homelessness in Santa Ana, California: A Case Study," *Clearinghouse Review*, v29/n8-9.

----------. 1996. "Municipal Regulation of the Homeless in Public Spaces," in Baumohl (ed.), *Homelessness in America.*

Slater, David. 1997. "Spatial Politics/Social Movements: Questions of (B)orders and Resistance in Global Times," in Pile & Keith (eds.), *Geographies of Resistance*.

Smith, David M. 1994. "A Theoretical and Legal Challenge to Homeless Criminalization as Public Policy," *Yale Law and Policy Review*, v12/p487.

Smith, Neil. 1984. *Uneven Development: Nature, Capital, and the Production of Space*. NY: Blackwell.

----------. 1992. "Contours of a Spatialized Politics: Homeless Vehicles and the Production of Geographical Scale," *Social Text*, v33/p54.

----------. 1996. *The New Urban Frontier: Gentrification and the Revanchist City*. NY: Routledge.

----------, and Peter Williams (eds.). 1986. *Gentrification of the City*. Boston, MA: Allen & Unwin.

Snow, David A., and Leon Anderson. 1993. *Down on Their Luck: A Study of Homeless Street People*. CA: University of California Press.

----------, Theron Quist, and Daniel Cress. 1996. "Material Survival Strategies on the Street: Homeless People as *Bricoleurs*," in Baumohl (ed.), *Homelessness in America.*

Snow, David A., and Michael Mulcahy. 2001. "Space, Politics, and the Survival Strategies of the Homeless," *American Behavioral Scientist*, v45/n1.

Soja, Edward W. 1989. *Postmodern Geographies: The Reassertion of Space in Critical Social Theory*. NY: Verso.

----------. 2000. *Postmetropolis: Critical Studies of Cities and Regions.* UK: Blackwell.

Solomon, Maynard (ed.). 1974. *Marxism and Art: Essays Classic and Contemporary.* NY: Vintage.

Sorkin, Michael (ed.). 1992. *Variations on a Theme Park: The New American City and the End of Public Space.* NY: Hill & Wang.

Spinoza, Baruch. 1991. *The Ethics of Spinoza: The Road to Inner Freedom.* NY: Citadel.

Spocter, Manfred. 2007. "The 'Silent' Closure of Urban Public Space in Cape Town: 1975 to 2004," *Urban Forum*, v18/n3.

Spradley, James P. 1970. *You Owe Yourself a Drunk: An Ethnography of Urban Nomads.* NY: Little, Brown.

Stamelman, Richard. 1993. "The Strangeness of the Other and the Otherness of the Stranger," *Yale French Studies*, n82.

The Stanford Daily (editorial). 1997. "'Sit-lie' Sits Poorly, Unfairly Removes Homeless," 4/3/97.

Steckner, Susie. 2001a. "Taking a Stand So Others May Sit," *Arizona Republic*, 3/23/01.

----------. 2001b. "Sidewalk Sitting Ban Stands Up," *Arizona Republic*, 5/16/01.

----------. 2001c. "Brickyard on Mill on Hold in Tempe," *Arizona Republic*, 6/4/01.

Steel, M., and M. Symes. 2005. "The Privatisation of Public Space? The American Experience of Business Improvement Districts and Their Relationship to Local Governance," *Local Govt. Studies*, v31/n3.

Stern, Ray. 2000. "Corporate World Invades Mill Avenue," *East Valley Tribune*, 4/8/00.

Stiles, Karen. 1998. "The Battle Rages On," *The Waltonian*, 10/98.

Stoner, Madelaine R. 1995. *The Civil Rights of Homeless People.* NY: Aldine de Gruyter.

Street Sheet. 2007a. "Lock 'em All Up!: Are Policing and Prisons the Solution to Homelessness?" *Blog Archive*, 11/1/07.

----------. 2007b. "Kamala Harris Wastes Too Many Resources on 'Quality of Life' Prosecution," *Blog Archive*, 12/1/07.

----------. 2007c. "How Much Does the Right to Sleep Cost?" *Blog Archive*, 12/1/07.

Subramanian, Ganga. 1999. "Mayor Covers Sidewalk Ordinance in Speech," *ASU State Press*, 2/12/99.

Svelund, Greg. 1999. "Sidewalk Ordinance Wrong," *Arizona Republic*, 1/19/99.

Tafari, Jack. 2005. "The Ongoing Transformation of Dignity Village," *Street Spirit*, March.

TCC (Tempe Community Council). *Homeless Task Force Report (Volume 1)*. 9/21/00.

----------. 2006. "Community News," *Network*, Fall.

TEAM. 2001. Interview on Mill Avenue. 5/16/01.

Teir, Rob. 1996. "Safety and Civility in Public Spaces," *Atlanta Journal & Constitution*, 1/24/96.

----------. 1998. "Restoring Order in Urban Public Spaces," *Texas Review of Law & Politics*, v2/p256.

Templar, Le. 2001a. "Things Looking Up These Days for Tempe Builders," *East Valley Tribune*, 4/30/01.

----------. 2001b. "Court Upholds Tempe Rule," *East Valley Tribune*, 5/16/01.

Thomas, Jim. 1993. *Doing Critical Ethnography*. CA: Sage.

Thomason, Art. 1998. "Bojangles is Not a Bum," *Arizona Republic*, 12/1/98.

Thoreau, Henry David. 1965. *Walden* and *Civil Disobedience*. NY: Harper.

Tobin, Mitch. 2000a. "Panhandler Law Put in Jeopardy," *Tucson Citizen*, 2/4/00.

----------. 2000b. "Sidewalk Law to be Discussed," *Tucson Citizen*, 3/6/00.

Trapenciere, Ilze. 2006. "Public Space, Homelessness, and Use of Public Space in Latvia," *European Observatory on Homelessness*, Dec.

Trujillo, Laura. 1999. "Sit-in Targets Tempe Law," *Arizona Republic*, 1/31/99.

Tucson Citizen (editorial). 2000. "Panhandler Law – Stop Overlooking Role of Police," 2/10/00.

Twaddell, Joanne C. 2007. "Homeless Teens: Some Kids Choose Streets Over Family Life," *Prescott Daily Courier*, 12/29/07.

UN News. 2005. "Growing Privatization of Property Among Reasons Driving Homelessness, UN Rights Expert Says," *UN News Centre*, 5/11/05.

United States Interagency Council on Homelessness (USICH). 2007. "Project Homeless Connect 'A Proven Strategy' to Help End Homelessness, Says Tempe Mayor," *USICH Newsletter*, 5/2/07.

Urquides, Heather. 2002. "Mill Avenue Merchants Bemoan Big-Time Status," *Arizona Republic*, 1/7/02.

VanderStaay, Steven. 1992. *Street Lives: An Oral History of Homeless Americans.* PA: New Society.

Verena. 2007. "Homeless in Osaka," *PingMag*, 2/13/07.

von Mahs, Jurgen. 2005. "The Sociospatial Exclusion of Single Homeless People in Berlin and Los Angeles," *American Behavioral Scientist*, v48/n8.

von Werlhof, Claudia. 1997. "Upheaval from the Depth: The 'Zapatistas,' the Indigenous Civilization, the Question of Matriarchy, and the West," in Lauderdale & Amster (eds.), *Lives in the Balance*, NY: Brill.

Wachholz, Sandra. 2005. "Hate Crimes Against the Homeless: Warning-out New England Style," *Journal of Sociology and Social Welfare*, Dec.

Wagner, David. 1993. *Checkerboard Square: Culture and Resistance in a Homeless Community.* San Francisco: Westview.

----------. 1995. "Beyond the Conventional Wisdom About the Homeless: 'Cultures of Resistance' on the Streets," *Research in Community Sociology*, v5/p127.

Waldron, Jeremy. 1991. "Homelessness and the Issue of Freedom," *UCLA Law Review*, v39/p295.

----------. 2000. "Homelessness and Community," *University of Toronto Law Journal*, v50/p371.

Ward, Colin. 1973. *Anarchy in Action.* NY: Harper & Row.

Waxman, Benjamin S. 1994. "Fighting the Criminalization of Homelessness: Anatomy of an Institutional Anti-homeless Lawsuit," *Stetson Law Review*, v23/p467.

Weber, Max. 1958. *The Protestant Ethic and the Spirit of Capitalism.* NY: Scribner & Sons.

Weil, Andrew. 1972. *The Natural Mind: A New Way of Looking at Drugs and the Higher Consciousness.* MA: Houghton.

Welch, Dennis. 2003. "Protesters March Peacefully in Tempe," *East Valley Tribune*, 11/16/03.

WFTV.com. 2007. "Group Intentionally Violating City Ordinance During 'Ladle Fest,'" 10/8/07.

Whisler, Brad. 1999. "Sidewalk-sitting Ban Calls for Political Action," *ASU State Press*, 1/22/99.

Wilber, Ken. 1977. *The Spectrum of Consciousness.* Wheaton, IL: Quest.

Wildermuth, John. 1997. "Friends of the Homeless Stage Palo Alto Sit-Down," *San Francisco Chronicle*, 4/25/97.

Williams, Brett. 1996. "'There Goes the Neighborhood': Gentrification, Displacement, and Homelessness in Washington, D.C.," in Dehavenon (ed.), *There's No Place Like Home.*

Williams, Timothy. 2002. "Homeless Give Officer $3000," *Arizona Republic*, 12/25/02.

Wilson, James Q., and George L. Kelling. 1982. "Broken Windows: The Police and Neighborhood Safety," *The Atlantic Monthly*, March.

Winford, Stan. 2006. "A New (Legal) Threat to Public Space: The Rise and Rise of the ASBO," *Parity*, February.

Wittenauer, Cheryl. 2003. "New Court Aims at Eradicating Pesky Behaviors in Downtown St. Louis," *Daily Courier*, 2/2/03.

Wolf, Jessica. 1999. "The Evolution of Mill Avenue, Tempe's Original 'Main Street': From Rugged Dust Town to Urban Center," *ASU State Press Magazine*, 10/14/99.

Wong, Edward, & Maria LaGanga. 1998. "Berkeley Poised to OK Crackdown on Homeless," *Los Angeles Times*, 12/8/98.

Wright, Talmadge. 1997. *Out of Place: Homeless Mobilizations, Subcities, and Contested Landscapes*. NY: SUNY Press.

----------. 2000. "New Urban Spaces and Cultural Representations: Social Imagineries, Social-Physical Space, and Homelessness," *Research in Urban Sociology*, v5/p23.

----------, and Anita Vermund. 1996. "Suburban Homelessness and Social Space: Strategies of Authority and Local Resistance in Orange County, California," in Dehavenon, *There's No Place Like Home.*

Yara, Georgann. 2007. "Mill Ave. Performers Help Create Happy Vibe," *Arizona Republic*, 8/2/07.

"Yogi." 1999. Interview on Mill Avenue. 1/19/99.

Zawicki, Neil. 2000a. "Residents Concerned About Changes on Mill," *ASU State Press*, 9/13/00.

----------. 2000b. "Taskforce to Propose City Homeless Shelter," *ASU State Press*, 9/22/00.

----------. 2000c. "Tempe Fences Out Homeless," *ASU State Press*, 10/16/00.

----------. 2000d. "Street Kids Struggle to Find Culture, Family of Their Own," *ASU State Press*, 10/23/00.

----------. 2000e. "Tempe Takes Down Spiked Fences," *ASU State Press*, 10/25/00.

Zerzan, John. 1994. *Future Primitive and Other Essays.* Brooklyn, NY: Autonomedia.

Zinko, Carolyne. 1997. "New Sidewalk Ban in Palo Alto Called Unfair to Homeless," *SF Gate,* 3/12/97.

----------. 1999. "Palo Alto Chief Orders Help, Not Handcuffs, for Homeless," *SF Gate,* 2/15/99.

Zoellner, Tom, and Elvia Diaz. 2001. "New Homeless Facility Still Faces Uphill Battle," *Arizona Republic*, 12/15/01.

Zukin, Sharon. 1995. *The Culture of Cities*. Oxford: Blackwell.

----------. 1997. "Cultural Strategies of Economic Redevelopment and Hegemony of Vision," in A. Merrifield & E. Swyngedouw (eds.), *The Urbanization of Injustice*, NY: NYU Press.

INDEX

CPSIA information can be obtained
at www.ICGtesting.com
Printed in the USA
LVOW12s1917240717
542441LV00002B/419/P